52115
£11
CW01638542

DEMO … ORY

In this philosophically sophisticated textbook analysis of democracy, J. L. Hyland explores in depth the concept which has come to reign supreme in the pantheon of political ideas.

He examines systematically the major topics and problems of democratic theory: the nature of democracy, majoritarianism, democracy and individual freedom, power and the relationship between socioeconomic factors and political equality.

In assessing the work of the major democratic theorists, whose accounts frequently conflict, the author seeks to answer the central questions surrounding the subject: What is democracy? What values does it provide? Can democracy fulfil its promise, or is it an unachievable goal to which we merely pay lip-service? Is democracy always justified? What are the counter-democratic features of modern society?

J. L. Hyland is a Lecturer in the Department of Political Science, Trinity College, Dublin

11/12/95

DEMOCRATIC THEORY

The philosophical foundations

JAMES L. HYLAND

MANCHESTER UNIVERSITY PRESS
Manchester and New York

distributed exclusively in the USA and Canada by St. Martin's Press

Copyright © James L. Hyland 1995

Published by Manchester University Press
Oxford Road, Manchester M13 9NR, UK
and Room 400, 175 Fifth Avenue, New York, NY 10010, USA

Distributed exclusively in the USA and Canada
by St. Martin's Press, Inc., 175 Fifth Avenue, New York, NY 10010, USA

British Library Cataloguing-in-Publication Data
A catalogue record for this book is available from the British Library

Library of Congress Cataloging-in-Publication Data
Hyland, James L., 1945–
Democratic theory : the philosophical foundations / James L. Hyland.
p. cm.
ISBN 0-7190-3941-X. — ISBN 0-7190-4517-7 (pbk.)
1. Democracy I. Title.
JC423.H95 1994
321.8'01—dc20 94-16673
CIP

ISBN 0 7190 3941 X *hardback*
0 7190 4517 7 *paperback*

Photoset in Linotron Joanna
by Northern Phototypesetting Co. Ltd, Bolton

Printed in Great Britain
by Bell & Bain Ltd, Glasgow

Contents

Introduction

Although I argue in Chapter 1 that political theory has to be thought of as an integrated synthesis of philosophical, normative and empirical analysis, the primary purpose of this book is to introduce students to a serious treatment of those philosophical and normative problems that lie at the heart of democratic theory and practice. Chapters 1 and 2 are methodological. In Chapter 1 I begin by arguing for a conception of political theory that is essentially normative. Political theory should be concerned with the evaluative appraisal of possible forms of political and social organisation and the principles upon which they are based. Such analysis can be neither purely philosophical nor purely empirical. The nature, value and realisability of social and political ideals can only be established by means of philosophical reflection, but a philosophical reflection that is continuously informed by empirical analysis. This conception of political theory immediately raises a major philosophical problem concerning the extent to which the value of social and political ideals can be subject to rational argumentation. At the centre of Chapter 1 is an account of the forms of rational argument that can, I claim, result in conclusions that are important and significant for the justification and choice of political and social ideals. I conclude the chapter by identifying the tasks of a political theory of democracy, those tasks being, in simple terms, to identify what democracy is, to specify the evaluative principles necessary to justify democracy and ask how justifiable those principles are and, finally, to determine the conditions required for the realisation of democratic ideals.

Chapters 2, 3 and 4 deal with the question of the nature of democracy. The first problem we encounter in attempting to answer that question is again a methodological one. The main purpose of Chapter 2 is to argue that identifying the nature of democracy should be conceived of neither as an investigation into the timeless 'essence' of democracy nor as an elucidation of some universal and timeless concept of democracy. The appropriate method, I will argue, has to consist in a construction of a concept of democracy, the justification of the specific construction lying partly in the ability of the concept to capture in a coherent manner significant and core elements of previous usages of the term and partly in the manner in which the concept as constructed enables a theorist to deal with the problems and concerns of democratic theory and practice. In Chapter 3 I begin to construct an account of democracy as political equality in all the moments of collective decision-making and I argue that we should conceive of this equality as effective equality, involving both equality of procedural entitlements to participate in a decision-making process and adequate access to that wide range of resources that would enable a person to utilise her or his procedural entitlements. I concentrate in this chapter on the problem of how we should conceive of the full range of procedural entitlements and rights that would be required to maximise political equality in any decision-making process. There are two particular problems that emerge in this context that require fairly detailed analysis and I move on in Chapter 4 to the treatment, firstly, of the problem of how far the degree of political equality in a society depends upon the number of people to whom rights of participation are extended and, secondly, how the maximisation of political equality within a decision-making procedure is affected by the technical voting rules. I am, in particular, concerned in this chapter to argue that any restrictions on the extent of the franchise diminish political equality and that the claims of the majority rule procedure to maximise political equality are unfounded. On the contrary, I argue that the realisation of political equality requires both the maximum extent of enfranchisement and the operation of a thoroughly proportional decision-making procedure and distribution of power. My argument up to this point, then, has been that we should conceive of political rule as being democratic to the extent that all those significantly affected by the decisions have equal and effective rights of participation at all levels of decision-making, with the understanding that this effectiveness is crucially dependent on adequate access to resources necessary to enable full and meaningful participation. The questions we then face are: how justifiable as a political ideal is such a conception of democracy and what are the social conditions required for its realisation?

Before approaching these questions directly, however, I examine in Chapter 5 a major alternative to the conception of democracy so far outlined, the conception that I refer to as the juridico-legal variant. There is a very influential tradition of political thought that argues, firstly, that democracy should be conceived of simply as that complex of juridico-legal rights that constitutes liberal representative government and, secondly, that the purpose of this complex of rights is not to ensure maximal participation in all levels of political decision-making but rather to preserve maximal individual freedom from governmental control. From this perspective it can be argued that the promotion of active political equality as an ideal will lead to a destruction of those values that democracy is meant to preserve. I argue in this chapter, firstly, that the question is not the semantic, conceptual one concerning which of the two opposing conceptions correctly identifies the real meaning of democracy, but the normative question concerning which of the two ideals is more justifiable. I subject the arguments in favour of the juridico-legal ideal of democracy to critical analysis that, at its heart, raises fundamental questions concerning freedom, autonomy, responsibility, coercion and constraint. Overall, the arguments in this chapter tend to the conclusion that, if the goal is to maximise the freedom and autonomy of everyone in a community, a wide range of collective affairs will need to be brought within the scope of collective decision-making and that, in that context, real ability to fully participate in political decision-making is going to be of critical significance.

A central question of modern political theory emerges in this argument, the question of whether there are strict limits to the legitimate scope of collective decision-making determined by inalienable individual rights, the infringement of which would render decisions illegitimate, no matter how democratic they were and no matter how beneficial the collective, aggregate consequences might be. I take up this question in Chapter 6 where, firstly, I look at the extreme anarchist position that would deny all legitimacy even to a maximally democratic government and, secondly, I examine the liberal democratic synthesis that postulates external determinants of democratic legitimacy deriving from individual rights. I argue that the anarchist argument is seriously flawed and that the liberal attempt to specify external determinants of democratic legitimacy is inevitably, in the last analysis, undemocratic.

This would constitute a criticism of the liberal democratic synthesis only if it could be shown that in the sphere of collective decision-making democracy was the uniquely justifiable procedure. I move on in Chapter 7 to the question of how a justification of democracy can be constructed. My argument falls into two major sections. In the first I claim that the justification of democracy depends on identifying a range of substantive values which, it is going to be argued, democracy promotes; but I go on to argue that the justification would be incomplete unless a basic egalitarian principle could also be established, a principle that claimed that the promotion of the substantive values was justifiable only if egalitarian. I examine in this section how such an egalitarian principle could itself be justified. In the second part of the chapter I argue that only a decision-making procedure that was thoroughly democratic would have any guaranteed tendency to promote substantive values in an egalitarian manner.

The final three chapters of the book concern the social conditions necessary for the realisation of democratic ideals. In Chapter 8 I look at certain theories that have played a prominent role in modern debates concerning democracy, theories that claim that the ideals of political equality and equal autonomy can be subtly subverted by extra-political structures of power and dominance. In Chapter 9 I turn to the question of whether, in particular, inequalities of economic power tend to undermine political equality and equal autonomy. And in the final chapter I examine the issue of the logical and organisational limitations of democracy. I argue that elite theories to the effect that there is, in complex organisations, an ineluctable tendency towards the emergence of oligarchies are, in fact, very strong and I conclude with a consideration of whether the significant realisation of political equality might involve a radical overhaul of political institutions as currently conceived.

1

Political philosophy and the tasks of democratic theory

It is hard to believe that as recently as 1966 Richard Wollheim felt it incumbent on him to write an article defending the possibility of political philosophy as a serious intellectual discipline that can, by rational argument, reach results that are relevant and important to the real world of politics.[1] Yet, as Wollheim documents in the introduction to his article, no major work in political philosophy had been produced since the 1930s in the British analytic tradition and, furthermore, most analytic philosophers were of the expressed belief that work in the traditional area of political philosophy was, in principle, impossible. While it is true that since 1966 political philosophy, even within the analytic tradition, has undergone a major renaissance, it still lacks a generally accepted systematically formulated rationale that clearly sets out its function, aims, methods and possibilities. This is not accidental; those aspects of analytic philosophy that originally led to the much trumpeted death of political philosophy are, to a large extent, still with us, and are not to be narrowly identified with, for example, the rather naive emotivism and excessively limited positivist account of the nature of philosophy espoused by A. J. Ayer in *Language, Truth and Logic.*[2]

There are, fundamentally, two elements of contemporary analytic philosophy that render political theory in the traditional sense problematic; namely, theories concerning the complex nature of value-judgements and a conception of philosophy as essentially a second-order conceptual reflective exercise that does not purport to establish or call on empirically based 'truths' and, in the famous Wittgensteinian formulation, leaves things as they were.[3]

Let us look, first, at the problems arising from the complex nature of value-judgements. Wollheim may be correct in his claim that T. D. Weldon's account of traditional political philosophy as the production of demonstrative arguments proving the unconditional superiority of some particular form of government is overly narrow, but it cannot be doubted that normative, evaluative assessment was, and still is, a central concern of political philosophy.[4] While very few contemporary philosophers would cavalierly reject value-statements as meaningless expressions of emotion not subject to any kind of rational debate, as A. J. Ayer had done, contemporary philosophers generally are well aware of the problematic nature of evaluative assessment that stems from the fact that such assessments must, in addition to calling upon non-evaluative accounts of whatever the object of evaluation might be, also invoke certain principles of value. For, as a matter of fact, different people, in different societies and cultures throughout human history have called on different, incompatible, sets of principles to evaluate and assess forms of social life. Furthermore, very few contemporary philosophers purport to be able to formulate demonstrative arguments establishing which set of principles *ought* to be used in such evaluations and assessments. It follows, inevitably, that a certain relativism is introduced into the process, for assessments will be valid, if at all, only relative to those people who just happen to share the same basic evaluative principles. But if there is an innumerable set of alternative principles, what is the point of evaluating from one particular perspective or of evaluating at all? Such questions pose serious problems for any conception of political theory that hopes to be more than a simply academic clarification of concepts.

The evaluative dimension of political theory generates further problems. While it seems to me misguided to think that there is a line of rigid demarcation between philosophical and non-philosophical questions and arguments, there is no doubt that, traditionally, philosophical investigation has been differentiated from those intellectual disciplines that call upon and put forward claims of a substantive empirical nature requiring experiential evidence for their support. What would actually be involved in any extensive assessment or evaluation of some particular principle of political and social organisation will depend, not only on the particular aspect of political and social organisation in question but also, of course, on the type of evaluative principle called upon. But what might be involved, and why this would be problematic from the perspective of contemporary philosophy, can be easily illustrated. Suppose one undertook an assessment of, say, democratic forms of decision-making utilising a utilitarian-type principle of assessment, which would rank one principle of organisation over another in terms of its greater contribution to general human happiness, or in the classic formulation, its contribution to the greatest happiness of the greatest number. It is patently obvious that such an assessment is going to have to rely upon some very substantive empirical theses concerning the consequences of the implementation and operation of various types of decision-making procedures, and, furthermore, attempt to estimate the consequences of these consequences for the happiness of individual human beings. It is, to say the least, difficult to see how armchair philosophical reflection, no matter what its profundity, could be the appropriate methodology here. It is true that a utilitarian-type principle of evaluation, being of an extreme consequentialist nature, puts the empirical determination of consequences centre-stage. But a moment's reflection is sufficient to establish that, irrespective of what measure of value we choose, very little serious assessment of principles of political and social organisation is going to be possible without thorough, and thoroughly informed, investigation of real-life political and social structures.

The problem of identifying the tasks and the appropriate methodology of political theory is exacerbated by a historically understandable but a theoretically unjustifiable carelessness of terminology, in which traditional political thought is referred to indiscriminately as either 'political theory' or 'political philosophy'. No harm would be done by such conflation if the term 'philosophy' was being used in a vague, non-technical sense that used to be common. But if, as is almost inevitable in a contemporary context, the word is taken as referring to a fundamentally non-empirical mode of reflection, the designation of traditional political thought as, exclusively, 'political philosophy' is seriously misleading. As mentioned above, the conflation is historically intelligible in that almost all the major traditional political theorists, from Plato and Aristotle on, were also major philosophers, in the modern technical sense of that term. And, of course, their reflections on politics contain elements that are what we would still call 'purely philosophical'. But that is not all they contain.

As a case in point, take the example of the political writings of Aristotle, from antiquity to the present day one of the most famous and influential political theorists. Aristotle was certainly a 'philosopher' in the modern, narrow, sense of that term. But it is well known that along with the other members of his school, on the basis of extensive and systematic empirical research, he produced detailed descriptive accounts of the constitutional political systems of no fewer than 158 Greek states, of which *The Athenian Constitution* is the only extant example.[5] And in a famous passage at the end of the Nicomachean Ethics in which Aristotle is beginning to take up explicitly political questions, he says:

> We should look at my own work *Collected Constitutions* and see from these what kind of procedures do in fact keep states and separate constitutions in going order, and what are those which bring them to a standstill, also what are the reasons why some states are well-run and others are not. When these matters have been examined, we should, I think, be better able to get an all-round view of such questions as what is the best type of constitution? What is the arrangement and structure of each type of constitution? What are their established codes of law and morals?[6]

Two things are evident from this passage; firstly, that the types of investigations into political and social structures that Aristotle is here referring to are not of a narrowly 'philosophical' nature; rather they are solidly empirical, and in addition to descriptive accounts are searching for empirically discernible structures and causes. Secondly, for Aristotle such investigations are an integral part of his political theory, which, consequently, cannot be understood as, exclusively, political philosophy, in the modern technical sense of 'philosophy'. But if political theory is not to be identified with political philosophy, what is political theory and what role does philosophy, in the more limited sense, play in it?

All of these problems, confusions and questions make it imperative, before proceeding to our examination of the political theory of democracy, to begin by giving a fuller account of what political theory is or ought to be, what its central concerns are and what the appropriate methods of investigation might be.

To understand the nature of political theory it is necessary to see it as, no matter how abstract or purely philosophical certain moments of it may be, essentially praxis-oriented. Its *raison d'être* and its very unity and identity consist not in the existence of an integrated set of phenomena that prove subject to a series of unified explanations, as in the case of a theoretical science such as physics, but rather in its role as, at least in intent, a directive influence on a set of unified human practices. I am drawing, in the above statement, on the Aristotelian distinction between a 'theoretical' and a 'practical' intellectual discipline.[7] A theoretical science, as Aristotle would have understood it, has as its single internal purpose the production of understanding through explanation of some unitary dimension of reality that proves subject to understanding by an integrated set of explanatory principles. A practical discipline is best understood as the intellectual dimension of a *techné*, where a *techné* is identified with a complex of human practices oriented to the achievement of some distinctive type of goal.[8] *Techné* ranges over everything from the set of skills required to play a musical instrument to medical practice. The central purpose of a practical intellectual discipline is the formulation of the principles that ought to be embodied in its associated *techné* or set of goal-oriented practices. There are many important dimensions of knowledge as practical that need not detain us here (such as, for example, the fact that its conclusions will always be 'inexact' and conditional, because individual instances of its associated actual practice will necessarily have to take place in widely differing circumstances, not all dimensions of which will be able to be anticipated 'in theory'). For our purposes, the most important features of a practical intellectual discipline, such as I am claiming political theory to be, are threefold. Firstly, it is essentially normative; its whole purpose is to formulate principles for the direction of action, to specify, that is, the norms that should govern its associated practice. Secondly, the formulation of such norms will be radically incomplete unless it is based on an experientially grounded understanding of the relevant dimensions of the concrete practices it is meant to direct. And thirdly, particularly when we are concerned with practices that have complex goals, these relevant dimensions can be many and diverse, resulting not just in the necessarily empirical substantive aspect of the discipline being integral, but also in the intellectual diversity of resources that need to be called upon. A good illustration of these three points is given by considering the academically respectable discipline of architecture.

Suppose one were to take a selection at random of some of the courses modern architectural students are required to study. One might be forgiven, at first, for thinking that they were studying some peculiar mixture of courses in theoretical science and mathematics; or, if you hit on the right ones, courses in the philosophical analysis of the aesthetics of large structures and the history of art; or some inexplicable combination of all of these. But, of course, the combination is perfectly understandable once it is realised that the students are not studying some one theoretical discipline, or a random selection of parts of different theoretical disciplines. Architecture as an intellectual discipline has its point and purpose in an associated complex of human practices, the designed construction of buildings. It also gets its constitutive identity from these practices and their aims. It is essentially normative, formulating the principles that should underly the practice. But the formulation of norms and principles is not just a question of abstract legislation for architectural practice. The normative dimension is itself ultimately regulated by the kind of demands people put on buildings and by the resources (including knowledge and skills) that builders have available. The two factors operating conjointly determine the substantive empirical intellectual disciplines that will be relevant to architecture itself. Questions that could be asked in a purely theoretical, non-practical context, (such as 'How much stress without breaking could a beam of a certain material, of certain dimensions bear?') become relevant to architecture if certain demands are being put on buildings and certain techniques and resources are potentially available. Though the two factors operate conjointly, evidently the demand factor is more fundamental; it is what makes various potential resources and techniques relevant in the first place. The complexity of the demand factor is also what renders the relevant intellectual resources that architecture has to draw on extremely diverse, a diversity that includes not only the 'hard' disciplines of physics, chemistry and mathematics but also philosophy, aesthetics, psychology and economics, to mention only the most important. A brief, cursory identification of the main categories of demand people place on buildings and their construction will illustrate this point. These categories would include, as the more prominent ones, the structural, the aesthetic, the functional and the economic. Furthermore, each of these categories is itself internally complex. Take, for example, the functional demands placed, in a modern context, on one particular type of building, namely, a house. People do not just 'live' undifferentiatedly in a house; they eat, sleep, relax, entertain, work, study, pursue various leisure activities, raise children and so on. A really well-designed house would attempt to meet these demands in a balanced way, that would also be integrated with the other types of demands. Consequently, good house design, from a functional perspective, must begin from a partly sociological, partly psychological, partly ergonomic analysis of these 'goals' of house usage and their interrelationship and prioritisation. The diversity of disciplines that a fully articulated architectural theory would have to draw on is evident. But it is not yet obvious that there is a 'philosophical' dimension. This is mainly dictated by the example we took and the perspective we viewed it from. With a house, most people are prepared to let its regulating functionality be consumer-led. If people do not want to use houses to entertain, then the construction of houses will be different. And no theoretical issues are raised by what we might call the optional alternative uses of houses. But if we think of other types of building, if we think of the external public dimensions of any building and if we think of buildings *en masse*, central questions of architectural practice are raised of a moral, aesthetic and environmental nature that are clearly philosophical. Admittedly, the ones discussed most by architectural theorists have been the philosophical aesthetic questions, but moral issues of resource allocation, city and rural planning, conservation and environment are becoming unavoidable questions for architectural theory. Of course, in practice, (and often in the formulation of theory) these questions are avoided by the simple expedient of accepting today's conventional wisdom, and if *de facto* goals, norms and standards are simply unconsciously accepted, the problems of design and construction become purely instrumental, technical problems in which the empirical dimension of architectural theory as based on mathematics and the physical sciences comes to dominate the discipline.

But a fully articulated architectural theory would logically require three moments or levels; the fundamental level would consist in the critical formulation and examination of the ultimate goals of construction, which goals, as already suggested, derive primarily from the demands people place on buildings. But a formulation of goals, even in quite specific terms, is a very different matter to the specification of the intrinsic features of structures that would enable them to approximate to the realisation of goals. It is one thing, again to take a 'homely' example, to postulate that a kitchen should be ergonomically efficient with respect to the preparation and presentation of food of certain quantities and types; it is quite another to specify the intrinsic features of a room, in terms of size, furnishings, light and layout that would render it so ergonomically efficient. The third moment consists in the specification of particular strategies and actions whereby that type of end-product can actually be constructed. In general terms, then, what is at stake is (a) the identification of end-goals, (b) the specification of the intrinsic features of structures enabling them to realise those end-goals and (c) articulation of concrete strategies of action that would bring to realisation those structures.

My thesis is that political theory should be seen as a practical intellectual discipline of exactly the same overall nature as architecture. In fact, the analogy is even closer. The associated practice of architectural theory is the design and construction of buildings; the associated practice of political theory is, of course, 'politics', in the broad sense that includes the constituting of fundamental structures of community life as well as any attempts to affect the day-to-day patterns of organised social life. Politics is essentially a second-level and, in a sense, parasitic practice. People have goals and aims and, just as it is assumed that the realisation of those goals and aims can be facilitated or hindered by the structures in which they live and work, so it is assumed that the structures of their co-operative life can facilitate or hinder the realisation of human happiness and well-being. Furthermore, just as in the case of buildings, it is assumed (by all except extreme anarchists) that appropriate structures of co-operative life, at least in some of their dimensions, will not emerge and operate spontaneously and so will demand the second-level activity of politics, concerned with the explicit structuring of patterns of community life, which second-level activity is itself likely to be organised and structured, rather than random and *ad hoc*. If we make the further reasonable assumption that the organisation of the political level, particularly its core, the making and enforcing of binding collective decisions, will have an important impact on the chances for the achievement of human well-being by members of a community, we can begin to get an idea of the area of concern for political theory. In short, it consists in the normative appraisal of patterns of social and, in particular, political activities in terms of their impact on human well-being.

This returns us directly to the problems with traditional political thought identified by analytic philosophers. Can philosophy as such have any particular competence in such appraisals? Simplifying matters, we could say that there are two main dimensions to political theory as so envisaged; firstly, the establishing of the appropriate 'goals', both of community life and the politically directive dimension of it, which goals will determine the relevant norms of appraisal; and, secondly, the study of actual or possible forms of social and political organisation with regard to their contribution, positive or negative, to the achievement of the goals. Modern philosophers, particularly those influenced by the analytic tradition, will not pretend competence in the area of legislating what the goals of life in general and social life in particular *ought* to be; that, surely, is the province of the political ideologue, the poet or the prophet. If it is argued that there is still a diminished role for what we might call 'hypothetical' political theory, in which certain goals or norms of appraisal are, *de facto*, accepted as the basis for an admittedly conditional assessment of political and social structures, the putative political philosopher is caught on the other horn of the dilemma; rational argumentation is here possible, but its form seems to be, definitively, simply empirical, falling in the province of the social sciences.

I will take up this second claim first. I have already insisted that such appraisals must, in fact, have a thoroughly empirical dimension. What I want to argue now, however, is that this empirical dimension, even if it is understood as producing only conditional assessment in terms of *de facto* accepted goals, is inseparable from and must be continuously informed by a philosophical dimension. There are two basic reasons for this; the first is concerned with the process of setting out the postulated goal or norms and the determination of precisely how and what empirical research would enable us to decide whether a particular policy or aspect of social or political organisation was in accordance with the norms or having a positive or negative impact on the achievement of the postulated goals. Unless the postulated goals were so ludicrously narrow as to render appraisal with respect to them irrelevant to anyone, unavoidable problems of a philosophical nature will accompany and inform the whole enterprise. Let me illustrate this by referring to a principle that has played a central role in most political ideologies since at least the end of the eighteenth century and is continually appealed to in real life contemporary political debate, namely the principle of 'equality', the principle that, formulated deliberately vaguely at first, no person or group of persons is, because of race, gender, age, appearance, etc. worth less than any other person or group. Now, remember, we are not concerned to question the acceptance of this principle as an appropriate norm for judging societies, nor are we even concerned with how far this principle should be limited by other possible values, goals or norms. We are simply postulating it as a basis for a conditional assessment. Can an empirical researcher go ahead directly to design tests that will decide how various alternative policies or political and social arrangements fare with regard to respecting and promoting 'equality'? The answer has to be a resounding 'No'; for what, exactly, would empirical research be looking for, what precisely is it supposed to test for? Not only, obviously, must this question be answered, but the attempt to answer it will throw the whole area into profound philosophical dispute.

Some political theorists[9] have argued, for example, that equality as a goal or aspiration of a society should be identified with equality before the law, equal legal status; so that, if we want to determine empirically how far any given society has progressed towards the achievement of equality, our research must be into the laws of that society, and at most into their implementation and practice. Others have insisted, however, that a person's status and life-chances are affected by much more than legal provisions and can be subjected to discriminatory practices falling well outside of the legal; so a person could have equal legal status but no real equality at all. Still further arguments have claimed that equality of status and life-chances, equality of the basic opportunities to achieve one's life goals must be interpreted in more positive ways; not simply as the absence of discriminatory practices but as the positive presence of the substantive preconditions of action. If large sums of money are required to obtain education, then inequality of financial resources will produce inequality of educational opportunity, even if there is a complete absence of legal and extra-legal discriminatory practices and attitudes. So, should equality be interpreted as full, substantive equality of opportunity, the provision of absolutely 'level playing fields' to use the currently favoured metaphor? But how level must a playing-field be to be really level? Should members of a group that has been disadvantaged and subjected to discrimination for generations be given a head-start by positive action programmes if real equality of opportunity is to be achieved? Or is this not subjecting other people to unequal treatment simply because they have been unlucky enough to be born in a group whose previous members in the past have been positively advantaged? Perhaps 'equality' should be interpreted, anyway, not as equality of opportunity but as equality of outcome? In the first place, unless we were to interpret equality of opportunity in a static and wholly unrealistic sense as being meaningfully measurable at an instantaneous moment in time, once we have begun interpreting that equality of opportunity substantively, it is debatable whether we can in fact separate it from outcome; for if outcomes, for whatever reason, are vastly unequal, along dimensions that affect opportunity, the two interpretations cannot usefully be distinguished. Secondly, could a society claim to respect and have achieved equality if, after having levelled the playing field it simply shrugged its shoulders at the plight of those who have, through no fault of their own, stumbled and ended up living lives of misery, deprivation and degradation? But if it is equality of outcome we are measuring, what constitutes that equality? It cannot, of course, be identity of outcome. Different people have vastly differing needs and perhaps we should interpret equality as equality of need-satisfaction. But what if some people have wildly extravagant aims that result in their needing far more resources than anyone else? Are they being treated unequally if they are not provided with everything that they need? How do we measure degrees of need-satisfaction anyway?

It should be evident by now that any attempt to forge ahead with empirical measures of degrees of equality independently of serious and searching answers to the above philosophical questions will inevitably produce appraisals that are naive in the extreme and, possibly, totally misleading. The idea and the ideal of equality are profound and complex; they embody deep and wide-ranging human aspirations and valuations and are embedded in whole ways of understanding oneself, society and the world at large, so that they are unintelligible in their true import and implications except as set against a background of understanding and self-understanding of a society and culture. The task of articulating possible political norms is not one that can be fulfilled either by simple empirical procedures or by the formulation of abstract semantic rules for the correct use of the relevant words. It is a task of reflective self-understanding that needs to be both philosophically sophisticated and empirically informed; political theory, even in its limited moment of merely formulating possible norms, must be a continuous symbiotic unity of many diverse forms of understanding directed by the overall philosophical goal of critical and reflective self-comprehension.

Even if one were to eschew conditional appraisal in terms of admittedly philosophically problematic norms such as equality, or justice, freedom, well-being and so on, and satisfy oneself with more piecemeal appraisals of policies and institutions by reference to narrower, more concrete goals, such as lowering the crime rate, ameliorating the unemployment situation and the like, it would still be my claim that such appraisals would have an unavoidable and integral philosophical dimension. I will illustrate this by referring to one central aspect of a famous and influential work of twentieth-century democratic theory, Joseph Schumpeter's *Capitalism, Socialism and Democracy*, to which we will be returning in later chapters.[10]

Schumpeter's concern, as far as it is relevant to our present argument, was to demonstrate the superiority of one particular form of democracy, the form that has come to be known as 'democratic elitism', in which the role of the people is reduced to simply electing leaders in free, competitive elections, without any pretensions to a more direct, continuous and participatory stance. One of Schumpeter's arguments in favour of the superiority of this type of leadership democracy centred on a particular substantive, empirical claim, namely, that no matter how intelligent and competent ordinary people were in their private life and their chosen area of professional expertise, when it came to politics such people would be only mildly interested and would lack any real competence. As Schumpeter states:

> Thus the typical citizen drops down to a lower level of mental performance as soon as he enters the political field. He argues and analyses in a way which he would readily recognise as infantile within the sphere of his real interests. He becomes a primitive again. His thinking becomes associative and affective.[11]

Schumpeter backs up and elaborates this claim by numerous references to crowd psychology, the Freudian 'unconscious', the roots of the irrational in human life and so on. It is worth noting, to begin with, the structure of Schumpeter's argument. Firstly, he has a particular functional criterion for appraising decision-making procedures; one procedure is superior to another if it, in general, produces better decisions. That does not get us very far, however, unless we have a criterion for determining what a good decision is. For our present argument we can simplify matters by imagining that we have only a very narrow, concrete concern, say, reducing the level of unemployment, and postulating that a better decision would be one that had a more desirable impact on the unemployment level. We have now not only a definite criterion to judge decisions, and consequently, decision-making procedures against but also one whose articulation is not philosophically problematic. The business of appraisal is reduced to studying the impact on the unemployment level of particular decisions and decision-making procedures. This study is simply a matter of empirical research. Schumpeter claims that good decisions are not likely without sustained interest, application and professional competence. On this issue we might agree with him. Secondly, as noted above, he goes on to assert that this interest, application and competence is not to be found in the typical citizen. Suppose Schumpeter were right about this (and, seemingly, establishing whether he is right is a matter of social research), is that the end of the argument?

In a noteworthy critique of Schumpeter's democratic elitism, Graeme Duncan and Steven Lukes argued, among other things, that there was a vicious circularity in this part of Schumpeter's thesis, deriving from the fact that Schumpeter uses an overly static and non-interactive theory of human nature.[12] Furthermore, there is even evidence that, on a general level, Schumpeter himself would accept the interactive theory favoured by Duncan and Lukes; he simply fails to notice its relevance and implications for this section of his argument. Schumpeter claims, as we have seen, that the typical citizen lacks interest, application and competence in the political field. But rather than assume that this is an unchangeable 'law of nature', is it not plausible to suggest that this incompetence and apathy derives from the elitist, non-participatory nature of contemporary political systems? If no demands are made on the ordinary citizen, if no opportunities are provided for active involvement, might not this result in the atrophy of whatever motivation and potential competence there might be? Apathy and incompetence might be a product of elitism, rather than a permanent justification for its continued existence. Schumpeter himself notes how many people are, in fact, perfectly sensible and rational, prepared and able to devote time and energy to detailed critical analysis of arguments in spheres of their life in which, because they have responsibility, they have a heightened 'sense of reality'. Perhaps their lack of this 'sense of reality' when it comes to politics should have been seen by Schumpeter to be connected with the lack of responsibility deriving from virtual exclusion from the political process.

There are two aspects of the Duncan and Lukes critique that are particularly relevant to our present concerns. Firstly, rather than a straightforward dispute over 'the facts', their argument concerns the circularity and possible inconsistency in Schumpeter's analysis, a typical critical, philosophical line of analysis. More importantly, the charge of circularity is based on the questioning, not of the immediate facts of the case, but of the fundamental background concept of human nature that Schumpeter is employing. Even in the absence of Duncan and Lukes' intervention, the philosophical dimension of Schumpeter's argument is evident. It occurs in a section that is significantly entitled 'Human Nature in Politics' and raises issues of the broadest philosophical nature concerning rationality, human attributes, the structure of the psyche and its operation. My general point is that even when we are appraising institutions in a fairly narrow, concrete perspective that does not itself raise philosophical issues, the empirical dimension of social research and analysis will continually bring into play and call into question fundamental background concepts, the critical analysis of which will give political theory an unavoidable philosophical dimension. So even if political theory is reduced to the conditional appraisal of institutions in terms of postulated goals and norms, it will still, necessarily, be that integration of philosophical and empirical analysis that I identified. The philosophical dimension would, of course, come more to the fore if we contended that political theory should go beyond this limited, hypothetical assessment; if, that is, we assigned to it the task of critical reflection on the norms and values themselves as appropriate for social evaluation. But if, as most analytic philosophers have argued, we cannot rationally demonstrate the unique moral correctness of any particular version of fundamental value or human well-being, is there any role for full-blooded normative political theory? My contention is that there is, and that it is precisely in this area that we have witnessed the most important renaissance of political theory, though, as suggested earlier, it is a renaissance that somewhat lacks a fully self-conscious rationale.

If normative assessment were to be identified with demonstrating the unique moral correctness of something, then, perhaps, traditional normative political theory would be impossible. But this is a too narrow view of the tasks of justification and evaluation in political theory.

There are, I would claim, four major dimensions of substantive normative political theory where rational argumentation and analysis are both possible and of the utmost importance, and can put forward considerations of great significance for making sensible and rational choices of political and social goals and principles. The first of these is a natural extension of the type of broad analysis of the meaning and implications of political goals or norms that I earlier argued would be a necessary dimension of the conditional assessment. However, there the purpose was simply to be clear about what empirical research in such conditional assessments should be testing for, whereas here the purpose of the analysis is to highlight features of such goals or norms that might be important for their desirability as guiding principles of appraisal and action. That such analysis can affect our evaluation of possible principles derives from the fact that it can bring to the fore implications in practice, background assumptions, the interrelations with other values and principles, all of which might be important determinants of our choice of principles. To illustrate this point, I will refer briefly to two famous pieces of contemporary political theory, each of which has at its core an analysis of the meaning of a possible principle but has, also, implications concerning the desirability of the principle as a basis for political action.

In the process of attempting to identify more precisely the meaning and implications of equality and liberty as political goals, many modern political theorists, most notably, perhaps, F. von Hayek, have claimed to have discovered an important tension between the two ideals and an incipient internal contradiction in the ideal of equality if it is interpreted as a commitment to equality of outcomes and substantive equality of opportunity.[13] The analysis focuses on liberty and begins by arguing that liberty as a political value is constituted by a complex of basic rights; in general, by rights to live as one chooses within the bounds of law and morality. Central among these rights is the right to acquire and dispose of economic goods. Given the plausible assumption that in the exercise of these rights people will make different choices with different intended outcomes certain consequences are inevitable, primarily the emergence of inequality of outcomes and inequality of substantive opportunity. Certain people are going to choose to be more parsimonious than others, more concerned with the efficient and productive employment of economic assets. Consequently, even if, at some notional point, we began with absolute equality of assets and opportunity, inequalities, as noted, will almost inevitably result. Particularly important for equality or inequality of opportunity is the right to dispose of economic assets. Most people will, naturally, be concerned with the welfare of their children and might choose to use their economic assets to provide for the best available health-care and education. They might also choose to give their children as they grow up a substantial financial helping-hand. All of this will obviously produce significant inequalities of opportunity. But if we gave basic priority to maintaining equality of outcome and opportunity, we could do so only by continually infringing some people's basic rights and liberty. Furthermore, it can be argued that not only does this not respect individual liberty, it is not even consistent with the principle of equality itself. Equality can mean, of course, equality of outcome and opportunity, and these things might be to some extent, valuable. But more basically, equality must be equality in fundamental rights, because it is by reference to equality in rights that one would justify whatever equality of outcome and opportunity one was aiming for. The point is, it is claimed, that giving unconditional priority to equality in these latter areas involves the infringement of equality in basic rights.

I am not claiming that the above challenge to the pursuit of equality is conclusive, but it is a serious challenge that a robust egalitarian has to meet and it stems, precisely, from claims concerning the meaning of equality and liberty, which claims, as can be seen, have important normative consequences.

My second example comes from Isaiah Berlin's famous *Four Essays on Liberty*, in particular, his distinction between positive and negative freedom.[14] People are negatively free when their actions are not subject to constraint or coercion by others; it is called 'negative freedom' because, in essence, it consists simply in the absence of such constraint, nothing being implied about the positive ability to do anything. That is, of course, the province of positive freedom, which is said to consist in people having the power to do various things. The basic point of distinguishing the two types of freedom lies in the thesis that negative freedom alone is only one, among many, preconditions of genuine free action, of a normal human life in which people's behaviour is a manifestation of free choice. Take the extreme example of a person paralysed, metaphorically, by neuroses and depression. Such a person may totally fail to act to achieve the many goals and aims that they have, not because they are subject to constraint and coercion by others, but because they lack certain internal preconditions of free, rational choice and action. The appeal of the idea of positive freedom is not, however, rooted solely in reflections on such 'extreme' cases. Rather, as Berlin himself argues, it stems from certain very common experiences concerned with self-control, or more accurately, lack of self-control. Now talk about self-control is very ordinary and widespread, but, it can be argued, it actually implies a profound and deep-seated conception of the self. For if, in the absence of interference by others, people can still be said to lack self-control in their life, this implies, firstly, a bifurcated image of the person, in which one dimension of the self can control or fail to control another dimension of the self. But more importantly it implies an evaluative ordering of these dimensions, according to which one side of the self is lower than, and ought to be controlled by, the other side. There are certain philosophical perspectives in which such assumptions are central. Take, for example, Plato, in whose work Berlin finds an early version of the ideal of positive freedom. In *The Republic* Plato argued that the human psyche was constituted of three independent sources of motivation, usually translated as reason, spiritedness and appetitive desires.[15] Furthermore, Plato was convinced that there existed an objective realm of eternal truths and ideals and that the only valuable life for human beings was one based on a full and rational understanding of such truths and ideals, which of course depended, in the first place, on reason being in control of the other dimensions of the psyche. If people's lives were dominated by irrational desire, they were 'unfree', in the now time-honoured phrase they would be slaves to their passions. Since Plato believed that there was a tendency for the irrational to be dominant in most people's lives, he concluded that a system of government such as Athenian democracy, which was based on and encouraged freedom, in the sense that ordinary Athenians were given control over their own destiny and their lives, resulted in 'unfreedom'. Genuine freedom and a worthwhile life for everyone were only possible when ordinary members of the State were unquestioningly subordinated to the rule of a wise elite, in whom reason, informed by the eternal standards, ruled.

Freedom, 'eleutheria' was an important value in ancient Greek culture, not least because its basic meaning was as the opposite of 'douleia', which meant literal slavery.[16] To be free was to be not a slave. It was generally recognised, however, that the important thing about slavery from the point of view of freedom was the coercive subordination to the master's will, and one could be coercively subordinated to the will of another while not, technically, being a slave. Consequently, the term 'douleia' became metaphorically extended to broader forms of coercive subordination to the arbitrary will of another, particularly to political subordination. And hence the correlative term 'eleutheria' was extended, particularly in Athenian democratic culture, not just to the free as distinct from the literal slave, but to the citizen who was not subject to political subordination. Plato is inviting us to extend the two terms further, by an extension of slavery to slavery to the irrational dimension of the self. Whereas the first extension is unproblematic, the second is highly contentious; firstly, because it is made possible only by the debatable theses that there are radically divergent 'parts' of the self and that one of these parts is evaluatively superior to the other. That second thesis is itself grounded on the further assumption of an objective basis for evaluative ordering in general.

The second contentious feature of the extension of the two related terms, freedom and slavery, consists in its implications for the relationship between the positive and the negative dimensions of freedom. It might have looked, to begin with, that positive and negative freedom were two necessary and complementary dimensions of 'freedom', negative freedom being an essential precondition of full freedom. Under analysis such as Plato's, however, it emerges that negative freedom can conflict with positive freedom, and, it is implied, since negative freedom is only justifiable as a precondition of full rational self-determination, when it does so conflict it can be justifiably suppressed, in the very name of freedom, which is, to say the least, paradoxical.

I have been content, so far, to let my account of these purported analyses of equality and liberty and the dimensions of freedom merely to suggest the normative implications, without attempting to identify precisely how those normative implications emerge from the analyses. Turning now to this task will both make explicit the methodology of this first type of substantive normative dimension of political theory and also provide a transition to the next dimension, which, to some extent, overlaps with the first.

There are three main ways in which, as our discussion illustrates, what begins as pure analysis can generate normatively relevant considerations. Firstly, as exemplified particularly by our discussion of positive freedom, questions can be raised about the acceptability of a norm or principle by demonstrating that on analysis the principle is only meaningful against a background of theoretical assumptions that are themselves questionable and open to debate. Anyone questioning the thesis of a bifurcated self and the evaluative superiority of one dimension of the self as grounded on the existence of an objective order of absolute values will find the prioritising of positive freedom untenable. Secondly, as both examples illustrate, analysis can bring into the open latent contradictions and inconsistencies. If an account of the meaning of equality and liberty such as Hayek gives is correct, it is clearly inconsistent to be unconditionally committed to substantive equality and liberty. One will have to choose which value is more fundamental and will limit the pursuit and implementation of the other. This is also the case with positive and negative freedom.

If we look again at Berlin's treatment of this tension, we will see clearly the third way in which normatively relevant considerations emerge. Berlin is clearly suspicious of positive freedom as a political ideal, not only because the ideal is meaningful only in the context of a world-view that he finds unacceptable but also because the acceptance of the ideal of positive freedom leads to a subordination of negative freedom to that ideal, which subordination can, as in the case of Plato, lead to a rejection of the value of negative freedom completely. The reason why this in itself raises doubts about the acceptability of the principle of positive freedom lies in the implicit priority given to negative freedom. In Berlin's evaluative framework negative freedom is clearly basic. Allowing for the rightful subordination of it to other values, even the value of positive freedom, would introduce the possibility of dangers too horrible to contemplate. What Berlin's analysis suggests is that holding to the more fundamental value of negative freedom involves rejecting the initially, perhaps, attractive idea that the fundamental value in this area ought to be the principle of positive self-determination. The argument is a typical example of what has come to be known as non-foundational moral argument, which, I would claim, is the second dimension of substantive normative political theory.

The basic claim of non-foundational theories is that even if one accepts the impossibility of formulating a universally valid, value-neutral philosophical proof of the superiority of some particular system of values, that does not entail the end of all serious substantive evaluation. There are two main forms of non-foundational assessment. The first is based on the plausible assumption that a set of values is going to be more than a simple aggregate of hermetically sealed principles, all of the same status or order of importance. On the contrary, an evaluative framework is likely to aspire to some degree of integration and internal consistency, and in addition, is likely to discriminate among its evaluative commitments, identifying some as far more basic and important than others. This opens up the possibility of identifying and articulating our most basic evaluative commitments and evaluating other putative elements of our normative framework in terms of those basic commitments. This, I would claim, is precisely what Isaiah Berlin is engaged in in his analysis of the meaning and relationship between positive and negative freedom. It is also the type of enterprise that is exemplified by works such as Robert Nozick's *Anarchy, State and Utopia*.[17] Nozick is not claiming to be able to demonstrate the truth of his fundamental assumption that human beings are the possessors of certain basic rights. What he is claiming, however, is that conceiving of human beings as characterised by a schedule of 'natural rights' is a fundamental element of our Western, twentieth-century evaluative framework, and further, that this conception, when articulated as Nozick articulates it, implies the moral objectionability of certain widely espoused conceptions of 'justice' and certain ideals of political organisation and action. To put it more positively, Nozick claims that if human beings are thought of as bearers of certain inalienable natural rights, we can go on to demonstrate the moral correctness of a particular set of political principles, namely the principles of extreme libertarianism. This demonstration of the moral superiority of libertarianism, even if valid, is, of course, conditional; but the conditionality is of a far different kind to the conditionality of that political assessment we referred to earlier as 'diminished political theory'. It pushes the frontiers of conditionality back from the postulation of specific principles of political assessment to an assessment of those principles themselves in terms of certain alleged fundamental values and normative commitments of our moral outlook.

The second form of non-foundational theory is more profound and more contentious. It is based on a rejection of one aspect of value theory that had become almost the universal orthodoxy in the analytic tradition, namely the claim that values, whether moral or otherwise, were always attitudes that were logically separable from our basic descriptive account of ourselves and the world, thus not being able to find any justificatory basis in descriptive accounts of ourselves and the world and, hence, being purely 'optional'. Theorists such as Bernard Williams, Michael Walzer and Charles Taylor[18] argue that though values might be logically separable from a *scientific* account of the world, such an account of the world is not itself logically fundamental and, both logically and in practice, has itself to be grounded in our fundamental conceptions of the world as we interpret it in our every day lives. Furthermore, such conceptions of the world and ourselves as persons in the world are inescapably infused with evaluative commitments and qualitative distinctions, without which we could not even conceive of what it was to be a person in the world, which possibility is itself necessary to our consciousness of being a person. To approach the matter from the opposite direction, the idea is that to be a person, to be a self-conscious, knowing, intentional agent in the world necessarily involves having an implicit conception of what a person is, which conception is inextricably evaluative. It will necessarily consist, in large part, of ideas concerning what it is right and wrong to do, what type of behaviour or life is worthwhile or valueless, which ideas themselves will involve evaluative, qualitative discriminations ranging across the 'world' itself. Further, as already stated, such evaluative discriminations will be an inextricable part of our fundamental conceptions of the world. These considerations imply that substantive evaluative issues are inescapable. The stance of value-neutrality, total scepticism with respect to all values, is not logically sustainable. In addition, a direction is given to substantive argumentation about evaluative fundamentals. We can explain, and to that extent justify, our fundamental evaluative commitments themselves by demonstrating their centrality to our fundamental vision of ourselves and the world. Such justifications are not in the nature of a neutral foundation for a specific set of values. Neither is it claimed that only one conception of what it is to be a person in the world is possible. Nor is it thought that any such conception and its integral schema of values is necessarily totally self-consistent, determinate and complete. And it is precisely this latter point that underlies the seriousness of such substantive evaluative analysis and argument. We begin, for example, by trying to explain why freedom is important by tracing the intricate connections between our concept of freedom and our basic understanding of what it is to be human. If we succeed, we demonstrate, at the very least, the impossibility of not taking freedom as a substantive evaluative principle without abandoning something central in our conception of the person. We could, in fact, contemplate that possibility, but only on the basis of offering arguments for transforming our idea of the person, which, if serious, would themselves have to draw on some aspect of what we think to be valuable and worthwhile. And given the possibility (indeed probability) of tensions within evaluative frameworks and conceptions of the world, such arguments are both possible and of the utmost seriousness. I used the example of 'freedom' in the last paragraph so as to allude again to our discussion of Berlin's analysis of positive and negative liberty, because on a deeper level, I would claim, Berlin is engaged in this second type of non-foundational theory.[19] Negatively, he is trying to show that positive freedom, certainly as it is interpreted by Plato, is a morally objectionable ideal because it conflicts, not just with some arbitrarily postulated value like negative freedom, but with our fundamental conception of what it is to be a person. Positively, he is attempting to show the point of negative freedom by demonstrating its centrality to our whole conception of the world and human life. Such arguments can never be ultimately conclusive, but they are unavoidable and have a substantive impact on our appraisal of principles and ideals of political and social organisation.

The third category of normative political theory is of a very different nature, it consists simply of non-moral evaluations, in particular, evaluations in terms of *de facto* individual personal good. This is not the appropriate place for a full analysis of the specific nature of 'the moral realm', except to say that for someone taking a set of values or rules to be moral values or rules they will at least be according those rules an overriding status with respect to other rules and values and an independence from particular *de facto* forms of human subjectivity such as specific desires, goals or aims. On the other hand, there are orders of value that are clearly rooted in, and derive their imperative force from, *de facto* complexes of desires and goals. The point, which is quite simple, though of fundamental importance, is that even for people with a robust system of moral rules and values that they treat with seriousness there will normally be vast ranges of their lives and actions in which choices are made from the perspective of values rooted in explicitly non-universal, 'personal' dispositions, preferences, desires, commitments and so forth. Anything which is an asset with respect to the realisation of such goals and aims will be positively valued, and even though the moral framework will be accorded superior status, such non-moral valuations will be of vital significance to people, for it is usually on the basis of such valuations that people choose and decide on their life-styles, their education, their occupations, their place of residence, their marital and sexual partners, the disposal of the core of their economic assets, and so forth. Now there is no doubt that people can and do evaluate everything from this year's budget right through to political systems as a whole from such 'personal' non-moral perspectives. Despite the fact that such evaluative strategies are both possible and important there is one obvious limitation on the significance of their results, namely that the results will have only personal relevance. It is clear that given that people will have different dispositions, preferences, desires and commitments and that people will be in different situations, what is good from such a non-moral perspective for one, may not be so for anyone else and almost certainly will not be so for everyone else to the same degree. There are, however, at least two types of theoretical approach that offer the possibility of basing evaluation on such personal individual perspectives but reaching conclusions with quite general relevance. The first approach notes simply that one can aggregate individual perspective evaluations and that there is at least the possibility that something can be shown to be a good from every individual perspective, and hence, the aggregated evaluation will be of, quite literally, universal significance. A few remarks should be made about such an evaluative strategy. Firstly, the aggregation in question is, in this context, not meant to refer to some form of mathematical addition of levels of individual satisfaction or well-being. It is evaluations that are being aggregated. From the perspective of person A, x is a good of high priority; *and* it is a good of high priority for B, *and* for C, and so on. Secondly, though scepticism about finding, say, political principles that could be shown to be goods of high priority from the perspective of everyone is in order, the strategy itself is perfectly coherent. Thirdly, if the strategy were successful, its results would be extremely significant, for it would be implied that everyone would have a very strong motivation for choosing such a principle. Fourthly, such evaluations are not necessarily meant to imply a resultant further evaluation from some impersonal, moral perspective. What is good for everyone is not necessarily good in some additional, impersonal sense. In fact, it would be quite possible for someone to be committed to an impersonal, moral framework that evaluated negatively that which had been shown to be good for everyone in the present sense. The moral framework might, for example, condemn certain *de facto* dispositions and preferences as corrupt. Finally, despite scepticism about the success of any specific attempt at evaluation of this type, it should be noted that many political theorists from Hobbes down to David Gauthier have in fact claimed to have successfully produced such evaluations.[20] For obvious reasons, such arguments tend to be based on distinctions between short-term and relatively superficial individual evaluations and evaluations in terms of factors claimed to be of much more fundamental, if not obvious, importance. Hobbes' argument to the effect that the institution of Absolute Sovereignty, where the sovereign has effective power to over-awe all, is in everyone's best interests is typical of such evaluations. Hobbes would admit that in actual practice the rule of any given sovereign will produce differential advantages, some benefiting more than others, some being, in fact, possibly severely disadvantaged. If such an oppressed group were to conclude that they would be better off with a weaker sovereign who could not oppress them as ruthlessly, they would, according to Hobbes, be gravely mistaken. Though a weaker sovereign would lighten the burden of oppression from the sovereign, it would also open them to victimization by their fellow citizens from which they are now protected by the sovereign power that over-awes all. Given the radical and ineradicable egoism of human nature that Hobbes postulates, such victimization would be inevitable and would inevitably initiate a self-perpetuating cycle of distrust, violence and enmity that would, sooner rather than later, undermine society totally and usher in the miserable chaos that is the natural condition of mankind. And the initially oppressed group would now be immeasurably worse off. Consequently, despite first impressions to the contrary, it is in everyone's fundamental interest to preserve the institutions of absolute sovereignty. Of course, hardly any theorist would agree that Hobbes' project of justifying absolute sovereignty by showing that it could be justified to every individual from the perspective of each individual's own good was successfully carried out. The argument would not even get off the ground without the debatable assumption of radical egoism. But Hobbes' failure does not imply the failure of all such projects. This is particularly the case if the project adopts the second approach mentioned above, which consists in weakening the aggregated evaluation, but in a way that still claims that the resultant aggregated evaluation has general significance.

What is meant here by 'weakening' the aggregated evaluation is simply that one aims at less than complete universality; one attempts for example, to show that something, while not a good of highest priority from absolutely every individual perspective, is such a good from most people's perspectives. If nothing determinate is implied about the value of the thing from the perspective of individuals here in the minority, allowing for the possibility that from some of their perspectives the thing in question has a high level of dis-value, then the generality of the significance of the result is destroyed. But a variety of qualifications and subsidiary considerations are possible which, it can be claimed, re-establish general significance, though still in a weaker form than the first strategy would produce if successful.

The first crucial factor here is that, particularly in the context of political theory, one is rarely ever evaluating only from the point of view of current instantaneous effects; the medium- and the long-term are also relevant. And the introduction of the medium- and long-term introduces uncertainty and the necessity of basing evaluations on probabilities. I will illustrate this point by a simple example of a distribution policy concerning a divisible good, such as money. Suppose we are evaluating two alternative policies, A and B, from the perspective of some particular individual X, and policy A is more immediately beneficial in its distributional implications for X. That is not necessarily the end of the matter. Simply from the perspective of X's own individual good, at least two further considerations are relevant. Firstly, X will have to take into account how he or she would evaluate the policies A and B if he or she were in a less advantaged position, because there is some probability of that in the future. Secondly, X will have to take into account such things as the indirect consequences for, say, social stability, of the two distributional policies. A distributional policy which, while not being from the perspective of the individual the best, or even close to the best, in terms of immediate advantages, might nonetheless be from everyone's individual perspective a good policy because it secured a reasonable level of well-being for each. Given the possibility that people may not be able to ensure the permanence of their current advantaged situation or the stability of a system with radically systemic advantage, such evaluations that take into account uncertainties and indirect consequences do have a high level of general significance. This is in itself an important conclusion and we need not spoil our argument by pretending to wring out of it stronger claims than are warranted by it.

The final category of substantive normative appraisal open to political theory is rooted in what Brian Barry refers to as the tradition of thought which claims 'there is a strong connection between morality and impartiality',[21] where the impartial, and hence the morally acceptable, is defined as that which could be justified to all affected, that which anyone affected would accept as reasonable. The basic idea behind impartiality is that no one is advantaged in a way that could not be defended to others who are also affected; as Barry puts it: 'if any other person could not reasonably be expected to accept it in the absence of coercion then the arrangement cannot be morally justified'.[22] This last quotation nicely encapsulates two fundamental problems involved in evaluations from the standpoint of impartiality. Firstly, Barry has elided talk about the impartial into talk about the morally justified. Now, though I would agree with Barry that in our contemporary moral outlook impartiality has become deeply entrenched as a necessary condition of moral justifiability, I would claim, firstly, that it cannot be maintained that it is a sufficient condition and, secondly, that there have been many systems of values that, both to ourselves and their holders, are in many ways recognisable as systems of morality that have not accorded impartiality such a central place. Hence, we cannot unproblematically identify the morally justifiable as such with the impartial. In fact, my own main argument concerning the importance of appraisals from the standpoint of the impartial will not rely on any alleged connection between impartiality and moral justification. The second problem centres on the notion of 'reasonableness'. It is particularly acute because the whole criterion of impartiality is a procedural one, internal to the group of those affected by whatever is being appraised; the impartial is that about which uncoerced consensus could be attained. Not every case of actual consensus or non-consensus can be interpreted as definitive demonstrations of impartiality and partiality respectively. Some people might be prepared to non-coercively consent to a proposal that was relatively disadvantageous to them because of the weakness of their original bargaining position or because they had been subject to (whether intentionally or otherwise) a process of indoctrination that had narrowed their expectations for themselves and induced in them a 'servile' mentality. On the other hand, others may be demanding special favours and refuse to accept what everyone else regards as an impartial solution; does the fact that a partisan minority refuses consent to what everyone else agrees on, because that minority is making unreasonable demands, demonstrate that the proposal is partial? It is for these reasons that a counter-factual element has to be introduced into such a procedural definition of impartiality, resulting in the postulation of an 'idealized' situation. There is nothing wrong in principle with this method, but in the present case it leads to a total indeterminacy in the concept of the ideally impartial; this is particularly damaging if 'the impartial as the result of the idealised debate reaching consensus' is the only criterion for specifying that which is acceptable in human affairs. This is because the idealised element in the situation is supposed to consist in excluding unacceptable, partisan, debating and bargaining conditions. There is, then, a straight circularity in defining the impartial as that which would attract uncoerced consensus in conditions that were impartial. Such a concept of absolute and universal impartiality is, then, fatally flawed.

Despite the unavailability of such a conception of 'ideal impartiality', we do continue to make and argue about judgements of partiality and impartiality, and such judgements carry great force. The obvious precondition of such judgements is a shared set of values and norms that enable us to determine reasonableness in conditions and demands and to unproblematically identify, in a whole range of cases, explicit coercion, duress and more insidious abnormal influence on belief and desire formation leading to serious deviations from what we consider normal individual autonomy. Against such a background, judgements of impartiality or otherwise become possible, having, admittedly, only a conditional and contextual validity. Furthermore, it is not difficult to understand their power. In the first place, the centrality of impartiality in our contemporary moral outlook makes such judgements a special case of non-foundational appraisal; this is all the more important because impartiality articulates the collective implications of human equality; to be morally unconcerned with impartiality, would be to be morally committed to a thesis that assigned greater intrinsic importance and worth to some specific group of people.

There is, however, a non-moral dimension to impartiality that lies simply in the polemical strength of such arguments, even when an implicit appeal to background assumptions of equal human worth is not being made. This polemical force is easy to demonstrate. Suppose two sets of social/political arrangements were, in some particular group of people, being considered and debated; and imagine, further, that one of those schemes was proven, admittedly in a conditional and contextual way, to be partial and partisan, advantaging one sub-group at the expense of others to whom the extra costs could not be justified. The second scheme, on the other hand, was proven not to place any more costs on anyone than on others in any way that could not be justified to everyone. Anyone persisting in supporting the first scheme could only justify their position in a frankly partisan way that would cut no ice with anyone else. Hence the polemical weakness of the first position and the corresponding strength of the second.

If it seems unduly cynical to identify the importance of impartiality with the *ad hominem* polemical strength of appraisals based on it, an alternative mode of formulating the same point will rectify matters. We can classify justifications as belonging to one or other of two fundamental types, the frankly partisan and the general. The frankly partisan type of justification purports only to address a specified group of people, either with regard to moral or impersonal values that they, as distinct from others, happen to share or with regard to interests that they have in common. It is relatively easy to provide such partisan justifications for almost anything. But when a policy, arrangement or principle is subjected to critical theoretical appraisal, when we ask, 'Is it justifiable in comparison to alternatives?', we are adopting the stance of the general. There are possible types of general justification that do not refer to or use impartiality. If there is general agreement on moral norms specific enough to produce a determinate justification of some arrangement, or the arrangement can be shown, in either the strong or the weaker form, to be a high priority good from everybody's non-moral individual perspective, the justifications in question would have the characteristics of generality. But when those forms of general justification are not available, the impartial is the only remaining form of generality. And that is the positive side of its polemical force, which is further strengthened if the requirement of impartiality is itself centrally rooted in the moral framework.

It is not my intention to imply that, in the absence of general justifications of the other two types, that which is impartial is, for everyone, demonstratively and uniquely 'the best', in the sense that we have proven either an overriding obligation or an overwhelming motivation to choose it. People can remain frankly self-interested in the face of the impartial or their moral values might be such that they dictate no compromise, even with the impartial. As in the other three areas of substantive normative theory, what I do claim is that appraisals from the perspective of the impartial generate considerations of extreme importance in the critical analysis of proposed norms, principles and social and political arrangements.

Another way of approaching the definition of political theory and its tasks is to relate it to the notion of a 'political ideology'. Since about the beginning of the eighteenth century organised mass action in pursuit of relatively pre-conceived and systematically formulated goals has been growing in importance. In that context, political theory has often tended to issue in political ideologies. A political ideology is a set of goals and principles propagated and publicised to galvanise and structure mass action in pursuit of the realisation of those goals. Orientation to practice is central. We can define political theory, in a more concrete way than previously, in relationship to political ideology and in so doing re-emphasise its ultimate orientation towards practice, while at the same time being able to specify its tasks more systematically and perspicaciously.

Though the details of a political ideology may remain fairly unspecified in the minds of many of its adherents, a fully articulated political ideology would, typically, operate on three interlocking levels. At the heart of an ideology is what I would call its identifying programmatic core, the set of social and political institutions and principles to which it is committed. It is these that give the focus and identity to political action motivated by the ideology. However, any political commitment that is allegedly ideological will claim that its support for the programmatic core is not just a matter of blind prejudice or partisan self-interest; on the contrary it will be implied that behind the particular political and social arrangements and specific principles that constitute its programme for action there are deeper principles and values that prescribe and justify its more specific commitments. This we can refer to as the evaluative or normative framework of the ideology. Furthermore, any political ideology will operate on a more diffuse third level that I will call the level of its theoretical underpinnings. It will consist of a set of theories, images, hypotheses or assumptions concerning society in its various dimensions, human beings and their nature, the nature of the world in which they live, ranging perhaps as far as overall conceptions of the nature of reality as a whole and the divine. This third level, then, encapsulates a particular vision of human beings, their societies and the world in which they live. It functions in two crucial ways with respect to the lower levels of the ideology. Firstly, it purports to explain and ground the evaluative framework. Just as with the specific political commitments, so with the principles upon which those commitments are based, the claim is that their adoption is not arbitrary; rather, they are grounded in and are explicable by reference to this wider vision of things. The second function relates to the implicit argumentative nature of an ideology. An ideology will, as we have said, claim that its normative framework justifies its specific political commitments; but to be credible it must do more than claim; it must argue, explain and attempt to convince. And all of this, directed as it is to specific forms of social arrangements and their underlying principles, will be possible only against the background of theories, explanatory schemata, hypotheses and other types of account of human beings and those dimensions of society that constitute the focus of any specific ideology. An ideology's attempt to connect values to specific implications may draw on theories of an even broader nature; it may draw on theories of history or even metaphysical and religious accounts of the nature of reality as a whole. Even the pragmatic and programmatically limited ideology, however, will not be able to get by in its attempt to justify its commitments in terms of its values without some background theories and explanatory schemata.

Any intellectual theorising that is directed towards a potential intervention in the articulation of a political ideology, whether its import is supportive or critical, is what I call political theory. In particular, the political theory of democracy consists in the critical investigation of possible democratic ideologies at each of the three levels that a fully explicit ideology must work on. On the first level, often referred to as analytic democratic theory, the task is to establish what, with respect to political and social arrangements, and principles of, particularly, the distribution of power in a community, a democratic ideology is committed to. This is often referred to simply as 'saying what democracy is' or 'defining the meaning of democracy'. As we will see, however, the task is more complex, primarily because we are interested not just in the abstract meaning of words but in the whole range of political and social aspirations, and their inter-connections, which might constitute the overall practical goal of anyone committed to democracy.

I have been implying all along that the three levels of an ideology form an interlocking whole, and it is evident that it would be difficult to say what a democrat is committed to without raising the question of what it is about the preferred political and social arrangements constituting democracy that a democrat finds valuable. The second major task of democratic theory is the critical appraisal of the possible normative frameworks for a democratic ideology. In simple terms: is democracy a worthwhile political goal? How would we attempt to justify democratic arrangements in comparison with possible alternatives? What principles and values might be brought forward to justify a democratic commitment, how are they related to each other and how defensible are they?

As I noted earlier when talking about political ideologies generally, an ideology's claim that its evaluative principles imply a commitment in practice to its programmatic core could only be made good against the background of certain theories and assumptions concerning the relevant dimensions of political and social reality. Paradoxically, in the light of democracy's growth toward unchallenged supremacy as an explicitly avowed political ideology, this third level of democratic theory has had to face in the last hundred years, a series of serious challenges to the adequacy and coherence of its theoretical background. These challenges have been directed to questioning the possibility, and sometimes the desirability, of any close approximation in reality to democratic ideals. They have been based on socio-psychological theories of human capacities and motivation, empirical studies of electoral behaviour and political culture, analyses of the structure of power and domination, accounts of the logic of organisation and collective behaviour and theories of the relationship between the political and economic dimensions of modern society. The final task of any political theory of democracy must be a critical appraisal of these challenges and an attempt to answer the question of whether democracy can be provided with an adequate theoretical grounding.

In summary, democratic theory, as we are going to develop it in this work, is concerned with what democracy implies in practice, whether and how democratic practices can be justified and, finally, whether a commitment to those practices can be provided with a theoretical grounding in adequate and valid theories of human nature and society.

2

What is democracy? The question of method

It has become a common-place of contemporary conventional wisdom from political philosophers to journalists that now, particularly after the collapse of the Communist regimes of the Eastern bloc, democracy rules supreme and unquestionable in the pantheon of political values. But there is a deeply problematic paradox at the heart of this nearly universal acceptance (at least in theory) of the unquestionable value and unique legitimacy of democracy. Everyone purports to be in favour of democracy, but there is little agreement over what democracy is. While the very terms 'democracy' and 'democratic' carry with them the honorific connotations of legitimacy, there are widely divergent and sometimes radically incompatible accounts both of the nature of democracy and of the reasons why democracy is such a desirable form of government. As Robert Dahl puts it in his *Democracy and Its Critics*:

> It may seem perverse that this historically unprecedented global expansion in the acceptability of democratic ideas might not be altogether welcome to an advocate of democracy. Yet a term that means anything means nothing. And so it has become with 'democracy', which nowadays is not so much a term of restricted and specific meaning as a vague endorsement of a popular idea.[1]

Dahl goes on to claim that the democratic tradition has been fed by many diverse and different tributaries, and this has resulted in the tradition being 'a jumble of theory and practices that are often deeply inconsistent'.[2] If even only a part of what Dahl claims is true one might be tempted to abandon the terms 'democracy' and 'democratic' as too irredeemably corrupt. That, however, would be a highly unwise move. The language of democracy is too deeply embedded in contemporary political discourse and is charged with such an enormous polemical force that it has become itself the inevitable and inescapable battleground for much contemporary political debate. If in popular usage 'democracy' is threatening to become little more than a polemical symbol with nothing but an emotivist connotation of alleged legitimacy and laudatory approval, it becomes all the more important for democratic theorists to attempt from the outset to answer as fully and as precisely as possible the question: just what is democracy?

The problem with this question, however, is that it is too deceptively simple. We need to go behind the question as so formulated and ask: what kind of a question is it and what are the appropriate methods for answering it? Most political theorists have by now assimilated the anti-essentialist lessons of modern analytic philosophy. In asking about the nature of something such as democracy, we have no warranty for assuming that there is some objective, timeless essence of democracy existing either in an unchanging realm of Platonic possibilities or as fully and identically embodied in every system of government popularly referred to as 'democratic'.[3] Consequently, the least misleading way of understanding the question is to treat it as a semantic question, a question asking what the word 'democracy' means and has meant. But this too has its dangers; we may be led to think that because we have had in modern languages for the last four hundred years or so the single general term 'democracy' and its equivalents, ultimately deriving from the ancient Greek 'demokratia', there must be a single, quite specifically definable meaning to be stated and described.[4] That belief itself might result in our adopting wholly inappropriate and inadequate methodologies.

The first temptation to be resisted is the etymological one. It is always interesting to trace the historical roots of a word, and it is sometimes enlightening. But it is a straight fallacy to conclude that because the ancient Greeks invented both the word 'demokratia' and the political system they so described, what they meant by 'demokratia' must be a pure and uncorrupted paradigm for what we should (and perhaps do) mean by 'democracy', and for what, as democrats, we should be committed to. Now I happen to believe that democracy in classical Athens, for example, despite certain features that we would nowadays consider totally undemocratic, such as the exclusion from political life of about 85 per cent of the total population, was both as a system of government and as a set of ideals similar in certain general respects to what I will be claiming should be our modern concept of democracy.[5] But that thesis can only be demonstrated by first giving an account of democracy now. If what we mean by 'democracy' now is similar to what the ancient

Greeks understood by 'demokratia', then, but only then, can the historical investigation have contemporary relevance for us. First, though, we must try to establish what we mean by 'democracy', independently of its etymology.

The second danger in treating our question as one about the meaning of the word 'democracy' is that we will treat it as a simple lexicographical issue, to be addressed by looking up a good dictionary that will articulate in a clear and precise manner the single correct meaning of 'democracy' which then *should* be what we take the word to mean, if we want to be using it correctly. There are many reasons why such an approach would be inappropriate and, on its own, wholly inadequate.

Firstly, there is the distinction between a dictionary definition and a conceptual analysis.[6] Even if there were no special and peculiar problems attaching to the language of democracy, a dictionary definition, giving, as it does, usually, only a relatively brief synonymous phrase or two, would fail to unearth the implicit complexity of most, even quite ordinary, concepts. The best way to think of the meaning of a term is as a set of rules determining its use. By definition, a competent native speaker of a language will have assimilated and internalised these rules; but normally the complex of rules governing any specific term will be present only tacitly in a person's practical consciousness. People, by learning through practice a detailed set of rules, are able to perform incredibly complex, rule-governed operations, often without being able, immediately, to articulate the rules in question. The conceptual analysis of a set of terms, such as those that we use in talking about the democratic character of a polity, consists in the attempt to lay bare the fundamental structure of the way that we conceive of a particular area of reality and to render it as intelligible as possible both by explaining its background assumptions and by investigating its necessary implications in varying circumstances. If the term whose meaning we are analysing is a general term, applicable to an indefinite number of particular situations, implying some set of characteristics that these situations have in common, at the centre of the rules determining the meaning of such a term will be an identification of this set of characteristics, together with a specification of those characteristics that would debar us from describing situations by means of the term in question. One method by which we will proceed is by a comparative reflective analysis of a hopefully representative sample of situations, some of which, as native speakers, we would unhesitatingly describe by the word in question, others of which we would judge not to be describable by the word. The purpose of this comparative reflection will be to articulate, as a hypothesis, the crucial principles of comparison implicit in the language-user's readiness to co-classify these and further relevant situations. The hypothesis must be tested by its ability to predict further uses of the word by competent speakers. We will be helped in all of this by our own tacit knowledge as competent speakers. But we can claim no infallibility for our efforts of reflective articulation.

Even an exhaustive and correct identification of the conditions for the accurate use of a word, an identification of what we could call the word's truth/falsity conditions, will, however, only constitute the beginning of that conceptual analysis whose purpose is, as I said above, to lay bare the fundamental structure of the way we conceive of a particular aspect of reality. What we need to investigate is the point or significance of categorising things and situations in this specific way, by relating the particular categorisation to the context of enterprises, both theoretical and practical, in which the word is used, and by relating this particular conceptualisation to other germane and relevant concepts. We need to investigate background assumptions and implications.

I will illustrate this by looking briefly at the language of freedom that we have already examined to some extent in the first chapter. In our ordinary, everyday speech we use the language of freedom unproblematically for the most part. We talk of someone having served a prison sentence being set free, we describe people who hand over £100 to someone holding a gun to their head as acting unfreely or under duress, and so on. Berlin, in his account of negative freedom, tries to capture the common characteristics of such situations by postulating the notion of external constraint. In the end he concludes, however, that we cannot identify something as a possible constraint except by reference to the possible choices that a person might end up making. This is something important about our concept of human freedom that does not become immediately apparent simply from a list of circumstances in which we would describe situations as 'free' or 'unfree'. There is a complex background assumption that gives significance and more precise intelligibility to our classification of circumstances. The assumption is that we are talking about human behaviour, where that behaviour is thought of as having its origin in choices that human beings make. To understand the point of differentiating between 'free' and 'unfree', we need to investigate what it is to choose and why we think that there is something especially valuable and important about chosen actions. Furthermore, 'free' and 'unfree' are only two of the numerous words that we use to describe human choices and actions from this general perspective; we talk about deliberate, purposive, intentional, voluntary, accidental, impulsive, reflex, to mention only the most obvious. For a full understanding of what we mean by 'free' not only must we situate 'free' in the context of an understanding of human behaviour but also we must trace its relationships of implication, inclusion, exclusion, compatibility and so forth with all these other aspects of human action that we conceptualise through this complex semantic field. Neither in the case of 'freedom' nor in the case of 'democracy' would any of this emerge from a simple dictionary definition.

Furthermore, in the case of 'democracy' even the most thorough conceptual analysis would fail to provide an adequate answer to the question 'What is democracy?' as raised by a political theorist. There are several reasons for this, the first being that, in accordance with the interpretations of the tasks of political theory as set out in the previous chapter, the political theory of democracy will be, in the first instance, an identification and critical analysis of what I called the programmatic core of democratic ideology, the whole complex of structures, institutions, procedures, rules and background conditions to which a democrat would be committed. The process of critically specifying this programmatic core will involve far more than abstract conceptual analysis of the meaning of the words 'democracy' and 'democratic'.

Before setting out systematically what further types of analysis will be required, I will illustrate why this must be the case by looking briefly at a problem that is central to democratic theory that we will be returning to later. Most dictionary definitions of 'democracy' begin with an identification of democracy with rule by the people, quite in accordance, in fact, with its ancient Greek etymology, 'demos' meaning 'people' and 'kratein' meaning 'to rule'. The problem that I am concerned with stems from the simple fact that the phrase 'the people' obviously refers to a group. There are certain types of activity that a group of people, precisely as a group or collectivity, can engage in, so that it is literally true to say that that group performed the action in question; for example, four people pushing a car. Each member of the group is doing the thing as described, and the overall effect of the collective action is a resultant of each person's contribution. Can a group of people, particularly 'the People as a whole' in a political community be capable of ruling in this collective sense? To rule is to exercise effective decision-making power from a position of authority over a political community. Ruling, consequently, involves making decisions, choosing between available options. When we are talking about a single person we understand quite well what choosing or deciding involves. But can a group of people decide? Well, we do say of a small group, such as a family, that they decided to do such and such, meaning that the group as a group decided, each participated and the resulting decision was agreed on. But there is something that we know about large groups of people that makes it almost impossible that a large group could be said to decide something in the way that a family might decide. What we know is that though absolute unanimity and consensus is not impossible, it is, in fact, on most issues highly unlikely. It is almost certain that on most matters there will be some disagreement. The very possibility of disagreement means that in the case of group decision-making there is a logical gap between each individual member of the group deciding which of the options to support and the decision of the group, *the* decision to be implemented. A collective decision-making procedure must have a rule that determines the decision to be implemented as a function of the decisions made at the end of the day by each participant. But what rule? There are, in fact, numerous alternatives and choosing which alternative will best implement our idea of democracy is no easy matter. The specification of this crucial element of what we mean by democratic decision-making, which, of course, if not undertaken leaves our notion of democracy radically indeterminate and inapplicable, depends not just on the general facts about the likelihood of disagreement just mentioned, but, as we will see, on certain more specific theses concerning how people will be likely to choose and even on some quite complex mathematical argument. My point here is that we cannot expect to produce a determinate account of what democracy in practice must be merely by an abstract reflection on the general idea of democracy. For a political theorist the question of the nature of democracy must be approached, in fact, on four decreasing levels of generality or increasing specificity.

Firstly, there will be the most general account of what we mean by democratic. Secondly, in the light of the fact that, as we noted above, democracy concerns the exercise of power and decision-making by a group, we will have to identify the specifically democratic structures by reference both to our general understanding of democracy and by reference also to what we know about group decision-making and the possible procedures. Thirdly, though in an extended way we talk about the democratic character of any decision-making procedure, as political theorists we are obviously primarily concerned with democracy on the level of the specifically political, and an identification of what democracy is will have to draw on an account of that power and decision-making that constitutes rule or government over a political community. Fourthly, however, political communities differ in many respects that are crucial to the way the structure of rule must be organised if democracy is to be realised. The organised, specifically political dimension of a community always operates in a wider social matrix that profoundly conditions its functioning. The overall nature of political power is a function both of its internal constitution and the wider social matrix. Consequently, if we are talking about two radically different matrices, what will be required if political power is to be organised democratically, both in terms of internal political structures and background conditions within the social matrix itself, might also be radically different. I will illustrate this point by mentioning two interrelated axes along which political communities can and have differed significantly in ways that centrally affect the conditions for democracy, namely size and media of communication. In ancient Athens the total citizen population entitled to participate in government is estimated by modern scholars to have been between 30,000–40,000.[7] One of the central organs of political decision-making was the Ekklesia or General Assembly of the citizen body, which met, debated on and decided all the important matters of political policy forty times a year. Though every qualified citizen was equally entitled to attend and speak to the Assembly and vote on issues to be decided, the evidence suggests that normal attendance was a little over 6,000. That number of people *can* gather together and listen to whoever wants to speak, consider the issues in hand and decide. If we are thinking of a political community of several million it is not equally feasible for them to be, even electronically, 'gathered together'; if any degree of democracy is to be achieved in such a polity, structures of representation are almost inevitable, structures that were, of course, utterly foreign to the ancient Athenians. Furthermore, the question of what democracy could mean in a large polity can only be answered by the investigation of the function, effect and preconditions of types of representation system. The numerical dimension of the social matrix is seen here to have crucial implications for the structures of democracy.

Related to the question of numbers is that of information. It is easy to see that the ability of a person to be a relatively autonomous, and hence genuine, contributor to a decision-making process is critically dependent on access to relevant information. In a face-to-face society whatever information there is can circulate easily and informally. It is inevitable that in a large society the distribution of information will have to be via some mass medium; it is for these reasons that almost all commentators have noted that, to speak loosely, 'the freedom of the press', not to mention its quality and who controls it, is and must be one of the fundamental elements of a mass democracy.

There will be many other relevant dimensions of the social matrix to consider, but the point here is the methodological one; since how a political system operates will be a function of its internal structure and external environment, an account of what is required for democracy cannot simply be a matter of abstract conceptual analysis but will have to be given by drawing on substantive information and theories of increasing concreteness. The conceptual analysis of our general idea of democracy, while important, can only be one element in a far more complex and substantive procedure.

There are, however, certain features of the way that the word 'democracy' is and has been used that render the task of defining democracy even more problematic. In the quotation cited above from *Democracy and Its Critics*, we see Dahl concluding that the word 'democracy' has lost whatever specific content it might have had, becoming more a term of approval or endorsement of nothing very specific, much like the modern use of the word 'nice', though the weight of approval in the case of 'democracy' is appreciably greater. Dahl might concede that the positive connotations of 'democracy' are, in fact, slightly more restricted firstly, in the domain of relevance of the term and secondly with respect to the type of reason lying behind the positive approbation than is true of a pure approbatory term such as 'nice'. 'Democracy', after all, even at its broadest and most vague, must be referring to some distributional situation among members of a group; and if it implies approval will do so on the basis of some degree of approach to 'equality', in some sense or other. But there is little here for conceptual analysts to get their teeth into. There is, however, one perspective from which it looks as though Dahl is wildly exaggerating; that is the perspective of thinking and sophisticated users of the term, whether they be theorists or political activists. Surely, if we look at what 'democracy' means in these contexts we will encounter a far more specific and precise meaning. And indeed it is true that when we look at both how the word is used and at accounts of its meaning in the works, for example, of political theorists we do find more precision and determinacy. In fact, however, our problems increase rather than otherwise, for along with the greater precision comes greater disagreement. This can be illustrated by looking at the accounts of democracy in the works of three twentieth-century theorists, Joseph Schumpeter, C. B. Macpherson and John Burnheim.[8] In his work *Capitalism, Socialism and Democracy*, Schumpeter, aware that previous writers had understood democracy differently, but claiming that those earlier conceptions were either ultimately incoherent or else wholly unrealistic, produced the now famous, quite precise definition of 'democracy':

> . . . the democratic method is that institutional arrangement for arriving at political decisions in which individuals acquire the power to decide by means of a competitive struggle for the people's vote.[9]

We are given by Schumpeter a precise criterion for deciding when a state is being governed democratically; if governmental office is allocated on the basis of competitive popular elections we have, unproblematically, a democracy. It is this characteristic that all democracies have in common and that non-democratic forms of government lack. Compare this, however, to the understanding of democracy developed by John Burnheim in answering the question 'Is democracy possible?'.[10] Burnheim argues that democracy is possible, but only if the following conditions are realised. Firstly, the nation state and national government must be abolished; any agency of rule claiming multi-competent sovereignty over the lives of people living in a specified territory being inimical to democratic self-government. Secondly, all decision-making must be radically decentralised along functional lines, decisions in distinct issue areas being made by autonomous bodies having competence restricted to their own areas. Thirdly, such bodies must be thoroughly representative of all who are affected by the decisions in question, the representativeness being achieved by selection of members by random lot, rapid rotation and short terms of service.

In some ways C. B. Macpherson's account of democracy is even more radically divergent from Schumpeter's than that of Burnheim. In his work *Democratic Theory: Essays in Retrieval*, Macpherson claims that the maximisation of democracy consists in the egalitarian maximisation of human powers,[11] where power is understood not in the conflictual sense of one person having power over another, nor in the limited sense of a person being able to affect the decisions of a body with the power to implement its decrees, but in the very broadest sense of human potentialities to engage in worthwhile activities. Democracy, according to Macpherson, is only achieved when all members of a community have, in an egalitarian manner, achieved maximum development of their potentialities, intellectual, aesthetic, moral, productive and emotional, to mention only the most important human powers.

Which, if any, of these accounts of the nature of democracy is correct? My claim is that the assumption lying behind that question, specifically that there must be a semantic/analytic method available to us which would allow us to identify a single precise and determinate meaning of 'democracy', is fundamentally mistaken. Failure to realise this leads to the danger of engaging in conceptual and normative legislation under the guise of neutral semantic analysis. There may be some justification for thinking that a term introduced by explicit definition into an artificial language, the users of which impose a strict and rigorous rule of precision and consistency, will have a single meaning constituted by precise and determinate rules of usage identifying in a completely unambiguous fashion the truth/falsity conditions for its application. Words in ordinary usage do not function in this fashion. They are best thought of as indicating a loose, not strictly pre-defined and potentially open set of what Wittgenstein called 'family resemblance' characteristics.[12] Just as we can co-classify a group of people between whom there is a family resemblance, without it being thought that there is a definite set of characteristics that each member of the group possesses identically and to the same degree as each other member, so in ordinary discourse we can operate with classificatory terms that are based on open-ended sets of relatively imprecise characteristics. Not all tables, for example, have the same set of identical characteristics and functions; but a kitchen table is in its structure and usage sufficiently similar to a dining table, which is sufficiently similar to a conference table, which is sufficiently similar to a work table, which is sufficiently similar to a telephone table, and so on, for us to usefully co-classify them. If people have roughly the same interests in the use they make of their classificatory systems, if they have roughly the same kind of experiences, and if no great evaluative weight rests on how something is classified, their personal networks of similarities will coincide sufficiently to underpin a not too ambiguous communication system. But indeterminateness and open-endedness can and do lead to semantic diversity. And semantic diversity cannot be legislated out of existence by linguistic fiat.

There was from the beginning an almost inevitable measure of indeterminateness in the language of democracy; and we should not find this surprising. Let me illustrate this by going back to the earliest extant use of the Greek word 'demokratia' in the works of Herodotus.[13] It was used to describe the system of government in Athens that had been initiated by the constitution of Kleisthenes in 509–508 BC and which was further modified throughout its nearly 200-year existence. Prior to this system of government the ancient Greeks were familiar with several types of government, such as the ancient constitutional hereditary monarchy, forms of aristocracy in which the major offices of state were the monopoly of a small number of noble families, and the self-appointed rule by a single leader, a tyrannos, though the ruler in question was not implied to be a 'tyrant' in the modern sense of that word.[14] The independent city-state of Athens had in fact been ruled by such a 'tyrannos', Peisistratos, in the decades preceding Kleisthenes' constitution. He had come to power via a military coup in a period of social unrest and civil strife. The traditional system of government in Athens, however, had been an aristocracy. There were two main loci of political power; a group of nine 'archons', officers of state appointed on a yearly basis, selected from the small number of noble families, and the Council of the Aereopagos, which was made up of ex-archons who became life members of the Council. Clearly, political power was concentrated in the hands of the nobility.

Kleisthenes' reforms severely curtailed the powers of the traditional officers of state. Furthermore, they instituted a new Council of Five Hundred, appointment to which was yearly by random selection from the citizen body as a whole. The new council had no independent decision-making power; rather it prepared the agenda for the Ekklesia, a general assembly of the people which all citizens were entitled to attend, which made all political decisions directly on the basis of a majority voting procedure. There were many other features of the system of government in Athens which a full description would have to mention.[15] But enough has been said to indicate that compared to the traditional aristocracy the Kleisthenian constitution gave to the ordinary citizens of Athens a really significant degree of political power. It is understandable that observers of these changes such as Herodotus should have thought that this system of government deserved a new name and so coined the word 'demokratia' from the two Greek words 'demos' meaning 'people', more usually 'common people', and 'kratein' meaning 'to rule'. But must those who coined the term have had in mind some highly definite and precise criteria that would unequivocally differentiate a democratic from a non-democratic city-state? Would they have been using the word in such a way as to enable them to determine logically whether Athens would have been more or less democratic if it had given rights of participation to women or non-Athenian resident foreigners? Or whether Athens would have been more democratic if there had been a council of *six* hundred, with *twice* yearly rotations? My suggestion is that the word was used to label states in which the 'demos' had a significant, with all the indeterminacy of that word 'significant', role in government.

When we ask the question: would such a society or political system be more democratic if . . .? we are, because of the modern heavy approbatory connotations of the term 'democracy', implicitly asking: would it be a better, more legitimate, a more consistent adherence to the evaluative principles that lead people to prefer democracy? When such questions are formulated explicitly it becomes obvious that they are substantive normative questions that could not, in the nature of things, be settled simply by reference to semantic rules. It is precisely because of the powerful polemical force of the term 'democracy' that there is such current diversity in its use. Different theorists want to capture the evaluative force for their own favoured political and social ideals. My claim, however, is that political ideals should be *argued* for on their merits, rather than being clandestinely legitimated by being smuggled into the supposedly neutral determination of what the word 'democracy' means. Even if we rigorously eschew clandestine legitimation, the semantic diversity renders the task of producing a single clear account of what 'democracy' means impossible to achieve by descriptive definition and analysis. Must we then leave the imprecision and diversity as it is and pass on? This would, however, result in our not being able to use the terminology of democracy in the construction of a systematic theory. But what alternatives do we have? There is, I would claim, one line of approach that is open to us, offering the possibility of introducing some level of precision in our use of the term 'democracy', as a basis for our further theoretical analysis. This consists in attempting to produce for 'democracy' what Rudolf Carnap called 'a constructional definition'.[16]

In some ways a constructional or constructed definition is similar to a pure stipulative definition by which a theorist simply postulates how the term in question is going to be used, irrespective of what its past meaning or meanings might have been. There is no rule to forbid stipulative definition or to determine the way a term is stipulatively defined. Because of this arbitrariness, which results in a stipulative definition being informative only about a particular person's linguistic intentions, answering the question 'what is democracy?' by a pure stipulative definition results in a radical re-(perhaps mis-) interpretation of the question; the question as posed by political theory is not meant to be about the arbitrary linguistic intentions of some particular theorist.

A constructed definition uses stipulation as one stage in a much more complex enterprise. Like pure stipulation it does not claim to be aiming for correctness in articulating precisely the previous meaning of a term. But it does claim to be related to previous meaning in both a backward-looking and a forward-looking way. Semantic diversity is sometimes no more than that, but sometimes it is both symptomatic of and the cause of conceptual confusion. Because of the semantic variation and indeterminacy at the heart of the language of democracy it is all too easy to slip unconsciously from the claim that some governmental system is democratic in the vague and imprecise sense to the conclusion that, as a matter of logic, such a system must then be characterisable by specific traits that have been incorporated into one of the more technical definitions of 'democracy'. It is even possible, then, to assume that anything characterised by one of the precise definitions is unquestionably good, since no one questions the value of democracy in some sense of the term. As we have seen, Dahl claims not only that the terminology of 'democracy' exhibits diversity and imprecision, but also that the democratic tradition has become 'a jumble of theory and practices that are often deeply inconsistent'.

It is in such a situation that a constructed definition can claim to be going much further than the personal solution of semantic diversity by the fiat of a stipulative definition. What motivates a constructed definition is the enterprise of adequately conceptualising and theorising about the whole range of phenomena and problems that constitute the domain of application of the varied uses of a term. A constructed definition is a stipulative definition put forward in association with a set of hypotheses; firstly, that the constructed concept, while not pretending to be *the unique* meaning implicit in all previous uses of the term, does capture some core elements of those uses in a coherent way; secondly, and this is the forward-looking aspect of constructed definitions, the definition will enable a clear conceptualisation of the whole area of concern in such a way that the central problems and questions about the area can be clearly formulated and fruitfully dealt with. It is this hypothesised theoretical fruitfulness that in the last analysis will constitute the criterion of adequacy of a constructed definition.

I will, then, be taking the question 'what is democracy?' not as a question about some objective timeless essence of democracy nor as a question of the correct meaning of 'democracy' as it has been used, but as a question about how we *should construct* a definition of democracy that will enable us to treat adequately of the problems, theoretical and practical, that have emerged as major concerns in the democratic tradition. Our definition, if it is to have relevance to the tradition, will have to claim to capture and fuse into a coherent whole certain core elements of previous understandings of democracy. Secondly, since democracy has been a political and social ideal, sometimes enthusiastically espoused, sometimes violently opposed, one crucial test of having captured core elements of previous understandings will be that the definition highlights those factors relevant to its normative evaluation; one aspect of its capturing core elements of past use will be its explanation of the underlying values of the democratic tradition. And, finally, as with all constructed definitions, the purpose of the whole enterprise will be to enable us to think coherently, clearly and fruitfully about the substantive problems of democratic theory.

Before moving on to the task of actually constructing a definition of 'democracy' in the next chapter, I will end this one by identifying, in advance, two general features of the definition that are specifically motivated by the methodological problems we have encountered. I have pointed out earlier the dangers attaching to a term like 'democracy' that carries heavy evaluative connotations. To ensure that substantive normative issues are not settled as though they were neutral semantic ones, my definition will attempt to identify democracy in as evaluatively neutral a way as possible, enabling us, when the time comes, to see as clearly as possible precisely where the substantive normative issues lie.

Secondly, I have been struck in my study of democratic theory by the amount of unnecessary confusion that has arisen from the naive assumption that all general concepts like 'democracy' must be what logicians call 'sortal' concepts, whose purpose it is to produce an exclusive categorisation of objects in a given domain into those which identically and unproblematically fall into the category in question and those which do not. In the case of 'democracy' the assumption would be that our definition would enable us, for any political system, to say simply: yes, it is a democracy; or no, it is not a democracy. In contrast to sortal concepts, we also have 'scalar' concepts, which always imply the presence of a characteristic or characteristics to a certain degree; they place things on a scale of 'more or less'. Thus, it is more accurate to say not that I am going to define what it is to be 'a democracy', but rather that I am going to define what 'democratic' is to mean, with the definite implication that, operating with a scalar concept, we will be locating things along the spectrum of the more or less democratic.

3

Democracy and political equality

In the dedicatory preface to his *Discourse on the Origins of Inequality*, Rousseau praises the independent republic of Geneva of that time as democratic, adding in explanation of the term that democracy consists in the identity of sovereign and subject.[1] While, in the light of the methodological problems raised in the last chapter, I am not claiming that Rousseau here manifests an accurate insight into the objective essence of democracy, I would claim that if we begin with Rousseau's pithy assertion, by analysis, elaboration and extrapolation we will be able to construct a concept of democracy that goes a long way towards satisfying our methodological criteria.

To begin this elaboration consider the following three scenarios, in each of which we will be imagining a group of, say, ten people who are subject in their lives to the results of an enforceable, authoritatively binding decision-making process. In scenario A the decision-making is located in a wholly external authority, say a single person, not a member of the group in question, who can and does make decisions binding on our ten people in complete independence of any input from them and without any consultation of their preferences or interests. In the second and third scenarios we postulate no agency external to the group to which the group is subject, the decisions by which each group is bound being made by the group itself. We have already encountered in a preliminary way, however, the problems attaching to the idea of a 'group' making decisions. A moment's reflection will suffice to convince us that one of the essential criteria of the externality of an authority, with respect to any individual member of an alleged group, in this context, consists precisely in whether or not the individual in question participates in the exercise of that authority. Consequently, to differentiate B and C from A we must postulate not only that there is no agency outside of our ten people but also that each member of the group participates in the decision-making to which they are subject, because if they cannot participate in the authority, the authority becomes external to them, the group becomes divided and there is no complete identity between sovereign authority and those subject to that authority. This illustrates Rousseau's point; it also demonstrates that according to this construal of democracy, the identity of sovereign and subject must depend on a real participation by subjects in the exercise of sovereign power. Further consideration will show, however, that more detailed internal elaboration is required before we can take the definition as adequate.

We have distinguished scenarios B and C from A on the basis of the absence in the former cases of any external authority, and we have argued that that itself should be taken to mean that the decisions to which members of each group are subject should be the result of participation by all members, otherwise the non-participating members will be subject to an authority of which they are not a part. But there are different degrees and levels of participation in decision-making, some of which can be exemplified by further elaboration of our postulated scenarios B and C.

Imagine that in situation B the ultimate decisions binding on the group are determined by a formal voting system, in which each member of the group has a vote, the result being decided on the basis of a simple majority rule procedure. However, two members of the group each have votes that count for three times more than the vote of each of the other eight members. Furthermore, though before a vote is taken there is free and open discussion of the options to be decided on, only the chairperson (one of the two with a triple vote) a position inherited for life, can decide the options to be placed on the agenda. Clearly, even on a superficial analysis, there are three levels of power within such a group, the chairperson's power, the power of the triple-voters and the power of the ordinary single-vote members. Ordinary group members do have a degree of power; they may, at times, if there is consensus among them, succeed in out-voting the two triple-vote members. Even then, however, they are only choosing between externally pre-set options. The chairperson can always ensure that alternatives to which he or she is opposed never get implemented, despite the overwhelming support that there might be for such options if they were put on the agenda, by the simple procedure of never including them.

Compare that distribution of decision-making power with the following, which we postulate in our third scenario, C. In C all decisions are similarly determined by simple majority. But unlike scenario B, in C each person's vote counts for one and one only. In addition, though there is a chairperson, the chair's power is limited to procedural matters, the chairperson is chosen by random lot and has no power to determine the agenda, any member of the group having the right to include whatever options on the agenda that they think ought to be debated and decided on. Such rules of decision-making do not give rise to any formal hierarchy of power such as was evident in scenario B. More importantly, however, it would be my contention that our pre-theoretical intuitions would lead us unhesitatingly to describe the structure of authority in C as more democratic than that in B. What we need to know is what lies behind this intuitive grading. The answer, I would suggest, lies in the concept of procedurally or institutionally guaranteed political equality where this is interpreted as equal effective rights to participate in the determination of the authoritatively binding outcomes. Equality of power in determining the outputs of the decision-making procedure is obviously at the centre of our intuitive differentiation of B and C. The element of institutional guarantee has remained so far implicit, because the only information we have been considering relates explicitly to institutional rules or procedures. Their importance, however, can be illustrated by considering a more concrete instance of the hierarchically systematic procedures of scenario B. When I differentiated in scenario B three levels of power I was speaking imprecisely; more accurately, what was being identified were three levels of procedural rights. But, as we will see in more detail later, having certain rights according to a set of rules does not automatically give one the effective power parallel to those rights. The hereditary chairperson might, for example, be permanently weak and indecisive, open to persuasion, cajolement or threat. And it just might turn out that our eight ordinary members, though their procedurally defined powers were limited to voting unequally on a pre-determined agenda, possessed great powers of persuasion, backed up, perhaps, with the capacity of wielding the significant countervailing power of forceful coercion. Suppose, for the sake of argument, we imagined that the informal powers of the ordinary members succeeded in balancing the procedural advantages of the minority, resulting in what was, for all intents and purposes, equality of effective power for each member of the group. Should we say then that the power structure of B was as unproblematically democratic as that of C? To follow such a strategy would, I think, be undesirable for three reasons. Firstly, it would conflate two important aspects of power, the procedural and the extra-procedural, which simply for conceptual clarity should be kept separate. Secondly, for several reasons that we will be examining when we turn to evaluating democracy, the procedural dimension of democratic power is particularly important. Finally, if we conflate the formal and the informal we would be led to certain results that would be confusing and paradoxical with respect to how we will want to use the concept of democracy in comparative political analysis. A political system that was constitutionally a monarchy but in which the monarch was either unswervingly benevolent and listened attentively to the views of her or his subjects or was at the mercy of an armed citizenry would be lumped together for analytical purposes with, say, representative republican governments elected by universal suffrage. For all sorts of theoretical purposes there are significant differences between such situations that will have to be marked. One way of marking such differences, with respect to our definition of democracy, is to clearly differentiate in that definition the two dimensions of political equality. One important focus of political theory is on structures or systems of rule; not just on *ad hoc* episodic exercises of power. Constitutive of such systems of rule will be procedural rights of decision-making. It is important, then, to begin our analysis of alternative systems by identifying the procedures of decision-making that will make a large contribution to the overall structure of power, while recognising at the same time that equality of procedural power can be either facilitated or undermined by extra-procedural factors. Both the procedural and extra-procedural conditions should be considered, however, as necessary constitutive conditions of that effective political equality with which I am identifying democracy.

We can summarise the results of our analysis of Rousseau's thesis that democracy is to be understood as the identity of sovereign and subject as follows.

With respect to a particular group of people democracy as so understood requires, firstly, that that group not be subject to any external authority. Secondly, since participation in the exercise of authority is itself a criterion of internality, each member of a group that is democratically organised must have rights of participation, otherwise the non-participants become subject to external authority, with which they are not identical. Thirdly, we recognised that participation in the exercise of authority was subject to differences of degree; and, I argued, our pre-theoretic intuitions suggest that the closer the approximation to political equality, equality of power in the determination of the final outcomes, the higher the degree of democracy. Finally, noting that when referring to systems of rule there are two dimensions to effective power, the procedural and the extra-procedural, I argued that the effective political equality with which I am identifying democracy should itself be understood as requiring, firstly, institutionally guaranteed equality in the procedures of decision-making and, secondly, the realisation of those extra-procedural conditions required to transform the procedural equality into fully effective political equality.

This last thesis raises two questions that are going to be central to the further elaboration of this concept of democracy. In comparing scenarios B and C, we identified various features, specifically, monopoly rights to determine the agenda and the differential weighting of votes, that led to a hierarchic asymmetry of procedural power. What we need to ask, however, is what a positive account of procedural equality would look like. Secondly, observing how institutionally defined power could be either facilitated or subverted by extra-procedural conditions, we must be led to ask: what background, extra-procedural conditions might, in general, be required to transform procedural equality into fully effective equality?

Before proceeding to these questions there is one further essential issue concerning the definition of democracy that can be highlighted by returning once again to Rousseau's dictum and our three scenarios. Given that the members of our group of ten in the third scenario had all the necessary powers to make use of their procedural equality, we would, if we adopted Rousseau's definition, be inclined to say that here was an example of a near perfect democracy. Suppose, though, that we were then informed that the group in question was a self-appointed military junta ruling ruthlessly over a population of millions. Would it remain obvious that we were examining a near perfect democracy? Evidently not, for reasons already implicit in Rousseau's concept of the identity of sovereign and subject. The group itself is not subject to external authority, neither is there an internal authority within the group of some over others. The group, however, though internally democratic is, we would say, ruling undemocratically over others. This situation highlights two aspects to democracy in the context of a political system as a whole that it is necessary to distinguish. We could call the first aspect the quantitative dimension and simplify the definition of this dimension by starting our analysis not with some vaguely referred to 'group' but by introduction of, at the outset, the idea of 'all those that are systematically subject to a decision-making procedure'. It is that specific group that constitutes, as it were, the conceptual domain of relevance of 'democracy'. From the quantitative perspective the structure of power will be more democratic the more widely distributed are the rights of participation. Though, as we will see in the next chapter, there are complex theoretical questions concerning the precise relationship between the degree of democracy and the extent of rights of participation, identifying this separate quantitative dimension of the coincidence of sovereign and subject does accord again with our vague intuitions that, to put it negatively, a society in which large segments who are subject to rule are excluded from participation is less democratic than one which extends participatory rights to such groups.

The second aspect we can call the qualitative dimension of democracy and depends upon the nature of the participation rights and not just on how extensively they are distributed. Crucially, the qualitative dimension is concerned with the effective political equality of the participants in a system of rule; the closer the approximation to real effective equality the nearer we get to perfect democracy from the qualitative perspective. It is worth pointing out that these two axes along which we can measure the degree of democracy within a society are conceptually independent; rights of participation could confer a high degree of equal effectivity on those who possess them, and yet that group could be a rather small proportion of all those subject to the system of rule in question.

As I said above, I will be turning to the theoretical problems surrounding the more precise specification of the quantitative dimension of democracy in the next chapter. But because the two dimensions are conceptually independent, we can raise now the question of the internal, qualitative dimension of political equality. I have argued so far that specifically political equality will consist in equal effectiveness in determining political outcomes, and that, for a system of rule to be democratic this equal effectivity will have to be mediated by decision-making rules guaranteeing procedural equality. But can we go further and say more explicitly what rules a decision-making procedure would have to follow if it were to confer an institutionally equal role on all participants? An adequate approach to this question will depend upon an initial analysis of what is involved in decision-making in general and in collective decision-making in particular. And it is to this that I will now turn.

A decision is the choice to implement one of several available alternative courses of action. In many situations individuals make decisions 'instantaneously' and perhaps, even, unconsciously. However, every decision has four logically distinct stages or 'moments'. By identifying these moments we will be able to see more clearly how decision-making must be structured if political equality is going to be approximated in a group making decisions collectively.

A decision is required when an agent is faced with several incompatible alternatives among which a choice must be made. The first moment of decision-making is the identification of both the necessity of choosing and the set of available options for choice. In the situation of collective decision-making, particularly when such decisions are arrived at by formal procedures, this first moment consists in the setting of the agenda, the identification of an issue-area in which it is proposed to make a decision and the laying down of the alternatives to be decided upon. As we shall see, it is a particularly crucial moment in the decision-making process.

When the alternatives are identified, we arrive at the stage of comparative assessment, the weighing up of the pros and cons of the various options according to whatever criteria are thought relevant. Even in the individual case this moment often involves explicit deliberation, and in the collective case the assessment typically takes the form of debate and discussion.

Evaluation is followed by the focal point of the decision-making process as whole, namely, the moment of choice in which the alternative to be implemented is chosen, in which, that is, the actual decision is made. When an individual person is deciding, this third moment is simple or unitary. The person arrives at the conclusion that this is what he or she will do. In the situation of collective decision-making this moment is internally complex and problematic. Though perhaps there is in theory the possibility of a 'mystical' feeling of collective unity in which each member of the group feels, simultaneously and in agreement with all other members, that *this* is what must be done, even here there is a logical distinction between one person choosing which option he or she would prefer to see implemented and the formal choice, the resultant collective decision. In practice, because of the possibility of individual disagreement over what is to be done, any collective decision-making must incorporate a mechanism by which *the decision* to be implemented is determined as some function of the individual, perhaps conflicting, choices among the available alternatives that people have made. When we are looking at collective decision-making from the perspective of maximising the equal effectiveness of each member, this internal complexity of the third moment becomes the site of a set of central and crucial problems in democratic theory.

The final moment of decision-making is the moment of implementation, when the choice arrived at is translated into action. This again is obviously a particularly crucial moment; decisions are directed to action, and freedom and self-determination, whether individual or democratically collective, will involve necessarily not only the effective right to 'make decisions', in the limited sense of the third moment of decision-making, but also the power to implement decisions in practice. The maintenance of effective equality at this level raises wide-ranging problems in the overall theory of democracy.

In the light of this analysis of the four moments of decision-making, how would the procedures of collective decision-making have to be organised if all participants were to be guaranteed equal effectiveness, so that no particular individual or individuals possessed asymmetric power over the determination of the outcomes that were going to be binding on all? Before looking at each of the stages in turn an important general point should be made, namely that, as we will discover, the overall equality in a decision-making procedure is not a simple arithmetic addition of equality at each stage. Rather equality at certain crucial stages is a necessary precondition for the achievement of any significant degree of overall equality.

This is particularly true of the first moment, the agenda-setting. If some sub-group were privileged at this stage by having, say, the exclusive right to determine what everybody else had to decide between, that would be a power to so pre-determine the possible final outcomes as to effectively nullify whatever equality the rest had at the other moments of decision-making. In the extreme, those with no agenda-setting power could be equally reduced to the position of slaves who were allowed the right to choose between trivial alternatives while being denied the power to decide anything significant. The members of such a group might have equal rights to debate and vote, but in effect they would be equal to each other only in their impotence as compared to the privileged agenda-setters. It follows, then, that overall effective equality requires, at the first moment of decision-making, equal agenda-setting rights.

Suppose, however, that such rights did exist, but that some sub-group had exclusive access to information needed to decide what the relevant options should be for the group as whole, or that some sub-group had the right to forbid the dissemination of such information. Despite the equal agenda-setting rights, the sub-group would again have power to manipulate the decision-making so as to effectively determine the outcome. The right of agenda-setting is ineffective without the relevant information. Consequently, if we are interpreting democracy as involving effective rights, equality requires in the first moment of decision-making free and equal access to relevant information. As Dahl points out in *Democracy and Its Critics*, given the inevitable relationship between general socioeconomic equality and equality of access to the wide ranges of information relevant to political decision-making, the effective rights to equal agenda-setting (and, obviously, to debate and discussion in the second moment) turn out to be very robust rights indeed, implying as they do the equal rights to free and extensive information.[2]

One element of such unconstrained access deserves specific comment. The freedom of the press is often cited as crucial to the adequate functioning of a democracy, and we can see from the present argument why this should be so and what that 'freedom' should actually amount to. The information and knowledge needed to be an equal participant in agenda-setting (and discussion and debate) goes far beyond what we normally associate with the mass media; its provision will depend upon a genuinely egalitarian educational system, which is why these rights are so robust. However, in a populous, complex society information concerning current affairs, relevant to political decision-making, will depend for its dissemination on channels of mass communication. The existence of such channels in a form in which they provide adequate access to information then becomes constitutive of equality in the first two moments of decision-making. But what is this 'form'? Even from the brief analysis given above we can arrive at a negative specification; control of the relevant information cannot be monopolised by some particular sub-group of the community, if everyone is going to have equal access. The incompatibility of monopoly control and equal agenda-setting powers would exclude not just the exclusive power of some official group of 'censors', it would also exclude *de facto* monopoly control based on such things as wealth; hence, the concern over small numbers of wealthy individuals controlling the major media of mass communication. This point becomes even more important, of course, when we make explicit that there is always likely to be genuine disagreements in perceptions of what is relevant and important, and hence multiple channels of articulation are going to be required to guarantee to all points of view the effective right to make their case to the people.

But should literally all points of view have this right? Furthermore, is it not plausible to suggest that some, perhaps minimal, censorship might be actually required for the protection of democracy? This, of course, is a view often supported and acted on by incumbent 'democratic' governments. Despite the high status accorded to 'free speech' in the pantheon of liberal–democratic values, there are very few governments that do not practise some restriction of access to information and censorship of some views. What can we say about this question from the perspective of the definition of democracy we are constructing, in which free access to information is a constitutive right?

The first point that needs to be made is a methodological one and it is that we should not confuse the important normative issue of whether it is ever justified to suppress information if it is believed to be necessary to protect the future of democracy with the semantic question of how such a policy is best described. Given the constructivist method that we are following, it is evident that we should not pretend to be able to settle the important issue of value and right by purely semantic legislation. Though it is the semantic question I am addressing here something can be said in clarification of the evaluative issue. Systems of values or prescriptive rules can be ranged along a spectrum, the two extremes of which we can call the *a priori* intrinsic and the radical consequentialist. If we value something in a radically consequentialist way we do so simply in terms of its consequences; the action itself, abstracted from the specific circumstances, is not considered to have any determinate value at all. An *a priori* intrinsic valuation, on the other hand, will categorise actions prior to and independent of specific situations and attach a definitive value to the categories of action. At the extreme, such values will be thought of as unalterable by the characteristics of the concrete situations in which instances of the action occur. If our approach to the justification and evaluation of democracy was predominantly consequentialist, it is easy to see how we would think temporary suppression of information or censorship might be justified precisely in the light of our commitment to democracy; if such censorship were in fact really necessary for the long-term preservation of democracy then it, like democracy itself, would be justified by its consequences, despite the fact that in the here and now it is contrary to the constitutive characteristics of a democratic structure of power in denying at least certain people equal participation in this exercise of power. If, on the contrary, one believed that certain undemocratic acts were intrinsically wrong, one would conclude that despite beneficial consequences, such things as censorship or the exclusion of certain minority views from having any influence in the decision-making process would be unjustified. What makes the question of censorship in the protection of democracy such a complex question in real life is, firstly, the fact that most people's systems of value are not at one or other end of our spectrum, but rather contain elements of the consequentialist and the *a priori* intrinsic. It is not at all inconsistent to think that certain types of action are intrinsically wrong or undesirable *and* that one might be justified in doing such things if the consequences were extremely important. The problem in practice is to determine the relevant priorities in specific circumstances. Though, as we will see when we come to discuss justifications of democracy, it is quite plausible to attribute a certain intrinsic value to democracy, it seems to me that very few people would give such unconditional intrinsic value to democracy that any deviation from democracy would always be wrong irrespective of the circumstances. Consequently, for most people consequences are going to be important. The problem is that our system of values may not specify in advance a determinate rule for identifying precisely when circumstances are extreme enough to override intrinsic value. Saving the whole human race from certain extinction would be extreme enough, but would the prevention of a merely possible future threat to democracy be serious enough to justify deviation from democratic practices here and now? My point is not to answer that question but to note that there is no reason to believe that our evaluative system will contain all the elements in advance to generate a determinate answer.

Secondly, as soon as we accept the relevance of consequences we run up against the problem of proof or corroboration of empirical predictions. Most disputes about censorship in the protection of democracy centre around the conflicting claims that the securing of democracy in the medium term requires the suppression and censorship of certain views in the short term and the claim that such censorship is either unnecessary for the protection of democracy or that it does more damage in the long term to the prospects of democracy than would the public airing of the censored views. The problem here is how you would prove one of these claims against the others.

Another important point of clarification can be made, however, by returning to the specifically semantic question of how we should describe such policies. The issue here is whether, granting that we are defining democracy as procedurally articulated equal effectiveness in determining the outcomes of decision-making and that we accept that this implies equal access to relevant information, is it ever correct to describe suppression of information as democratic, if it is necessary for the future preservation of democracy? We could, of course, simply stipulate that by 'democratic' we mean to indicate either that decisions were arrived at by a distribution of political power in which all those affected by the decisions had equal effective rights of participation in the making of the decisions *or* that, whatever the distribution of power lying behind the decisions, they were intended to bring about, at some future date, a distribution of power that would be democratic in the first sense. It seems to me, however, that such a definition, apart from being totally unnecessary, would engender, almost inevitably, conceptual confusion and, possibly, moral hypocrisy. Since there is no reason to believe that only decisions that were democratic in the first sense would be democratic in the second, we would be classifying together structures of power with radically different intrinsic features. Secondly, such a semantic conflation is unnecessary; we have a perfectly adequate way of describing a power structure which, while not democratic in the first sense, is genuinely intended to bring about at some future date a democratic distribution of power. We can say that the exercise of such power is democratic *in intent*, though not, here and now, in fact. Providing the intention is genuine it is entirely appropriate to describe such situations as 'democratic in intent'. An extreme example would be the unforced abdication of an absolute monarch, with the intention of preparing the way for a democratic constitution. Though democratic in intent, such a decision is obviously not one arrived at by a procedure in which the outcome is determined on the basis of the equal effectiveness of all who are affected.

An important further point needs to be made, however; it is that not all actions intended to 'secure the future of democracy' can be regarded as unproblematically democratic in intent. This is the point of clarification referred to above concerning debates about censorship and the suppression of information. Compare the following two types of situation. In the first type of situation a definite, but temporary, deviation from the intrinsic conditions of full democracy is envisaged, with the intent of securing the future implementation of fully democratic structures. As we have already noted, we can describe such a situation as, unproblematically, democratic in intent. Suppose, however, that censorship and the restriction of access to certain information are envisaged as permanent possibilities, always necessary to preserve 'democracy' or the security of the 'democratic state', as they usually are in most modern states with respect to certain 'extremist' views and secrets of state. Such actions should not, I would contend, be described as unproblematically democratic in intent, because the 'democracy' that is being secured is not full democracy. It is more honest in such circumstances to admit that full democracy is not a secure, self-recreating system. One might be genuinely committed to democratic ideals and regret that their implementation would be self-defeating; one then might be democratically justified in sacrificing a certain amount of democracy so as to secure a viable but less democratic structure. But wish and reality are radically different.

According to our definition then, the qualitative conditions of full democracy require, in the first moment of decision-making, equal effective rights in agenda-setting, which implies equal access to relevant information. Consequently, any restriction of access, no matter how justified by democratic or other considerations, has to be seen as a deviation from full democracy. It is evident that everything that has been said about access to relevant information in the context of the first moment of decision-making is equally applicable to the second moment, the moment of assessment and deliberation. Overall political equality would be subverted if equality in agenda-setting was followed by lack of access to the relevant information for deliberation and assessment. Specifically, if some sub-group could manipulatively control information, disseminating only that that would lead to the decision that it favoured, effective political equality would be destroyed. Hence, equal and open access is as critical here as it was with regard to agenda-setting. In most decision-making bodies this second moment is, like the first moment, not just a conceptually distinct aspect of decision-making but an actually separate stage, usually characterised by discussion and debate. There is an important point to be made about the openness of discussion and debate in connection with access to relevant information and equal effectivity at this stage.

In ancient Athens major political decisions were taken by the Ekklesia, or the Assembly of the people, in which all citizens were entitled to participate and that met forty times a year, four times in each of the ten administrative periods into which the year was divided. The agenda for the meeting was drawn up by the Council of Five Hundred, or the Boule, as it was called. However, this council itself was selected by lot from the citizen body each year, term of office was for one year, and no person could serve more than twice in a lifetime. Furthermore, though it was the Council's responsibility to draw up the agenda, private citizens could and did present to the Council issues that they wished to be debated, and amendments could be made from the floor on the day of the Assembly. Once a motion was put to the Assembly every citizen had the right to address the people. This was known as Isegoria, or equality of voice. For the Athenians this equal right to voice one's opinions was one of the central elements of their demokratia.[3] The first point to be made about free and open debate is that it is a central and efficient way of ensuring equal access to relevant information; in simple matters, each decision-maker might be fully informed on all relevant matters before the decision-making. But when an issue is complex it is likely that the relevant information is available only fragmentedly to most decision-makers. One way of facilitating fuller and more equal access is through publicity of debate. There is, however, another aspect to open debate; it derives from the fact that deliberation is not only a matter of information but also of evaluative perspective. The Athenians sometimes expressed their commitment to demokratia as a worship of 'Pythia', a personification of 'persuasion'; they viewed participation in decision-making as a process of persuasion, each participant being entitled to put forward his point of view. To be an equally effective participant in a decision-making process must involve in the moment of deliberation not just the right of receiving the relevant factual information or important evaluative considerations. A deliberative assembly that, by its procedural rule, was forced to 'deliberate' in silence, would not only be deprived of an efficient means of disseminating information but it would also deny equal effectiveness to those members who believed they had information or points of view that were important but were not generally known about. Freedom of speech has to be a constitutive element of a decision-making procedure that purports to embody the principles of equal effectiveness; to deny someone the right to voice her or his opinion is to that extent to deny equal effectiveness in the determination of the eventual outcome.

When debate and discussion are over decisions have to be made. Although I have been at pains to emphasise that effective equality has robust conditions in the first two moments of the decision-making process because the power to significantly determine the eventual outcome lies partly in those moments, it is more than obvious that if a person's power were confined to the first two moments, if, that is, a person had no right to register the decision he or she had made and have that decision entered as a determinant of the final outcome, equal effectiveness in determining that final outcome would be seriously undermined. It is, of course, for this reason that democracy is popularly identified with 'one person, one vote', the centrality of voting as the embodiment of equal effectiveness makes such an identification intelligible if not wholly justifiable from the perspective of the definition that we are constructing. Even confining ourselves to the third moment of decision-making, the formula 'one person, one vote' is an inadequate formulation of the conditions of political equality. The first inadequacy stems from the possibility of the differential weighting of votes. Although in modern representative democracies differential weighting is not a common procedure, such respected 'democrats' as John Stuart Mill seriously proposed it.[4] From the perspective of equal effectiveness, however, it is evident that differential weighting would be a serious deviation, and hence the formula 'one person, one vote' is an adequate articulation of the conditions of political equality only if it is made explicit that 'one vote' means 'one weight'; each person's vote must be given the same importance in determining the decision to be implemented. That, however, is only a statement of the problem, not a solution. There are an indefinite number of 'vote aggregation' procedures and, firstly, unless one is specified, no decision is determined by individual participants casting a vote for their preferred options. Secondly, we need to ask which procedure accords most with the condition of equal effectiveness. This is a complex question with which I will be dealing at length in Chapter 4, but to illustrate the kind of issue at stake here consider the following possibility. One procedure for determining the outcome decision as a function of the votes cast is the unanimity rule. Requiring unanimity is, of course, equivalent to giving each voter an absolute veto; it is the system of voting operative currently (1993) in the EC Council of Ministers and in the United Nations Security Council. Evidently, the unanimity rule privileges no particular voter; it is true, equally, of each and everyone that her or his counter-vote would be sufficient to ensure a negative outcome. Further, if a positive outcome does result on the basis of actual unanimity, each voter can truly say that her or his vote was crucial in determining that outcome. It is equally true of each that had that person voted differently the outcome would have been different, hence each person's vote was equally influential in determining the outcome. What more could we look for in the matter of equal effectiveness? The issue, however, is not so simple. And it is not just the practical difficulties of achieving consensus that causes the problems. Consider the situation in which the vast majority vote in favour of a proposal and, at the extreme, a single person votes against. Clearly, it is that person's vote that determines the, albeit negative, outcome. The votes of the vast majority in favour of the proposal are, in that instance, ineffective. So how can we say that each voter has equal effectiveness? The position is made even worse when we take into account the fact that it is an easily demonstrated theorem of probability theory that if preferences are distributed randomly, consensus is one of the least likely outcomes and the improbability of consensus increases in direct proportion to the number of voters. Therefore, such a system if operative in a numerous group of decision-makers would, in the long run, be biased in favour of dissenting minorities, reducing the vast majority, in most cases, to ineffectiveness. As can be seen, the question of which vote aggregation procedure most accords with guaranteeing long-run equal effectiveness raises numerous issues to which we will return later. All we can say at the moment is that the basic principle, from the perspective of the definition of democracy that we are constructing, for the selection of a vote-aggregation procedure is obviously the principle of maximum equal effectiveness. We will be dealing later with the detailed implications of this principle.

In the normal course of events decisions are intended to be implemented, implementation being, in our schema, the fourth and final moment of the whole process. No matter what degree of equality is achieved in the first three moments it counts for nothing towards effective political equality if the outcome in the issue area in question is not determined by the decision arrived at in the third moment but rather is the result of the activity of some other agency, whether intentional or not. This reflection results, on the level of procedures, merely in the truism that the outcome implemented must be the decision arrived at. Equality at this stage concerns not so much the equality of people as participants in the decision-making process, but rather the autonomy of the decision-makers in controlling their own affairs. Such autonomy, and hence equality, would be undermined by the existence of a structure of countervailing power rendering the decision-makers impotent in the implementation of their decisions. One major dispute in modern democratic theory concerns the contention of some theorists that countervailing structures of power, particularly of economic power, can all but negate the putative equality of citizens as participants in political decision-making, by determining a whole range of outcomes of vital importance to citizens independently of official decision-making. But does this imply that citizens through the channels of political decision-making should be able to control all aspects of society? Though this might be thought of as simply the contention that the authoritatively binding procedures should in fact be sovereign, it has the ring of totalitarian socialism that does not sit well with the orthodox assumption that legitimate democratic government must, if the very ideals of democracy itself are to be achieved, be constrained by the principles of liberal respect for individual freedom and rights. To deal adequately with this matter will involve us in complex questions of both a normative and empirical nature which we will be investigating in later chapters.

I have been putting forward in this chapter the hypothesis that we will be able to construct the best and most serviceable concept of democracy by elaborating Rousseau's understanding of democracy as consisting in the identity of sovereign and subject. More explicitly, this involves treating as democratic a power-structure that operates through authoritatively binding decisions if all those who are subject to the decisions have equal effective rights in the determination of the decisions to which they are subject. This, as we saw, has a quantitative and a qualitative dimension. The quantitative dimension of democracy depends on the ratio between the number of those affected by decisions and the number of those affected that have effective rights of participation in making the decisions. The qualitative dimension of democracy is determined by the degree to which the conditions of effective political equality are realised in the four moments of decision-making and consists both in procedural rights and the powers to effectively utilise those rights.

I have explicitly stated all along, both in postulating the basic definition and in specifying its implications, that the enterprise is one of hypothetical construction, though I have obviously been guided by earlier theorists such as Rousseau and by pre-theoretic intuitive usage. It is worth pausing at this stage to consider how far our method in practice has conformed to the principles elaborated in the previous chapter and also how we could justify, in accordance with those principles, the specific content of the constructed concept.

Firstly, the very explicitness of the method saves us from the illusion that we are, once and for all, correctly describing the objective essence of democracy or identifying the necessary elements of the unique concept that has, supposedly, always informed every use of the term 'democracy'. Ultimately, if it is to prove acceptable the construction will have to demonstrate that it can deal in a theoretically fruitful way with the range of problems and concerns that have been central to democratic theory and practice.

One beneficial consequence has already become apparent; we

have been able to differentiate clearly between the semantic question of what we are going to understand by 'democracy' and the substantive normative issues concerning the rightness or desirability of those structures of power that satisfy the conditions that have been specified. The postulated concept of democracy is meant to enable us to identify and compare structures of authoritative power with respect to those features that have been thought particularly significant from both explanatory and normative perspectives in debates concerning democracy. But we cannot, and do not, pretend to be settling important evaluative questions by definitional fiat.

A further related point should be made here about the definition given that has not yet been emphasised; it has been constructed to aid descriptive categorisation and comparison, and has been formulated in terms that do not depend upon normative concepts or values. It is intrinsically non-evaluative; I have not defined 'democracy', for example, as a *fair* distribution of political power, or as that system that accords with the *natural rights* of human beings. As I argued in Chapter 1, the purpose of political theory is to produce evaluative appraisals of possible forms of social organisation. To accomplish this in an orderly and coherent fashion, we need ways of describing and comparing these possible structures that do not already presuppose an evaluation of them, though our concepts need to highlight, as was said above, those features of social organisation that are likely to be relevant to evaluative appraisal. It is my contention that the definition given does just this.

Moving away from evaluative problems, a fourth advantage of our definition is what can be called its sophisticated scalarity. Referring back to the distinction between the quantitative and the qualitative dimension, and, within the qualitative dimension, the distinctions between the conditions of equality at different moments of the decision-making process, it becomes obvious that a system's being democratic is a matter of degree, and a matter of degree measured along multiple dimensions. It is true that the language of democracy is sometimes used categorically, to identify, that is, the category of governments that are considered to be, simply, democracies, over against another category of non-democracies. This, I think, is far too simplistic, blurring as it does important similarities and differences. Furthermore, it leads into insuperable definitional problems. Suppose it is assumed, as it would have to be if the defined concept was going to relate to previous usage at all, that the criteria for and the level of enfranchisement were going to be relevant to a system's being a democracy. How would we, in a non-arbitrary way, determine the minimum cut-off point? The same question arises with respect to the nature of the participation rights or decision-making powers. Much greater clarity is produced if we construe talk about democracy as describing where, on the relevant scales, a particular system lies. This accords with a wide range of pre-theoretic usage in which, as was the case in the comparison of the different decision-making structures discussed at the beginning of this chapter, we want to say not that this is a democracy and that is not, but that this is more democratic than that. In addition, the explicit multi-dimensional scalarity of the concept facilitates the highlighting of numerous relevant features of a power-structure, thereby making possible sophisticated and nuanced comparisons. It will never be a case of this system being a democracy and that system not, nor even of this system being, in an undifferentiated way, more democratic than that. If we say that this system is more democratic, we will have to specify the precise dimension along which we are measuring. And it has been noted that high levels of equality in one dimension do not necessarily imply high levels in the other dimensions; consequently, a full assessment of the degree of democracy necessitates analysis of a power-structure in all its dimensions.

It would be correct to point out that all of these arguments for the definition relate to its formal structure and not to its specific content. How would we justify the specific content? How would we justify making equality of power in determining political outcomes the central element in the construction? How would we argue in favour of the claim that an integral element of such equality should be what we have been calling the quantitative dimension? How should we substantiate the claim that not only are procedural rights central to a democracy but also the effective powers to utilise those rights? As I said above, a full justification will depend on the adequacy of the whole theory of democracy being developed on the basis of the definition. However, even at this stage it can be argued that the very use made in constructing the definition of reflection on some previous theoretical and pre-theoretical usages demonstrates that the definition not only falls well within the parameters of previous usage but also goes a long way toward explicating that usage by making explicit the principles upon which it was based.

A further mode of justificatory argument for the definition would be by means of a critical comparison with plausible alternatives. A good place to start such a comparison is with Austin Ranney and John Kendall's 'Basic principles for a model of democracy', firstly, because their formal approach is similar to the one adopted here in being explicitly constructivist and in assuming that the concept constructed should be scalar, but, secondly, because their model of democracy is apparently more complex than the one formulated in this chapter.[5] A critical analysis might demonstrate that we have been too minimalist. Ranney and Kendall postulate four essential factors in their model of democracy; popular sovereignty, popular consultation, majority rule and political equality. Is it desirable to include, in addition to the political equality that I have made the core of my definition, these three further elements? I will argue that when we examine in detail what these other conditions of democracy are supposed to amount to we will discover that they are either completely redundant in being reducible without remainder to political equality or else they constitute factors that would be wholly inappropriate as elements of a concept of democracy.

It cannot be denied that talk about popular sovereignty or the will of the people has an honoured place in the rhetoric of democratic politics. I will claim, however, that unless such phrases are interpreted as equivalent to political equality understood in the decidedly disaggregated and individualist manner of my definition where it is made plain that we are talking about each individual having equal effective rights of participation, popular sovereignty is either a vague and dangerous myth or something that one would be ill-advised to include as a central element of our definition. Ranney and Kendall expand on what they mean by popular sovereignty by saying that in a democratic polity the sovereign power of ruling must lie fundamentally with 'the people as whole'. As hinted at above, this can be construed as a vague but harmless allusion to political equality: every member of 'the people' has rights of participation, and those rights being equal, no particular sub-group is especially privileged. But does this not imply that in some sense, particularly if all do participate, the resulting decision can be said to emerge from 'the people as a whole' or even be said to express 'the popular will'? For is it not true that everyone is participating in the making of the decisions in question?

This last formula contains an important ambiguity, the ambiguity between participating in the decision-making process and participating in the making of the specific decision that is the outcome. To see the importance of this distinction consider the only two possibilities relevant to this argument; the case in which there is literally complete unanimity on a particular decision and the case where there is a dissenting sub-group. In the situation of literal unanimity it is literally true that everyone participates in making this particular decision, it is literally true that 'the people as a whole' decided this. When there is dissent, however, this is not the case. A dissenting group opposes a particular proposal, fights against that proposal right up to the point of voting against it. They may remain implacably opposed even after the decision has been taken, though they may, as the lesser of two evils, consent to its implementation as a condition of the preservation of the democratic system. But if they have used all the powers at their disposal to prevent the decision being made, it is simply obfuscation to include them as members of 'the people as a whole' that made the decision. In this regard, Lord Bryce's definition of democracy as 'rule by the will of the qualified *majority*' is more honest.[6] The danger of conflating participation in a decision-making process with participation in the making of a particular decision lies in the powerful ratification given to a decision if it can be construed as a decision of 'the people as a whole'; the implication is, if this is the will of the whole people, who can be legitimately opposed to it? The second danger lies in the implicating in a specific decision of those opposed to it in the following way. I am a participant in a decision-making process; the resulting decision, to which I am opposed, is seen as a decision taken by the people as whole; being a member of that group, it is implied that in some sense this is *my* decision, and hence, rather than being opposed to its implementation, I should be committed to it, since in part, it is *my* decision. Now it may well be the case that if a decision-making system is genuinely and fully democratic this implies an obligation to accept the results, even if one was opposed to a specific decision. This, however, is a difficult evaluative question and, as I will be arguing later, such obligations are arguably not absolute but conditional and cannot be proven on the specious basis that for each individual, since the decision is a decision of the whole people, it is also her or his own decision. If there is dissent, one group will propose and another oppose; if the opposing group, despite each member having the same effective rights as all the other decision-makers, is ineffective in preventing the opposed outcome that is precisely what they are in this context, ineffective. They have not, through the exercise of their equal powers, determined this precise outcome; the powers of others have prevailed in determining the decision-outcome, and that decision is decidedly not the decision of its opponents.

As I noted above, when there is actual unanimity on some issue, it is literally true that the decision was made by all the people. But I take it that Ranney and Kendall are not claiming that we should postulate actual unanimity on every issue as a defining characteristic of a democratic system. Might it not be plausible, though, to postulate a second level unanimity as such a condition, that is, unanimous consent to the procedures? If unanimous consent to the procedures is seen as a condition of democracy, would this not imply that even when there was disagreement on specific issues, the decision that resulted from the procedures was, in an indirect sense, the decision of, literally, the whole people, since the whole people, literally everyone, had decided on the procedures to be followed in arriving at particular decisions? The concept of consent has played a major role in liberal-democratic theory from at least the end of the seventeenth century to the present. I am not raising here the question of whether consent should be thought of as required for the legitimacy of a system of rule. I am, firstly, questioning whether it should be thought of as a necessary or sufficient condition of democracy. That it should not be thought of as a sufficient condition is easily established. If the whole population of a state believed unreservedly in the theory of the divine right of kings and also in the infinite wisdom and benevolence of some particular claimant to the throne, and have willingly consented to being ruled by an absolute monarch this would not transform absolute monarchy into democracy. Our sensible reluctance to conflate such absolute monarchy with democracy indicates that what we should be concerned with in specifying the conditions of democracy are the intrinsic features of the on-going structure of power through which political outcomes are determined, not whether such structures are consented to. Rather more surprisingly, I think it can be shown that consent should not be treated as a necessary condition either. Supposing some decision-making procedure satisfied our conditions of quantitative and qualitative equality, everyone in the society having equal effective rights of participation. A minority within the society, say the descendants of a former aristocracy, refuse to accept the legitimacy of the new order. Would the structure of equal rights be less democratic, simply because 'the aristocratic party', all of whose members have the same rights as everyone else in the society, refuse to consent, wanting a monopoly of political power for themselves? Again, what is suggested by this case is that in comparing systems of rule our concern should be with the distribution of effective power articulated through the systems in question.

There is one final argument that we should look at purporting to show that in a democracy the implemented decisions are in some real sense the responsibility of the people as a whole. It could be claimed that even if we accept that we should not enter unanimous consent to the procedures as a necessary or sufficient condition of democracy, it will normally be true in democratic societies that, as a matter of fact, there will be at least near unanimous consent to procedures, and would that not imply that when this is the case it is justified to speak of the decisions arrived at being, indirectly, consented to by the entire community? The analogy usually appealed to here is that of a person issuing a genuinely blank cheque; by issuing the cheque the person has given consent 'in advance' to whatever figure is entered, even if there is no participation in the determination of the figure. Similarly, it can be argued that anyone consenting to certain decision-making procedures is giving consent in advance to whatever the results of those procedures might be, even if there is no participation in the positive determination of a specific decision, either because the person abstained or voted for a defeated alternative. The problem with this conclusion is that it assumes that there is only one form of consent, namely absolute or unconditional consent. One can, of course, issue genuinely blank cheques, that is, totally unconditional ones. But one can also constrain the possible users by placing any number of conditions on the amount to be entered or the uses to which it can be put. I will be arguing in Chapter 6 that there is no reason, either in principle or in practice, why it should be thought that democratic procedures should command or require unconditional consent. And it is in fact likely that very little actual consent is ever wholly unconditional. I conclude that there is no literal way in which we can truly claim that a democratic decision must be seen as a decision of the entire community.

I should make it clear that I am not accusing Ranney and Kendall of succumbing to the myth of a specious 'popular will' in talking about the people as a whole, although they are given to such locutions as: 'Democracy, in other words, is one among several ways of organising the State, one among several answers a *community can make* (emphasis added) to where within it sovereign power is to be lodged.'[7] When it comes to a more detailed formulation of the conditions of popular sovereignty, however, they make it clear that what it implies is that *all* members of the community share in power and no class or group is privileged in its access to the ruling power in a community. My complaint here is simply that this is identical to political equality and, hence, redundant as an independent principle or condition of democracy.

Exactly the same can be said about popular consultation. If by political equality we mean more than some legal fiction, if we mean, as Ranney and Kendall put it, 'Each member of the community must have the same choice as his fellows to participate in its total decision-making process', then no separate condition of consultation is required.[8] Participating in the determination of the agenda, in the debate and discussion, and in voting for one or other of the options simply is the mechanism whereby the opinions, preferences and judgements of members of the community are made manifest and determine the eventual outcome. It makes no sense to say that people should be equal in this precise way and also that their opinions should be consulted in the decision-making process. It would seem that the reason popular consultation is cited as an independent factor is that Ranney and Kendall assume that democracy must be representative, for in their explication of this factor they say:

> In democratic government, that is to say, the people must be 'consulted' about the policy they wish those in power to pursue in a given matter – and the holders of office, having learned the popular desire, should proceed to do what the people want them to do. Thus 'popular consultation' in this sense requires three attributes: (1) on matters of public policy there must *be* a genuine popular will; (2) the office holders must be aware of what that will require; and (3) having ascertained the nature of the popular will, they must then faithfully, and invariably translate it into action.[9]

(I will not comment again on the specious unity such language seems to imply.)

Although it is obvious that all governments in the modern world claiming to be to any extent democratic are 'representative' governments, it does not seem desirable to specify an element that derives from a specific form of democracy as a necessary condition of democracy itself. Even when a government is representative, if there is political equality among citizens, this must be constituted by effective rights to determine who the office-holders are to be and, to some extent, what decisions and actions those office-holders must take. Equality in determining outcomes is constituted by those outcomes being determined by the expression of preferences and judgements by the members of the community. Popular consultation is merely a tautological reformulation of this condition. Although it is, perhaps, helpful to emphasise that when government is allegedly 'representative' it is not rendered democratic simply by the assertion of the minority of actual office-holders that, in some mystical way, they are representing 'the people'; for there to be any degree of democracy at all, according to our definition, members of the community must have equal effective rights of participation, the exercise of which is institutionally guaranteed to equally determine to some extent the outcome of decisions.

The majority rule condition is a more complex matter to deal with. I will have a lot more to say about majority rule in a later chapter, in which I will claim that the near definitional equivalence of democracy and majority rule often postulated is a fallacy. We have already seen the appropriate place for the discussion of majority rule, namely in the context of the determination of the conditions of political equality in the third moment of decision-making, specifically at the point of vote aggregation. If the arguments for the majority rule principle as the uniquely democratic decision procedure were correct, they would be so because they demonstrated that such a procedure was the articulation of political equality at the point of vote aggregation. That this is how Ranney and Kendall view the matter is evident from the fact that all of their objections to any alternative to majority rule come down to the claim that such alternatives give a privileged position in the decision-making process to a minority or minorities. In other words, non-majority rule procedures are not instances of political equality. It is again political equality that emerges as the single, though as we have shown, internally complex condition. The other elements, if they are justifiably included in the definition of democracy at all, should be viewed as elaborations of what I am postulating as the core of democracy, namely equal effective rights of participation in the making of those decisions to which a person is subject.

4

The quantitative and the qualitative dimensions: the extent of the franchise and majority rule

In a recent work on Athenian democracy[1] the American classical scholar and historian Chester G. Starr raises a problem that anyone studying the history of political thought in ancient Greece has to confront, namely: granted the exclusion from participation rights of women, resident foreigners, slaves and males under the age of eighteen, is it not more appropriate to refer to the Athenian political system as a broadly based oligarchy rather than, unqualifiedly, as a democracy? Even with a relatively low estimate for the slave population[2] and the failure to add in any estimate for resident foreigners Starr concludes that 'about 18.5% could have been voters'.[3] He deals with the problems that this raises by comparing that percentage to the estimated 20 per cent who were entitled to vote in the United States presidential election of 1860, adding that 'American citizens would by and large indignantly deny that their government was not a democracy.'[4]

There are two interrelated problems with this way of dealing with the question. Firstly, a modern feminist and/or critic of racist oppression might just as indignantly assert that the system of government in the United States in the nineteenth century, far from being democratic in any unqualified way, was a white, male-supremacist oligarchy. Secondly, if we are to get any further than assertion and counter-assertion, we will need a detailed analysis of the complex implications of the concept of democracy as political equality. In this regard, to claim, as Starr does, that 'democracy, after all, is a system of government in which those who are generally considered capable of assessing political issues for themselves have the ultimate voice'[5] is wholly inadequate. To begin with, we must differentiate between:

(a) the internal democraticness of a decision-making procedure, as constituted by the equality of effective power shared by those entitled to participate, and

(b) the democraticness of the distribution of political power in a society as a whole.

As we saw in the previous chapter, the latter constitutes the quantitative dimension of political equality and raises the following theoretical question that lies behind the historical one concerning Athens: assuming that the complex of effective rights constituting a decision-making procedure meet our criteria of political equality, how is the degree of democracy in a society as a whole related to the proportion of the total population to which those rights are extended?

A first approach, which is, in fact, the assumption made in Chapter 3, would be to suggest straightforwardly that the degree of democracy varies directly with the number of those enfranchised as a fraction of the total population. There is, however, a problem with this suggestion. All democratic systems, it can be argued, have operated with some exclusion principle that specifies who should be included/excluded from the franchise; modern-day Western democracies exclude non-nationals, children, the certified insane, for example. It is often claimed that such justifiable exclusions do not affect the democraticness of the political system. It would be ludicrous, it might be argued, to claim that a society in which there had been a 'baby-boom' had become less democratic. The difficulties posed for the straightforward approach become acute when we take into consideration the fact that different societies have used different principles of exclusion, which principles have seemed as justifiable to their holders as ours do to us. Once it is accepted that certain exclusions are, because justified, irrelevant to the question of democraticness, it has to be further accepted that there is an ineradicably evaluative dimension to the concept of democracy. The concept of democracy becomes like, say, the concept of murder, which has a definite descriptive content only when the relevant evaluative/legal dimension of the concept is specified. The problem for the concept of democracy, however, is that there seems to be no agreement on which principles of exclusion are justified and, hence, can be included in the definition. In deciding whether a particular political system is democratic, which set of exclusion principles should be used?

There are, basically, only two ways of answering this question, the moral imperialist approach and the relativist approach, though the former can occur in a diluted 'liberal' guise. The moral imperialist will see no difficulty in producing a definition of democracy incorporating her or his exclusion principles, believing that the whole enterprise can be justified by reference to the normal criteria for definitional construction and the assumed 'rightness' of the evaluative principles called upon. The more liberal version takes into account the possibility of bias and ideological distortion. A set of exclusion principles may be believed to be justifiable when in fact they are little more than a means to facilitate egoistic sectional power-grabbing by providing a cloak of moral rectitude. The liberal will, consequently, argue that seeing as some reference to principles of exclusion is necessary we should insist in our definition of democracy on two things: (i) that the principles be minimally restrictive, and (ii) that implementation be maximally liberal in the sense that we operate with the assumption that people will satisfy the inclusion criteria so that a *special* case has to be made for each specific exclusion.[6] As a political principle in contemporary democracies such a suggestion is admirable; it is, however, theoretically unsatisfactory. Liberal 'minimalist' values are still values; *their* incorporation into the definition needs to be justified as against alternatives. To a person already imbued with liberal, pluralist values, and consequently sceptical of too substantive moral stipulations, minimalist principles will be appealing. But to others holding to a more robust ethical system, such minimalist principles will seem wholly inadequate. Both are offering differing normative perspectives and have to face the fact that for the normative perspective adopted to be incorporated unproblematically into the concept of democracy to the exclusion of alternative perspectives, some fundamental justification of the preferred perspective is needed.

Now, even if one were prepared to consider that one did have an objectively valid, absolute and conclusive proof of one's own normative principles, it would still be the case that those who disagree with one's ethical base would dissent from the definition of democracy that incorporated those principles. In the light of this *de facto* variation some theorists have adopted a plainly relativist position, saving the universality of the definition of democracy by relativising the normative content. 'Democracy' would be defined as, say, popular rule, where 'the people' is specified not objectively and, in descriptive terms, identically for all applications of the concept, but by reference to the principles of exclusion *accepted as valid* in the particular society to which the term is being applied. Schumpeter (though not defining democracy as popular rule) is a perfect example of such an explicit relativist position:

> The salient point, to repeat, is not what we think about any or all of these possible disabilities. The salient point is that, given appropriate views on those and similar subjects, disqualifications on grounds of economic status, religion and sex will enter into the same class with disqualifications which we all of us consider compatible with democracy. We may disapprove of them to be sure . . . Must we not leave it to every populus to define himself?[7]

The problems with the relativist solution are, however, even more devastating than those undermining the moral imperialist stance.

In the first place, the universal univocity of the definition is secured at the expense of emptying the concept of democracy of all definite descriptive content. We can only know whether or not a specific power structure is 'democratic' when we know which of the indefinite number of possible exclusion principles the relevant reference group considers justified. It consequently becomes completely impossible to discuss 'democracy' on a reasonable level of generality; we cannot ask about its conditions of emergence, operation or stability, we cannot raise questions about its likely consequences in society or how it might be justified. Without reference to the specific relevant exclusion principles 'democracy' does not refer to any particular power structure; when specific exclusion principles are called upon in differing applications of the term we can easily end up referring to radically different political power structures.

Consequently, the term ceases to have analytic usefulness, for it can no longer be used to classify and compare different structures of political rule in a generally acceptable manner. In its general form the term has no definite descriptive content, while in its specific applications its descriptive content will vary with the varying normative principles of the relevant reference group.

One consequence of this variation in meaning in specific applications is that 'democracy' threatens to become all-embracing, being applicable to any distribution of political power providing only that the relevant reference group believes the exclusions and consequent restrictions of political power to be justified. In limiting cases the relativist definition produces extremely paradoxical results: an extreme relativist would have to apply the term 'democracy' to, let us say, a monarchy if there existed in the monarchical community a general belief that the tradition-determined sovereign was the only person competent to rule.

A final problem concerns the conflict between the relativist definition and certain central popular usages of the term 'democracy'. While not accepting that popular usage should be taken as an infallible guide in the construction of a definition, some attention should be paid to the core, paradigm uses. Now, if we took the example of an organisation that accepted fairly narrow assumptions of competence (e.g. the Catholic Church, in its restriction of power to bishops and pope) popular usage would deliver the unequivocal verdict of 'not-democratic' irrespective of the sincerity, generality of belief in, or even truth of the competence assumptions in question.

We seem to have arrived here at a genuine impasse that threatens to destroy the coherence of the concept of democracy. Because it appears so obvious to us that the exclusion of certain categories of people does not in any degree affect the democraticness of a political system, we feel it incumbent on us to include a reference to 'justifiable exclusions' in our definition of democracy. But we have to accept as a fact that to other societies it has seemed equally obvious that other categories of people (women, slaves, people of non-Athenian stock) could be excluded 'democratically'. But neither the relativist nor the moral imperialist approach is able to produce an operationalisable, analytically useful or coherent concept of democracy.

The way out of this dilemma is to deny that normatively justifiable exclusions are relevant to the degree of democraticness; to put this more positively, we need to define democracy independently of all normative frameworks, so that the degree of democracy will depend only on the actual proportion of those enfranchised. It might be objected that this move is made inadmissible by our previous concession that some exclusions quite obviously (to us) do not affect democraticness. The belief, however, that this concession implies the necessity of incorporating a normative framework into the definition of democracy is mistaken. The mistake stems from a failure to distinguish between two quite different, though easily confused theses. The first thesis is that exclusions of people from political power that are normatively justifiable do not affect the degree of democraticness. The second thesis is that the concept of democracy is such that the exclusion of certain people from political power in a given organisation is conceptually irrelevant to the democraticness of that organisation.

All concepts have intrinsically determined domains of relevance. The state of things outside such a domain is conceptually irrelevant to the application of the concept or the degree to which the concept is instantiated if it is subject to degrees. To begin with, let us take a simple mathematical example, the concept 'prime'. It is evident that this concept has a 'relevance domain' that restricts its possible application to integers. In considering its actual applicability we need not take other types of number into consideration, nor need we examine trees, stars or whatever. To illustrate the point further, take a concept with more normatively political relevance, the concept of racial justice. In deciding the extent to which a given society can be said to be racially just we do not need to look at how that society treats animals. This irrelevance (of how animals are treated) to the application of the concept of racial justice does not rest on a normative assumption concerning what rights we should concede to animals. The most fervent animal liberationist will not think that how we treat animals is relevant to racial justice. My argument is that the concept of democracy also has such an intrinsically determined domain of relevance. The thesis that we must include a reference to norms of justified exclusion in our definition of democracy is based on the claim that we indubitably accept that certain justified exclusions – e.g. very young children, non-resident non-nationals – do not affect the degree of democraticness. My counter argument is that the exclusion of such categories does *not* affect the degree of democraticness not because such exclusions are justified but rather because the status of such categories of people is conceptually irrelevant to the application of the term democracy.

To demonstrate this thesis I will have to formulate a definition of democracy from which the determinants of its domain of relevance will be evident. I will then show that the irrelevance of exclusion from political participation of categories of people outside this domain is completely independent of whether such exclusions are also believed to be justified. I will then look at some of the positive merits of the non-evaluative definition of democracy proposed.

I have defined democracy as a system of decision-making in which all those who are subject to the decisions made have equally effective power to determine the political outcomes of the decision-making. This definition provides two determinants of the domain of relevance; (a) those who are subject to the decisions, and (b) those who can participate in making the decisions. Anyone to whom one or other of these conditions does not apply is outside the relevance domain. This enables us to deal unproblematically, by calling on the first determinant, with the exclusion of non-resident foreigners that are in no way subject to the decisions made. Their exclusion from participation does not lessen the democraticness because they are outside the relevance domain of the concept. This conclusion is completely independent of whether or not we think such exclusion normatively justified. Most people would probably think that anyone not systematically subject to decisions would have no right to be consulted. My argument is that it is not their not having such rights that makes their exclusion irrelevant. To see that this is so imagine a case being made for the justifiability of their inclusion. A Platonic paternalist might think it perfectly justifiable to give political power to an outside society of wise philosophers; even Plato, however, would not have thought that excluding such philosophers was undemocratic; he would simply have thought it unwise. The point I am making is that whether or not the exclusion is thought justified, it is irrelevant to the application of the concept of democracy in that those who are not subject to a power are outside the relevance domain of the concept of democracy.

Let us take, now, an example of a category of people excluded by our second determinant of the domain of relevance, the ability to participate in the making of decisions. I should emphasise that what is being referred to in this clause of the criterion is *the ability to make a decision*, not the ability to make a possibly sensible decision, or a reasonably informed decision. Exclusion from formal rights of participation does not affect democraticness, according to this clause, when formal inclusion would not be capable of producing real inclusion; when, that is, the person formally included could not be said to be making a decision at all and, hence, could not be said to be participating in the exercise of power. Very young children (under the age of two, perhaps) would fall into this category. It is instructive to compare the exclusion of such children with the exclusion, let us say, of 12 year olds. There is no doubt whatsoever that 12 year olds are subject to decisions made in a society. It seems to me equally obvious that they are capable of participation in the making of those decisions. A community might think, however, that in general there is a high probability that 12 year olds will not be capable of making reasonably informed, sensible, independent decisions and might believe that, consequently, a good case could be made for justifiably excluding them. My argument is that we should, in accepting the non-evaluative definition of democracy proposed, accept that such exclusions are undemocratic, though perhaps justifiably so. Whereas the exclusion of the very young is not undemocratic, because it is a conceptual impossibility to include them. It is precisely by confusing these two radically different types of exclusion that the whole problem arose in the first place.

It might, perhaps, be worth pointing out a possible subterranean motive for the persistence of this confusion. Given the generally honorific associations of the term 'democratic' in the modern world, if we can pretend that real exclusions do not affect democraticness by confusing them with domain-relevance exclusions, this handily relieves us of the responsibility for the serious normative consideration of exclusions, which would be unavoidable once those exclusions were admitted as undemocratic.

The first major merit of the non-evaluative definition proposed is that in so separating the semantic from the substantive evaluative issues it allows us to focus on the important evaluative questions that should be raised about democracy, rather than tying up the whole debate in a tangle of circular definitions.

Secondly, of course, the non-evaluative definition, in escaping the dilemma of relativism or moral imperialism, produces a concept of democracy that is operationalisable and can be generally used for the analytic task of comparing and classifying different types of political power structure.

Thirdly, as I have already argued, the non-evaluative definition does correspond with certain central cases of ordinary usage which, in some important contexts, will accept that a justifiable deviation from democracy, justifiable because of a lack of competence, is still, even though justifiable, a deviation from democracy. I refer to the example previously cited; even the Catholic Church does not believe itself democratic, though it does believe that its bishops and pope are the only group with competence to make important decisions in faith and morals.

As I began this discussion with a reference to 'Athenian democracy' it would be appropriate to conclude by noting that contemporaneously with that 'democracy' Aristotle had developed a set of distinctions that would have enabled him to provide an account of the degree of democracy existing in Athens that would accord perfectly with the approach adopted in this work. In *The Politics* Aristotle distinguishes between three forms of rule or, more accurately, three ways in which one can be subject to power.[8] These he refers to as the master–slave form of power, paternal power and 'political' power. In each of the three cases those who come under the power are, equally, subject to the power in question. The master–slave type is identified by two factors; the slave does not participate in the exercise of the power and the slave's interest is not taken into account in the exercise of power. With respect to paternal power, those subject to it (typically, according to Aristotle, women and children) also do not participate in its exercise, but their interests, as articulated by the paternal power-holders, are held to be the prime determinants of the decisions made. The third type of power, 'political', Aristotle thinks of as appropriate in a community of equals, and is constituted by the fact that those subject to power also participate in its exercise. The reason we put 'political' in inverted commas is that one of Aristotle's reasons for making the distinctions was to enable him to say that actual structures of political power were in fact sometimes instances of master–slave, sometimes instances of paternal and sometimes instances of 'political' power in his technical sense. Aristotle thought it obvious, for example, that Plato had been recommending that political power should be of the paternal type. I am suggesting that Aristotle would have found no difficulty with describing the power structure in Athens as democratic with respect to Athenian males over the age of twenty but also as paternal and/or master-slave with respect to all others systematically subject to its rule. That conclusion would have remained unaffected by how justifiable he might have considered the different types of rule to be in the circumstances.

The quantitative dimension of political equality should, then, be defined as being dependent on the simple ratio between those affected by decisions and those with effective power to participate in the making of the decisions. Given the plurality of possible principles of justified inclusion and exclusion, any alternative definition will result in incoherence. I pointed out in the previous chapter that the quantitative and qualitative dimensions of democracy are conceptually independent; given the treatment of the quantitative dimension we can formulate the following complex answer to the question of how democratic ancient Athens was, using, of course, our own concept of democracy. Firstly, from the quantitative perspective the Athenian political system was not as democratic as it would have been had, for example, women and resident foreigners been granted political rights, though it was far more democratic than the political system in existence before Kleisthenes' constitution when the lower orders of Athenian society were excluded from significant political power. From the qualitative perspective, for adult Athenian males, political equality was of a very high degree, arguably much higher than the degree of political equality achieved in modern systems of representative government.

I have already spelt out the basic dimensions of qualitative political equality, but there was one specific problem that I left unsettled; namely, the precise conditions for maximum political equality in the third moment of decision-making. The problem arises because of alternative procedures for aggregating votes. The question must be asked: do some of those procedures guarantee higher levels of qualitative political equality than others? In particular, what is the democratic status of the majority-rule procedure?

It is undoubtedly true that in the popular mind democracy is often identified with simple majority rule. Furthermore, within academic contributions to the democratic debate there is a strong tradition that identifies democracy with political equality and political equality with institutionally guaranteed equality of weight in the decision-making process. Influential and widely cited works such as R. Dahl's *Preface to Democratic Theory*, J. Lively's *Democracy* and A. Ranney and W. Kendall's *Democracy and the American Party System* explicitly argue that simple majority rule is, at the very least, a necessary condition of democracy.[9]

In spelling out this explicitly posited relation each of these works notes that this procedurally guaranteed equality, interpreted in a radical sense as applying to each issue decided upon, has itself certain necessary conditions. In the first place, a fair procedure of popular consultation (assuming universal suffrage) is required, giving each person in the community the real chance of manifesting her or his preference with respect to possible political outcomes. Furthermore, each person's manifested preference must be given the same weight by the procedure that is accepted as determining the outcome; as it is normally put: 'one person, one vote; one vote, one weight'.

It is, of course, well known that a decision-making procedure that perfectly satisfied the above slogan need not be either a simple majority system, nor, for that matter, be fully democratic. 'One person, one vote; one vote one weight' is only a necessary, not a sufficient condition, of simple majority rule. In Lively's formulation, such a condition guarantees only *prospective* equality; i.e. prior to a decision being made, no individual has any greater chance than any other individual of determining the outcome of the process.[10] This criterion would be satisfied, for example, by a procedure that randomly selected one person's manifested preference, and allowed that preference to determine the outcome. While we would admit that this procedure does not favour *in advance* any particular person, there is a stage reached in the application of the procedure at which the preference of only one person is taken as determining the outcome. Looked at retrospectively, such a procedure actually guarantees that in the determination of any particular outcome it is the preference of one single person that is effective. As Dahl formulates the matter, our normal intuitions concerning the distribution of power required by democracy demand not only initial equality but also a procedure that guarantees that the most preferred alternative is the one to be implemented; furthermore, he argues, assigning equal weight to each vote implies that the most preferred alternative is the alternative preferred by *most*:

> The only rule compatible with decision-making in a populistic democracy is the majority principle . . . The principle of majority rule prescribes that in choosing between alternatives, the alternative preferred by the greater number is selected.[11]

The problem is that procedures that give initial equality of opportunity to determine outcomes can differ significantly in the way in which, at a later stage of their application, they select manifested preferences as determinants of outcomes. In view of the likelihood of several incompatible alternatives gaining some support, it would seem inevitable that any workable procedure would have to have a later-stage selection of a particular group of preferences as determining the outcome. Granted the enormous difficulties in registering and aggregating intensities of preference, the only available criterion for aggregating and comparing groups of preferences is one based on the number of votes cast for each of the alternatives. Consequently, the later stage selection of a set of preferences as determinant of the outcome can only be formulated as a numerical quota. But which numerical quota criterion is most in accordance with our intuitions concerning democracy? Let us examine Lively's way of dealing with this question; it is extremely lucid and relatively non-technical.[12]

According to Lively later-stage numerical quota criteria can be grouped into four mutually exclusive and logically exhaustive categories; namely stipulated majority criteria, simple majority criteria, simple minority criteria and stipulated minority criteria. The latter two would seem to be intuitively undemocratic and anyway, as Lively argues, would become, in practice, equivalent to the first two; since if it were generally known that a version of the minority criterion was the operational one voters would vote for the least preferred alternative in an attempt to push it over the minority limit, hence transforming the minority system into its mirror image majority system. Consequently, the two majority systems seem to be the only serious contenders. Can we say which of these procedures is the more democratic, the more in accordance with maximal political equality? Suppose, for the sake of argument, that some form of minority system was workable. It would seem to follow that the smaller the determining minority, the less democratic would the system be; certainly, the smaller the determining minority, the further away would the procedure be from Dahl's criterion of the alternative preferred by most. In view of this, it might at first seem that if some form of majority system were used, democraticness would increase in direct proportion to the level of stipulated majority required. Lively's analysis neatly shows the fallacy in this assumption. For, as he points out, the higher the stipulated majority required, the more likely will it be that a dissenting minority will block the implementation of a highly supported majority preference. In fact, any stipulated majority system will increase the probability that it will be the preferences of a minority that will, at least negatively, determine the outcome. Consequently, if we accept both the undemocraticness of minority determination of outcome, and the logically exhaustive four-fold categorisation of possible procedures, the only democratic procedure is the simple majority one. Lest this seems like a too begrudging acceptance of simple majority rule as the least of four evils, we could attempt to put the positive side of the argument by looking at the demand for political equality in a historical context. The demand for political equality has always been a protest against inherited minority political privilege. From this point of view it could be plausibly argued that the one continuous thread in the whole democratic tradition has been the rejection of minority rule. What can be said, then, in favour of a simple majority system is that in the context of maximising prospective equality it is the only system that guarantees the impossibility of minority determination of political outcomes; the very facet that we have claimed as the central core to all democratic movements.

As has often been pointed out, however, the situation is not quite so straightforward; majority rule, the operation of the simple majority system, may lead, in certain circumstances, to consequences that seem on the one hand so socially unacceptable as to be describable as majority tyranny, and on the other hand simply undemocratic. The problematic circumstances usually referred to are those in which (1) there is a large dissenting minority on a certain issue that for them constitutes something absolutely fundamental to their well-being; or (2) there is a large permanent minority whose interests coalesce around fixed sets of alternatives that range over the whole spectrum of political outcomes. In each of these cases the straightforward application of the simple majority system would involve the total disregard in practice of the central, fundamental interests of a group in the society. In the second case, in particular, the minority group would be so aware of its identity in opposition to the majority on practically all political issues that it could not fail to be aware also that the formal equality of opportunity to influence outcomes via the simple majority procedure would not in actual practice *ever* give them any power to realise their major political objective. It would seem at least plausible to claim that permanent minorities do not have any real power to determine outcomes, since over the whole range of outcomes preferred by the permanent minority none of their preferences is ever effective. Their formal prospective equality is never in fact translated into retrospectively establishable determination of outcomes. They have, and they know they have, no power at all. The later stage selection of the majority as determinant of the outcome excludes the minority preference from having any influence. If a minority is permanently excluded then how can we say that there is anything like an equal distribution of effective power? There is an initial equal opportunity, but this initial equality is given the lie by the selection at the later stage.

There have been four types of considerations forwarded to deal with this apparent dilemma in democratic theory:

1. Dahl's 'minorities rule' thesis.
2. Buchanan and Tullock's 'log-rolling' hypothesis.
3. The consolations of democracy argument.
4. The reassessment of the value of democracy.

I will deal with each of these in turn.

Dahl's solution to the problem of the possibility of majority tyranny consists, fundamentally, in the claim that it is a pseudo-problem based on a set of false assumptions concerning the actual mechanics of political decision-making in functioning 'democracies'.[13] He claims that his own 'minorities rule' thesis more accurately represents the normal process of policy determination and that in the light of such a thesis we see that the real determinants of political outcomes are not tyrannical majorities but rather intense minorities whose effectiveness is a function of their active organisation that itself is a function of the intensity of their interest. Paradoxically, the end result is claimed by Dahl to be basically in accord with democratic requirements since each potential minority interest has the same (equal) opportunity and the same (roughly) access to resources necessary to make its preference, if intense enough, effective. The 'minorities rule' thesis is equivalent, I think, to three subtheses concerning:

(a) the relation between interest groups and society as a whole;
(b) the relation between interests themselves;
(c) the role of minority groups in the determination of political outcomes.

It is usually false, according to Dahl, to see society as a set of individuals uniquely assignable to a set of interest groups differentiated from each other along a single axis. A society is not usually made up of a set of subgroups with exclusive memberships determined by reference to mutually exclusive interests. Rather, we should see conflicting interests of a certain sort as grounding *one* way of subdividing society into groups with a conflicting interest, while another type of interest grounds another way of subdividing the society into groups whose membership will not necessarily (probably will not) overlap with the membership of the groups defined by reference to the first type of interest. And so on, for the myriad other interests that individual people will have. The membership of interest groups defined with respect to interests of different types is not likely to encompass the same set of individuals.

It is easy to fall into the fallacy of assuming that with respect to some particular issue, A, if there is a minority that is intensely pro-A, there must be a majority that is intensely anti-A. Whereas, according to Dahl, it is perfectly possible for the anti-A majority to be not all that concerned about A. Incompatible preferences are not necessarily clashes of equally intense or fundamental interests. Not all interests are equally important.

In the normal run of events a well-organised active minority of quite a small size can play a decisive role in the determination of a political outcome. In fact, according to Dahl, in the normal run of events *it is* well-organised active minorities that do play the decisive role in the determination of outcomes that are of particular relevance to them. The basis of this likely effectiveness of organised minorities can be derived from points (a) and (b) just discussed. Within a democratic/representative context an incumbent government will have to have secured 'majority' support. In the light of points (a) and (b), however, it is unlikely that this majority will be a monolithic group all sharing a widespread set of interests in common and having no interests in common with the minority opposition supporters. It is much more likely that the majority will be made up of a relatively unstable coalition of interest groups, many of which will have interests in common with members of the opposition supporters. Now, it is obvious that a government need only alienate a fairly small percentage of its supporters to fail to maintain its winning coalition. An intense minority, active and well-organised, can threaten this failure directly, if its electoral support is needed, and indirectly by undermining the popularity of the government with a sufficient number of its supporters who may not, on the particular issue, have any fundamental interest at stake but who may nevertheless be turned against the government by a well-organised barrage of anti-government propaganda. Providing that an intense minority is not faced with an equally intense and vocal majority, the minority cannot be easily ignored by the government. We need only add to this the thesis that the intensely interested are more likely than not to be the well-organised and intensely vocal to derive the full thesis that intense interest groups are likely to be the central agents in the day-to-day determination of political outcomes.

This polyarchal or pluralist dissolution of the problem of majority tyranny has come under much criticism. Even were we to grant that the official political forum was the major locus of power in society, the solution of the problem of intensity/fundamentality of interests would only be solved if we assumed that a group whose fundamental interest was at stake on some issue would almost always realise this and develop an intense preference in the area in question. Secondly, intensity of preference would have to be fairly readily transformable into vigorous political activity and, thirdly, there would have to be a relatively high probability that this would result in a well-organised campaign that would itself result in a high probability of success. As many of Dahl's critics have pointed out,[14] a great deal has to be assumed if we are to be in any way confident about the general probability of this sequence being realised. It has been claimed with some justification that Dahl's dissolution of the problem of majority tyranny over intense minorities replaces the problem with one of the tyranny of a few well-placed, well-organised minorities. It should be obvious, however, that whatever the merits of such criticisms, Dahl's solution works for our problems only by defining them out of existence. If there *are* permanent minorities whose interests converge over a wide-range of social issues, the preconditions of pluralism are just not realised. Neither are they realised in the simpler situation of a minority on some issue that is seen as absolutely fundamental to them faced with an equally intense majority.

We can deal fairly briefly with Buchanan and Tullock's conception of log-rolling, since, in terms of its relevance to the present problem, it can be considered a special case of minorities rule theory, being distinguished by its specification of a particular mechanism, vote-trading, by which an interested minority might be enabled to secure its preferred outcome in the face of initial majority opposition. Buchanan and Tullock present their elaboration of the concept of log-rolling in the context of outcomes being directly determined by majority voting.[15] A minority that is intensely pro-A will, of course, by definition, be faced with a majority that is anti-A. Buchanan and Tullock note, however, that the oppositional majority is not necessarily monolithic; in particular, a minority subset of the anti-A may be a minority that is intensely pro-B, such that they would prefer the combination B and A, to the combination not-B and not-A. Providing that our original pro-A minority would prefer the combination A and B, rather than not-A and not-B, despite being anti-B, a coalition is possible between the pro-As and pro-Bs, each party trading its vote on the issue that is of less relevance to them, creating, if they are sufficiently large minorities, the requisite majority in each case.

There is no doubt that the possibility of such coalitions is an important mitigating factor in the application of simple majority procedures, guaranteeing, whenever such coalitions are possible, the partial effectiveness of minority preferences. Being a special case of the minorities rule thesis, however, it suffers most of its defects as a solution to the problems I am considering. It offers no direct solace to a minority fundamentally affected by a majority decision that is not considered negotiable in exchange for minority support on other issues, nor, *a fortiori*, to a permanent minority faced with a permanent majority that does not need minority support on the whole range of social issues over which it holds sway. It is the realisation of this that turns many democratic theorists to our third attempted solution.

By 'the consolations of democracy', I am referring to a set of considerations that attempt to show that in all probability the disvalue to a minority group stemming from the fact that its preferences are not effectively influential in determining the content of a set of political outcomes will be outweighed by the more indirect, positively valuable consequences on the group of having a democratic procedure for conflict resolution. The type of consequences usually referred to can be distinguished into two categories: (i) the long-term political outcome consequences, and (ii) the wholly indirect consequences. In category (i) I am thinking of the possibility that though a group is an ineffectual minority with respect to a set of specific issues, it might, in the future find itself part of an effective majority on other issues, and it might, furthermore, find itself able in the future, whether by lobbying, vote-trading or rational persuasion, to get the decisions from which it currently dissents reversed. In category (ii) I am referring to values that are secured by democracy independently of any particular political outcomes, such things as equal legal status, freedom of speech, association and opposition, the existence of institutions enabling peaceful and orderly succession of governments. It is undoubtedly true that all these things are realised in a properly functioning democracy and it may even be true that their realisation may be valuable enough to a minority group to outweigh the dis-value of the non-satisfaction of certain of its specific interests. The problem is, however, that it may not be. The general values of democracy may pale into insignificance for a minority compared with what it sees as some massive injustice or, in the case of the permanent minority, the continuing injustice of its exclusion from power by the operation of a majoritarian system. It is such possibilities that lead on to the fourth attempted solution.

The revaluation of democracy that I have in mind is characterised by a certain hard-headed realism that is a useful counterbalance to the all too usual unthinking acceptance of democracy as the universally highest, perhaps only, value to be achieved in political life. In a Schumpeterian spirit it is pointed out that democracy is a particular *method* of arriving at political decisions; no more, and no less. As a decision-making procedure its claimed value must be demonstrated by reference to its capacity for achieving other, more fundamental, values. Consequently, there must *be* other, more fundamental, values; freedom, autonomy, human development, community, equality and access to material and cultural resources, justice, and so on. Even when it is accepted that democracy may produce some of its valued consequences indirectly, i.e. by the fact of its existence rather than by the content of its outcomes, it must still be recognised that democracy's capacity to achieve these desired goals needs to be demonstrated. Secondly, so this revaluation approach argues, it must be recognised that the relationship between democracy and most of these sociopolitical goals is a contingent one, and being contingent it can on occasion fail. If it does fail, if democracy as majority rule produces, for example, a permanently oppressed minority, there is nothing inconsistent in arguing that for the sake of more important values democracy must, perhaps temporarily, be deviated from. Such is the revaluation of democracy that insists that democracy ought not to be the be-all and end-all of political and social ideals, and, consequently, is prepared to condemn democracy as majority rule when it leads to injustice.

I have a great deal of sympathy with each of these approaches. It seems to be essential to realise that a majority-rule system *can* produce so grievously oppressed minorities as to be challengeable on the grounds of its injustice. But it is also important to realise that the indirectly produced values of democracy should not be lightly dismissed and that it will always be extremely difficult to decide whether the unjustness of a particular series of outcomes outweighs these indirect, and rather amorphous, benefits. Furthermore, it is also necessary not to make too much of the problem of the possibility of majority tyranny, for, despite defects, the arguments and analyses produced by Dahl and Buchanan and Tullock do demonstrate the varied ways in which intense minorities can have an effective voice in the political process. There still remain, however, the situations, particularly that of the permanent minority, in which these considerations seem to fail to reconcile democracy and justice. I will argue, however, that what cannot be reconciled with justice is not democracy as political equality, but majority rule. For, I will maintain, the identification of political equality with majority rule is fallacious. It is fallacious in a very simple way. The argument attempting to show the 'democratic' superiority of the simple majority system, as outlined earlier, contains a crucial premise, the claim of logical exhaustiveness for the four-fold classification of procedures that determine which group of votes will determine the outcome. This premise, I will show, is based on a further background assumption that is never articulated. Furthermore, this background assumption is, in most cases of political disagreement, invalid. Only by falsely assuming its validity can theorists like Lively, Dahl, Ranney and Kendall be misled into thinking that equal weighting of preferences must, to maintain overall political equality, imply selection of outcomes on the basis of a simple majority. Once we see exactly what this unformulated background assumption implies we will be able to appreciate that when it does not hold, which, as I have said, is the normal situation, there are numerous alternative procedures available for relating preferences to the procedural determination of outcomes. Furthermore, I will argue that some of these procedures will immediately appear as immeasurably nearer to the optimalisation of political equality than the simple majority system that comes about the lowest in the ranks of the potentially democratic. Rather than simply stating baldly the questionable background assumption, and proceeding immediately to a demonstration of the fallaciousness of the simple majority argument by proving the contingency of its assumption, I want to situate the discussion in a wider context by examining briefly certain normative elements of the democratic ideology that will be appealed to later in the argument.

From a normative perspective, as we will see in Chapter 7, democracy is grounded upon general egalitarianism, the principle of the non-discriminatory distribution of social goods. The Aristotelian 'activist' tradition of ethics would view the active participation in the directing of communal affairs as intrinsically worthwhile, hence as itself a social good and hence as not to be discriminatingly distributed (without some weighty overriding justification, which, as a matter of fact Aristotle himself thought only too easy to find in the case of women and slaves). Power, however, is also an instrumental good, the present capacity to achieve future apparent goods as Hobbes described it,[16] in the light of which a different type of egalitarian argument can be brought into play. The basic egalitarian principle insists that no one person's interests deserve any greater respect than the interests of any one else; more positively, each person's interests should be treated with equal respect in the determination of political outcomes. Consequently, in so far as having an equal say in the determination of political outcomes is relevant to the ensuring that those outcomes give equal consideration to interests, political equality becomes important. In other words, political equality is justifiable instrumentally only if it can be shown to be relevant to the achievement of equal respect for people's interests in the content of the political outcomes produced.

Let us imagine, as a deliberate utopian fantasy, a community of perfect democrats; not simply a community that holds steadfastly to accepted democratic procedures, but a group of people imbued with the egalitarian principles outlined above as part of the normative rationale of democracy. Suppose that in some particular fundamental issue area a genuine conflict of interest emerges. Group A, let us say 70 per cent of the population, see option A as most in accordance with their interests, while a second group see option B, an option wholly excluded by A, as, with respect to their own interests, clearly the most preferable. What will group A do? Will they rub their hands with glee at the fact that they are in the majority, put the matter to a vote and send group B off to read Dahl on the power of intense minorities as a consolation? If they were imbued, as imagined, with the democratic ideology, they will realise that maximising their own interest satisfaction would lead to the complete denial of interest satisfaction on the part of group B. On the basis of their hypothesised internalisation of the principle of equal respect for fundamental interests, we can deduce that instead of pushing their majoritarian advantage to realise their own interests at the expense of the minority, they will give equal consideration to the interests of that minority and sacrifice the maximisation of their own interests for the sake of allowing the minority interest some influence in the determination of the outcome and hence some satisfaction by the outcome. A utopian fantasy! No system of decision-making can rely on goodwill and the internalisation of egalitarian respect; and, furthermore, even if it could, procedures are necessary to expedite decisions. But, suppose that we had a decision-making procedure that institutionalised this arrival at compromise. Would we not thereby circumvent the necessity for reliance on goodwill and at the same time expedite the process of deciding? In principle, yes; but, it will be argued, any decision-making procedure to be democratic will have to embody political equality. This will have to be achieved by giving everyone the opportunity to manifest their preference and then by giving equal weight to those manifested preferences in the determination of the outcome. If there is, as we are imagining there to be, a difference of preferences, some procedure will have to be adopted that will assign one group of expressed preferences the role of determining the outcome, as a choice between the mutually exclusive possibilities. We have now, of course, come full circle; we are faced with Lively's argument that such procedures are classifiable into four groups, etc.

Our digression into the utopian fantasy has, however, not been without purpose, for it will enable us to formulate with precision the background assumption, referred to above, which is necessary for the validity of the majoritarian argument *and* it will enable us to see clearly how limited in applicability that assumption is.

The assumption required to render the majoritarian argument valid is that in the problem area addressed by the decision-making procedure there is only a limited number of mutually exclusive possible outcomes, one of which will be implemented at the expense of all of the others. The reason why we could imagine our utopian group implementing an informal decision-making procedure that allowed some influence to the expressed preference of the minority was that we assumed that between the outcomes A and B, most preferred by the majority and minority respectively, there was at least one other possible outcome, the compromise outcome.

The argument of the simple majoritarians completely depends upon the assumption that, in the nature of the case, a typical political conflict is necessarily a winner-takes-all situation; that is, a conflict in which, irrespective of the nature of the decision-making procedure, there are a limited number of possible outcomes, each of which gives the maximum pay-off to one group and zero pay-off to the other group. Far from this being typical, it is almost impossible to describe a situation in which a political conflict must of necessity be resolved in one of only a limited number of mutually exclusive ways; perhaps issues of war and peace might be one example, though even here there are degrees and types of both war and peace. It is *much more* normal for it to be the case that in an area of political disagreement there are numerous possible outcomes, only a few of which are the most preferred outcomes of the conflicting groups. The illusion that, in the nature of the case, political disagreement is a winner-takes-all game is created by the fact that when decisions are made via a majoritarian system the decision-making procedure *itself* transforms the disagreement into the limiting case of zero-sum conflict in which the most preferred option of the majority is implemented, with maximum pay-off to the majority and zero pay-off to the minority. There are normally any number of alternative possible outcomes that would distribute the pay-offs more evenly.

It might be conceded by the simple majoritarian at this stage of the argument, that we have demonstrated the intimate connection between majoritarianism and the by no means always justified winner-takes-all construal of political disagreement. But we can only overturn the majoritarian principle if we can show that when the winner-takes-all assumption is not warranted there will thereby be made applicable alternative decision-making procedures that will incorporate prospective equality and achieve retrospective equality to a higher degree than simple majoritarianism. But what would these decision-making procedures look like? To make the answer to this question obvious we need only take one particular area of democratic decision-making that is perfectly familiar, the decision by the electorate as to who will represent them in government.

Suppose that we have an electorate of 100,000 and that it is decided that the ratio of electorate to representatives should be 10,000:1, giving us ten representatives for the total electorate. The candidates for election, let us imagine, belong to three competing parties, A, B and C, with a support in the electorate of 60 per cent, 30 per cent and 10 per cent respectively, spread evenly throughout the 100,000. A simple method of deciding on the final list of representatives would be to break the decision down into yes/no choices for each candidate, the yes/no option being determined by simple majoritarian procedures. It is clear that, granting a vote along party lines, the candidates from party A will be elected. It is a winner-takes-all game, with the majority getting 100 per cent maximum pay-off and the minorities' returns being zero. A simple-minded simple majoritarian might say that this is, perhaps, unfortunate, but democratic; more democratic, certainly than the 30 per cent getting its way or the 10 per cent getting its way. But, of course, these are not the only possible outcomes; the possible outcomes include all the possible permutations and combinations of candidates in the ten places to be filled. What is more, there are any number of well-tried proportional representation election procedures (e.g. making the 100,000 a ten-seater constituency with an election quota of 10,000) that could produce results that would give the minorities a retrospective influence proportional to their numerical weight.[17]

It is not my intention to enter the debate concerning the merits of various proportional representation election systems in the whole context of problems raised by the functions of national government, coalitions, continuity and coherence of policy, constituency representation, accountability and so on. I have taken the case of election of representatives as a clear example of a 'democratic' decision that could have many possible outcomes but that is rendered a winner-takes-all game by the simple majoritarian procedures. The central point that I want to emphasise is that in such cases there is *no justification whatsoever* for the claim that simple majoritarianism is the only system consistent with political equality. Let us remind ourselves that all the procedures we are considering are 'one person, one vote; one vote, one weight' and hence are identical with respect to prospective equality. With respect to retrospective equality, proportionality systems score far higher than simple majority systems, with the plurality system so low on the scale as hardly meriting being classified as a system of retrospective equality at all.

My central theoretical conclusions are as follows:

1. As a general argument, Lively's identification of political equality with simple majority rule is invalid.
2. When the potential outcomes of a political decision are possibly composite or subject to degrees (as most distributive outcomes are) a decision-making procedure that guarantees an influence in determining the outcome proportional to numerical weight will

be far higher on the scale of retrospective equality than either a simple majority or a plurality system.

3. A simple majority system is only justifiable from the point of view of political equality when, in the nature of the case, the only possible political outcomes are winner-takes-all outcomes.

In conclusion, let us look at some of the more specific implications of these theses that identify political equality with proportionality of influence. I want to look at three areas. First, by way of a possible counter-argument, the anarchist-inspired claim that full retrospective equality would imply the legitimacy of individual dissent from *any* governmental outcome, itself implying the lack of legitimacy of any centrally imposed decision. Secondly, the question of the appropriate scope for central imposition of order, and thirdly, the question of the optimal structures of government decision-making from the perspective of maximum retrospective equality.

It is easy to appreciate the plausibility of the anarchist argument based on the fundamental value of political equality. A political outcome exists, in the last analysis, in the structure of the action and interaction of individuals. If a political decision, no matter how arrived at, is imposed from the centre against *any* dissent, it contravenes absolute political equality, for those in favour deny any influence to the dissenters. There is no doubt that this is the case. Where the anarchist argument falls down, however, is in its claim that if each individual is allowed, by means of tacit individual mutual accommodation, to act as he or she thinks best the end result will be optimal political equality. The mistake in the argument stems from the failure to appreciate that owing to the interdependence of people's choices the simple absence of a centrally organised decision-making process will not prevent the asymmetry of power and influence; some will have more accommodating to do than others. As Bernard Shaw argued in his Fabian Tract against the American individualist anarchist Benjamin Tucker, if we think that a majority will use its power to dominate a dissenting minority via the process of a 'democratic' decision, it will have, if anything, more chance of being dominant in the absence of a centrally imposed order.[18] If the decision-making mechanism institutionally guarantees *some* influence to minorities, it is more likely that their voice will have a degree of effectiveness than if outcomes are left to the informal process of mutual accommodation. The point is that whether formally decided upon or not it is both necessary and inevitable that, owing to the interdependence of all members of a community, there be some areas of social life that are structurally determined. This raises our second question, can we determine whether, from the point of view of political equality, there *are* other areas of life that are better left to individual decisions?

Taking our cue from the observed weakness in the anarchist argument, we can reverse the consideration and state a general criterion for excluding some areas from central decision-making. If the action of an individual or group does not either illegitimately or significantly restrict the range of options open to others then, from the point of view of maximising political equality, the anarchist argument is valid; maximum retrospective equality is achieved by allowing the outcome to be determined by individual choice. This conclusion parallels, of course, the classical liberal thesis, the freedom of each is to be maximised consistently with the guarantee that no one's freedom interferes with the freedom of others. What is novel in the way in which our conclusion is arrived at is that instead of respect for the individual's conscience being seen as a legitimate liberal constraint on the implementation of democracy, we have argued for it from the perspective of democracy as political equality itself. Majorities have no rights to monopolise political power. Majoritarianism is justifiable, as all the arguments in its favour demonstrate, only by appeal to the more fundamental value of political equality. In areas where, from the nature of the issue, there need not be a general societal rule, political equality is maximised by the social outcome being the result of individual decisions. How, precisely, the boundary between these two areas is to be drawn is a question that will be taken up in Chapter 6. When a general societal rule is required, equality is maximised by institutionally guaranteed proportionality. Only in the limiting case of the issue being of its very nature a winner-takes-all issue is simple majoritarianism justified as the lesser evil.

What, finally, in institutional terms would proportionality imply? It would involve maximal proportional representation in the electoral system. It would also involve the continuance of proportional influence into the decision-making mechanisms of the legislature, for example, by the allotment of cabinet posts on the basis of proportionality and perhaps, even, proportionality in the control of government spending. It might involve giving temporary veto power to minorities in the legislature as a way of, while not guaranteeing final proportional effectiveness, increasing the countervailing power of minorities. Some of these measures have, in fact, been adopted in the consociational democracies, as Lijphart has described.[19] And while it is important to recognise that there are values other than political equality to be considered in the normative analysis of any system of rule, I think I have shown conclusively that the identification of political equality in theory with majority rule is fundamentally misguided. From the perspective of the qualitative dimension of political equality, insofar as this depends on each person having an equally effective say in the determination of the outcome of the decision-making process, proportionality vote-aggregation procedures will tend to maximise such equality far more so than majoritarian alternatives.

It should be noted in conclusion that, as with my argument concerning the quantitative dimension of political equality, the present claim that proportionality procedures are more democratic than majority procedures is not meant to be a directly evaluative claim. Majority procedures, as has often been argued, simplify decision-making and may lead to more coherent approaches to political issues and these benefits might, in fact, justify sacrificing some degree of political equality and democracy for the sake of efficiency. It is, however, important to realise that such a sacrifice is being made; it is important not to confuse democracy with efficiency.

5

The liberal variant: democracy as rights

> Full equality for most cannot but mean the equal submission of the great masses under the command of some elite who manages their affairs. While an equality of rights under a limited government is possible and an essential condition of individual freedom, a claim for equality of material position can be met only by a government with totalitarian powers.[1]

This passage is indicative of a completely different approach to the understanding of democracy. This approach would judge my definition over-inclusive. According to my definition the political equality constituting democracy must be articulated through equal rights of participation and equal rights to access and express relevant information; but in addition I have included whatever background conditions might be required to make those rights effective. In certain limited and very specific situations the necessity of such background conditions is uncontentious. To illustrate the point let us restrict ourselves to the simple right to vote, normally exercised by going to a polling station and marking a ballot paper. Consider the following two situations. Firstly, a poll is being held and the people entitled to vote set off for the polling station only to find that they are physically prevented from entering by an armed gang who admit only those that they are sure will support their own favoured proposal. The possibility of democracy promised by the constitution remains unrealised; the result is determined by the coercive force of an armed minority, rendering the rights of equal participation ineffective. What is required for the realisation of democracy here is the enforcement of democratic rights. Even Hayek would have no difficulty agreeing; rights imply the illegality of attempts to interfere with their exercise and hence the necessity of enforcing those rights by preventing such interference. The background condition required to render democratic rights effective is a negative condition; the absence, enforced if necessary, of attempts to prevent their use. A second example would be the case of voters with severe physical disabilities. The right to vote by marking a ballot paper in a polling station requires the capacity of physical movement; the physically immobile are systematically excluded from participation unless otherwise provided for. Such provision, however, could be made on the purely procedural level by allowing a postal vote or, perhaps, in our technologically advanced age, by allowing voting by electronic mail. This is simply a matter of being imaginative about the mechanism of voting. The real problem begins to emerge only when we start taking into consideration the more diffuse and wide-ranging conditions necessary to make rights of participation in collective decision-making fully effective in an equal way across the whole community. As we have seen, full participation in a decision-making process requires not just access to the relevant information in the limited sense of having a right to such information, but also the capacity to assimilate and appraise such information. The scope and complexity of decision-making by modern governments are so enormous that the capacity of full involvement is inconceivable save on the basis of a far higher educational standard than achieved by most people of lower socioeconomic status. Furthermore, the conditions of life of the relatively economically disadvantaged are themselves implicated in the inability to benefit from educational opportunities. Only if the economic well-being of the less well-off was to be vastly improved and then became itself a basis for a high level of educational achievement that could be utilised in the form of a thorough understanding of public affairs would equally effective participation in political decision-making become a reality. Are we then to say that a system of rule, the structure of power that determines political outcomes in a society, does not approach anything like high levels of democracy unless the socioeconomic, cultural and educational conditions for full and equal participation are realised? It is at this point that thinkers such as F. von Hayek would demur. Democracy should be thought of as a system of rule and, as such, is constituted by the complex of defining rights of participation in the process of ruling. If for some reason the rights of participation are not taken up, this is a matter not of the system not being democratic but rather of the democratic system not achieving, perhaps, what people might desire of it. From this perspective democracy should be defined as the set of legally enforceable rules that guarantee the rights of citizens to equal participation, a conception that emphatically does not include reference to socioeconomic and educational background conditions.

There is, in fact, quite a plausible semantic argument for this position. The main use to which the concept of democracy is going to be put is in the comparative analysis of political systems such as monarchy, aristocracy, etc. Suppose we take the example of monarchy and imagine a political system that is monarchical, in which sovereign power is vested in the legitimate hereditary king or queen. Suppose further, however, that the incumbent is so weak and indecisive that he or she becomes simply a puppet of a group of *eminences grises* who, behind the scenes, constitute real power in the state. What we have here is still a monarchy, though in this instance an ineffective one. Does this not demonstrate that concepts categorising political systems are framed in terms of legally constituted rights of rule? And should we not, therefore, restrict ourselves to such complexes of rights in the definition of democracy?

This argument, however, is not conclusive. If the powerlessness of a particular monarch was systematic and persistent, we would be equally inclined to describe the situation as a 'monarchy' in name only, implying that when we used the word unqualifiedly we were indicating substantive power that was here absent; though, because the power of the court clique was not itself constitutional, we would still retain the label 'monarchy'. Adding, 'in name only' highlights the anomaly of the situation. For a structure of power to be a political system it must be articulated through rights of rule; in the absence of a sociological understanding of the constraining effect on the utilisation of such rights by the social matrix within which the political dimension of society operates, and with rights of rule where we can assume the existence of background prerequisites as normal, the reference to such conditions can remain tacit. But if we are interested in the systematic determination of political outcomes, as we must be both from the explanatory and the normative perspectives, our concepts of comparison should point up all those features that constitute the power structure expressed through the mechanisms of authoritative decision-making. Consequently, I would argue that our concept of democracy, while including equal rights of political participation should also make explicit the necessity of the effectiveness of those rights. If the effectiveness of political rights is systematically undermined for certain groups, we would then judge the actual process of determining political outcomes as deviating from full democracy.

I would admit, however, that simply from the point of view of semantic clarity either alternative would be acceptable, provided that we were perfectly clear which alternative had been accepted. If we define democracy, or any other political system, in terms simply of constitutional rights without any implication that those rights actually structured the process of political decision-making significantly, we would, when rights were ineffective, describe the situation as constitutionally democratic, adding that democracy here, however, was ineffective. If we included effectiveness in the definition we would refer to such situations as 'democracies in name only'.

Behind the issues of semantic clarity and consistency, however, lurks a deep evaluative divide. Anyone left-of-centre of the political spectrum would probably be outraged at the suggestion that democracy had been achieved when the constitutional form of rule granted equal political rights but when the actual structure of power consisted in a minority rule because large sections of the population were rendered, in effect, incapable of participation through economic and educational disadvantage. On the other hand, offence would be caused on the right of the political spectrum by the allegation that a society was not really democratic at all, despite its constitutional guarantees of equal rights, if in fact economic and educational inequality lead to a differential utilisation of those rights. The proximate cause of the passion aroused in this debate concerning the definition of democracy is the confusion of semantic and normative issues. The confusion is not, however, accidental. It is, of course, logically ludicrous to think that what gets included in the definition of a term on the basis of semantic considerations should become automatically transformed into an article of political faith. But the logically ludicrous is polemically serious. The positive evaluative overtones of the terminology of democracy are so strong that whichever political ideology manages to capture that terminology has gone a long way towards making itself popularly acceptable. But if what is fundamentally at stake is a clash of ideologies, and, in particular, a conflict of core underlying values, it follows that though the battleground is semantics the real issues cannot be adequately dealt with on the basis of merely semantic arguments. Since the underlying ideological conflict is one of the most important matters in contemporary political debate, and since it impinges directly on democratic theory, we cannot simply leave the issue aside, noting that it cannot be settled by means of a debate concerning the meaning of words. We need to confront, head on, the rival ideological claims.

When we penetrate beyond the confusing semantic veil these rival ideological claims can be formulated as follows. On the one hand it is argued that rights, no matter how robust in content or how strongly legally entrenched they are, will be next to worthless to someone who does not have the background prerequisites necessary to utilise the rights. From this perspective, it follows that a political programme committed to the provision of a set of rights ought also to be committed to the provision of the enabling conditions that alone would make those rights worthwhile. What is the point of providing rights that are not usable, that cannot be taken up? A useful way of formulating this side of the argument is to say that rights, in this context the democratic rights of participation, should be viewed as positive rights. A right is best thought of as the correlative of enforceable obligations. My right to life, say, consists in obligations on the part of others not to take my life, obligations that are rightfully enforceable. If the correlative obligations are, as in the above formulation, negative in character, if, that is, they are the obligations not to do certain things, the corresponding right is a negative right. But the right to life could also be interpreted positively; it could mean, that is, that there were enforceable obligations incumbent on other people to provide me, under certain conditions, with the means of survival. Whenever a right is thought of as implying that others are enforceably obliged to positively act in such a way that the possessor of the right is a beneficiary of their action, the right in question is a positive right. In fact in most contemporary advanced societies the right to life, and even the right to life of a relatively high quality, is interpreted as a positive right. When people are unable to provide for themselves, their right to life is thought to imply the obligation on the part of public authorities to provide something above the means of mere survival. Interpreting the commitment to democracy as a commitment to equal effective rights can be seen as the extension of the positive interpretation of rights to the area of democratic participation. From this point of view, saying that everyone is equally entitled to rights of democratic participation implies that there are obligations incumbent on a society as a whole, and ultimately on the government of that society, to ensure the provision to everyone of all those conditions, economic, educational and cultural, necessary to render effective political participation possible for all. If we are committed to the value of such participation, we should be committed to the provision of all the necessary preconditions, and not just to the removal of negative constraints; we should be committed to, in the terminology now fashionable, the positive empowerment of citizens. This is taken to involve the construal of democratic rights as positive rights and to imply a vigorous programme of affirmative action.

It is at this point that theorists such as Hayek would disagree. The problem lies not in the belief that positive empowerment is more valuable than the mere possession of formal rights, but in the conclusion that this is thought to entail, namely that rights should be interpreted as positive rights and, hence, the collective authority of the state should be permanently mobilised for the purpose of providing people, if necessary, with the extensive range of economic, educational and cultural resources that would constitute their empowerment. It is not the goal of positive empowerment that Hayek rejects, but the proposed means, namely state action. He rejects those means because he believes that extending the scope of collective authoritative decision-making into the area of the provision of these positive conditions of empowerment will be inefficient, democratically counter-productive and, finally, subversive of the fundamental value that democracy itself is meant to serve, namely, the value of individual liberty.

Many democratic theorists who interpret democratic rights in a much more extensive and positive manner than Hayek would agree that personal autonomy plays a central role in the justification of democracy. The relationship between the value of personal autonomy and the justification of democracy is not, however, unproblematic. Firstly, valuing personal autonomy is a basis for justifying democracy only if combined with an egalitarian commitment in this regard. Secondly, complete and unconstrained personal autonomy is obviously as incompatible with democratic government as it is with any other form of government, since being subject to government consists in being constrained by decisions that are not necessarily one's own, in the straightforward individualist sense of that phrase. Thirdly, even in the absence of constraint by authoritatively binding decisions, personal autonomy cannot be realised in a completely maximal fashion for every individual, unless individuals lived in total isolation from each other. Evidently, each person's choice and action can, and often does, constrain, either intentionally or otherwise, the freedom of choice and action on the part of others. It is the complex interplay of all of these factors that constitutes one of the central problems of democratic theory in relation to freedom, liberty or personal autonomy, whatever we want to call it.

Hayek quite clearly ascribes a more fundamental importance to individual liberty than he does to democracy:

> We have no intention, however, of making a fetish of democracy. It may well be true that our generation talks and thinks too much of democracy and too little of the values which it serves. It cannot be said of democracy, as Lord Acton truly said of liberty, that it 'is not a means to a higher end. It is itself the highest political end'. . . . Democracy is essentially a means, a utilitarian device for safeguarding internal peace and individual freedom.[2]

But how does democracy serve individual freedom, when it necessarily involves a circumscribing of that individual freedom by enforceable law? This, of course, is the crux of liberal democratic theory from the time of John Locke to the present. The basic structure of the liberal democratic argument for the restricted surrender of freedom to democratic government is as follows.

Suppose we begin with the premise that everyone has an equal right to freedom. Under the normal interpretation of 'right' this will imply two things. Firstly, that any individual's liberty is constrained by the corresponding rights of others, for those rights imply correlative obligations. Consequently, just as any given person's liberty consists in the correlative obligations on the part of others, so also that person's liberty is rightfully exercised only within the bounds set by the obligations they are under to respect other people's rights. Secondly, since we are postulating liberty as a right, the correlative obligations are enforceable. Consequently, equal liberty does not imply the complete illegitimacy of coercion; in fact coercion is justifiable if it is aimed at the prevention of, or at the redress of, infringements of other people's rights. A person's freedom can be constrained by another's action in two importantly different ways that I will call directive and non-directive. Directive constraint exists where there is the deliberate intention on the part of a person to get someone else to act in a manner that they would not otherwise choose and where the intention is realised through the use of, or the threat of the use of, force of some kind. Non-directive constraint occurs as an unintended consequence of the action of one (or more) person(s) which, though unintended, significantly restricts or constrains the options open to another person. To illustrate the distinction, consider the following situations. A house comes up for sale in some neighbourhood and a potential buyer puts down a bid. The current residents of the neighbourhood consider the potential buyer 'undesirable' and make known their desire to have the bid withdrawn, backing up the demand with threats. Here we have a clear case of directive constraint. In the second situation, no one threatens the potential buyer, he or she simply finds that they have been outbid by, let us say, a person completely unaware of the existence of the first bidder. The first bidder's freedom of action is in this context non-directively constrained by the results of other people's actions. Of course, mutual interpersonal non-directive constraint is an unavoidable fact of life in any community of interactive persons.

We have been talking so far only of constraints on freedom of action. But most people will think that a wide range of directive constraints are actually also infringements of people's rights to liberty; furthermore, even some non-directive constraint, if significantly detrimental to a person's well-being or freedom, might be thought of as infringing the person's rights. If constraints are in fact perceived as infringements of liberty, then, by the logic of rights, coercive prevention or redress of such infringements becomes legitimate. The problems for the maximisation of individual liberty, as classically identified by Locke, arise from two sources. Firstly, there may be no one with sufficient power to prevent or redress potential infringements; and, secondly, there may, and probably will, arise practically insoluble disputes between people over whether certain constraints actually amount to infringements of rights. If an independent agency were created with the power to settle such disputes and to enforce respect for rights via the making of collectively binding decisions, then, though those subject to those decisions would in that precise respect have their liberty curtailed by directive constraints, the overall consequence might be the achievement of higher levels of effective individual liberty than otherwise. This would be the case if the agency confined itself to the minimum directive constraint necessary to eliminate, or at least minimise, illegitimate infringements of liberty.

The potential dangers of this solution, however, have been well recognised in the liberal democratic tradition. An agency capable of undertaking these tasks will need to have two very considerable powers; the power to define people's rights and the consequent legislative framework of interpersonal obligations and the power to enforce such laws. The dangers lie in the potential for tyranny that these powers entail. The specifically liberal response to these dangers operates on three levels. Firstly, there is the elaboration of a theory that attempts to demonstrate the illegitimacy of governmental action except when it is strictly limited to the enforcement of people's rights and the securing of the fundamental conditions of basic social stability, and when it pursues these tasks through 'the Rule of Law'. Secondly, there is a specification of institutional mechanisms that might, in practice, ensure these restrictions on governmental power. The core mechanisms suggested are the strict constitutional delimitation of the legitimate scope of governmental action, the separation of powers among executive, legislative and judicial branches, and various other more specific 'checks and balances'. Thirdly, there is what we can call the theory of the necessity of non-governmental countervailing powers. The plausible contention lying behind this theory is that the institutional mechanisms designed to limit governmental power will on their own be ineffective unless there are loci of power in the community independent of government. The three central countervailing powers are, firstly, an amorphous 'spirit of freedom' and independence among citizens, secondly, access to economic resources independently of governmental control and, thirdly, a free press.

In addition, within the democratic tradition it is suggested that making governmental decisions subject to popular control by those bound by the decisions will itself help to ensure that the power of authoritative decision-making will not be abused by infringing people's liberty. It follows that the ability to participate in making those decisions to which one will be subject is doubly valuable, even from a predominantly liberal perspective that gives priority to individual liberty. By participation one can attempt to ensure that individual liberties are not encroached upon by governmental action. Secondly, it is evident that if a person, for whatever reasons, is unable to participate in such decision-making, that person will necessarily be subject to directive constraint by an agency which, owing to the person's non-participation, is wholly external. As a consequence, individual liberty is limited and threatened in two ways. As I said above, Hayek would not disagree with the claim that positive enablement to participate fully and equally in collective decision-making is an important value. The question is, however, whether extending the scope of collective decision-making into the area of the positive provision of the resources required for full participation is the best method of ensuring the optimal provision of those resources. We are now in a position to understand Hayek's negative answer to that question.

As indicated above, Hayek employs three distinct types of argument, the first of which is purely economic and derives from his well-known support for the theory of the superior economic efficiency of the operation of competitive market forces. There is no doubt that the capacities required for full and equal participation in democratic decision-making involve not only high levels of educational and cultural development but depend crucially on access to economic resources. And, as Dahl puts it: 'From ancient times to the present day, however, virtually all thoughtful advocates of democratic and republican government have strongly emphasised how democracy is threatened by inequalities in economic resources.'[3] Hayek's basic claim, however, would be that to attempt to address this problem by means of extensive governmentally dictated redistribution and provision of the required resources would be economically counter-productive. An economic system with significant levels of state intervention would lose both the economic benefits of competition and even the alleged benefits of thoroughgoing planning. As Hayek says in *The Road to Serfdom*:

> Although competition can bear some admixture of regulation, it cannot be combined with planning to any extent we like without ceasing to operate as an effective guide to production. Nor is 'planning' a medicine which, taken in small doses, can produce the effects for which one might hope from its thoroughgoing application. Both competition and central direction become poor and ineffective tools if they are incomplete . . .[4]

Of course, Hayek believes competition to be the more efficient method of ensuring high levels of production and economic well-being. This belief is based partly on the standard economic theory of the beneficial effects of competition in lowering prices, raising standards of productive efficiency and meeting complex demand-functions in a continuously flexible way, and partly on the theory that no central planning agency could conceivably gather and adequately appraise all the information necessary to efficiently organise a massive modern economy. And the experience of communist rule in the former Soviet Union and the Eastern European countries would seem to bear this out. But do we have here the basis of a purely economic argument against the wisdom or desirability of extending the scope of authoritative collective decision-making to cover the provision by those means, if need be, of the resources necessary for full and equal participation? My claim is that the plausibility of Hayek's argument as a purely economic argument rests on two questionable assumptions. The first assumption is that the deductive consequences of the pure theory of economic competition can be directly relevant to concrete political problems. The second questionable assumption is that overall economic efficiency should be given a higher priority than ensuring adequate access to the resources required for full democratic participation.

Consider first the claim that a perfectly free and competitive market system would be more, and significantly more, economically efficient than either of the two alternatives, namely a planned economy or a market economy subject to relatively high levels of government intervention. What weight can that claim, even if uncontended, carry in any conceivable practical situation in which the issue emerges of whether it is desirable for government to act so as to offset the effects of economic forces on those left in a disadvantaged position? How would the claim constitute an argument against such governmental provision? Clearly the alleged undesirability of such intervention depends on the claim that it would result in a less efficient economy overall. What we need to ask, however, is, less efficient compared to what? If the answer is: less efficient compared to a completely free market, there is hardly any situation in which this could be a relevant consideration. The reason for this is that no economic system has ever approached or is ever likely to approach the pure model of a free market. Systems of economic production and distribution operate in the context of constraining environments constituted by their specific histories, the impacts on them of external economic systems, physical conditions and significant levels of already existing governmental intervention. For the argument against a specific case of governmental intervention to get off the ground the relevant comparison has to be not with the superior efficiency of an absolutely free market, but with the relative levels of efficiency of concrete possibilities, all of which are, from the perspective of the pure theory, distorted by exogenous factors. This renders any general argument about the economic undesirability of bringing the provision of the background resources necessary for effective citizenship under collective decision-making radically inconclusive.

Such general arguments, however, suffer from an even more serious defect, the questionable prioritising of overall economic efficiency above the ensuring to all of the economic, educational and cultural resources needed for full democratic participation. Even when we are dealing with a maximally efficient absolutely free market, there is no assurance, according to Hayek himself, that distribution will accord either with need or desert. Hayek accepts the inevitability of individuals or groups suffering 'diminutions of their income which although in no way deserved yet in a competitive society occur daily . . . losses imposing severe hardships having no moral justification yet inseparable from the competitive system'.[5] He is prepared to concede the necessity of providing 'security against severe physical privation and the certainty of a given minimum of sustenance for all'[6] though he adds somewhat ominously that 'there is particularly the important question of whether those who thus rely on the community should indefinitely enjoy all the same liberties as the rest'.[7]

Suppose, for the sake of argument, we assume as the status quo a perfectly free market, resulting in maximum overall economic efficiency. Following Hayek we can also assume that the distribution of the efficiently produced economic assets will leave some groups suffering 'severe hardships' and, *a fortiori*, lacking the economic background conditions to full democratic participation. Let us also accept that the attempt to remedy this situation by intervening in this free market will result in a considerable lessening of overall economic efficiency. It is evident that if that fact alone were taken to be a decisive argument against intervention the implied evaluative principle could only be that overall economic efficiency, irrespective of distribution, was more valuable than ensuring the provision to everyone of the conditions of effective citizenship. But how could such an evaluative principle be justified? We need to approach an answer to this question, of course, in the light of our discussion in Chapter 1 of the possibilities for normative argument.

Though as we will see shortly, the philosophical investigation of the complex of concepts and assumptions expressed in our language of liberty and personal autonomy is centrally relevant to a full discussion of this question, the limited issue of prioritising economic efficiency raises the normative question directly. How could we justify the value placed on overall economic efficiency? Obvious though the point is, we should begin by reminding ourselves that though general economic efficiency is an impersonal systemic property of an economy, it is not at all plausible to think of it as an impersonal intrinsic *value*; its value will be instrumental, consisting in its impact on the economic well-being of individual persons. This highlights the important point that the conflict of values that we are dealing with is not a conflict between the partisan economic and political disadvantage of one group compared to the general and impersonal, and hence impartial, value of economic efficiency, but the partisan economic advantage of the well-off compared to the disadvantage of the less well-off. If we temporarily sidelined the distributional issue and considered the matter from the explicitly moral perspective of the intrinsic worth of higher levels of economic well-being compared with economic well-being as a precondition for the effectiveness of democratic participation, it is not plausible to rank the former over the latter. As we noted above, even in a predominantly liberal scheme of values, inability to participate in collective decision-making is a very serious disadvantage, resulting as it does in the person's being under the directive constraint of a wholly external agency in those areas where authoritative decisions are currently made and also in the complete inability to protect whatever negative liberties are currently enjoyed.

From the perspective of impartiality, the prioritising of the high level of economic well-being of some over the economic conditions of democratic effectiveness of others is even less justifiable. To demonstrate the impartial value of economic efficiency one would need to prove that we could justify to the less well-off the principle that while it was legitimate to expect them to sacrifice expectations of higher economic and political well-being for the sake of maintaining the high levels of economic well-being of the rich, it was not reasonable to ask the rich to sacrifice some economic well-being at the margin for the sake of securing the conditions of democratic effectiveness to the poor.

The final form of justification is one that attempts, superficial evidence to the contrary notwithstanding, to show that prioritising economic efficiency is actually better for everyone, even for those who temporarily suffer from its distributional consequences. There are two possible forms of this argument. The first would be purely economic and would attempt to prove that the putative increase in the welfare of the less well-off envisaged as the result of distributional intervention would, even for the less well-off, be undercut by the decline in overall efficiency, with the effect that the least well-off would be worse off than they previously were. Obviously, this argument depends on proving the thesis that governmental intervention will result not just in the loss of some efficiency, but will bring about such a disastrous decline in efficiency that the envisaged redistributional benefits to the less well-off could no longer be provided. In fact Hayek never attempts to prove this precise point. He admits that even in the context of very high levels of governmental planning 'some workmen will perhaps be better fed'[8] but at this point he argues that this undoubted economic advantage will be purchased at the cost of individual freedom, an argument to which we will return.

The second form of the argument appeals to the possibility of those who are temporarily disadvantaged directly benefiting in the future from the policy of prioritising efficiency. The point here is that it may be rational to choose the principle of overall economic efficiency over the principle of governmental intervention even when it is acknowledged that the first principle involves the possibility of being adversely affected by its distributional consequences, if there is also the possibility of directly benefiting from the efficiency. In concrete terms, even a person who is currently disadvantaged might rationally prefer the organisational principle of efficiency in the light of the possibility of future direct benefits. Abstract though this argument is, it should not be dismissed out of hand. In the present context, however, it suffers two weaknesses that render it less than persuasive. Firstly, the rationality of the preference crucially depends on the comparative probabilities. This is particularly telling when we are considering actual current disadvantage. It is not at all evident that the mere possibility of future benefits outweighs the actuality of current disadvantage, especially when we accept, as does Hayek, that though those who start poor *may* end up significantly wealthier, the abstract probabilities are against such an outcome. This point is reinforced by a second, namely, that what we are comparing are not just different levels of economic well-being; in the context of the present argument concerning the conditions of effective citizenship, the actual situation of the disadvantaged is one in which they suffer not merely economically but in terms, also, of political impotence. It would be hard to demonstrate the rationality of sacrificing current political effectiveness to the mere possibility of future economic benefit. I conclude that there is no purely economic argument that should convince us of the necessity of giving maximum efficiency a priority above ensuring to all the economic, educational and cultural conditions of full democratic participation.

As indicated above, however, purely economic considerations constitute only one strand in Hayek's argument against the extensive use of government action to attempt to achieve substantive justice. The second strand of his argument is particularly relevant in the present context; it consists precisely in the claim that in so extending government action the level of actual and effective democratic accountability will, far from being enhanced, suffer radical decline. Consequently, the attempt to secure that dimension of substantive justice that consists in actual access to the resources required for effective participation will be, inevitably, democratically counterproductive. The basis of the argument can be set out briefly. Though governmental decision-making that undertakes on a permanent basis the responsibility of ensuring the egalitarian distribution of the resources required for effective participation may succeed, and may even do so without seriously affecting overall economic efficiency, new factors will inevitably have been introduced into the decision-making process that will render it relatively impenetrable to democratic control. This will undermine the democratic effectiveness not only of those who were previously disadvantaged but also of practically everyone in the society in question. The features of the extended decision-making leading to this consequence are, firstly, the sheer mass and complexity of matters brought under government control; secondly, the changed nature of the content of the decisions, since there will have to be a tendency away from making very general decisions typical of 'the Rule of Law' towards the appraisal of specific cases; and, thirdly, the necessary creation of a vast administrative apparatus required to implement the new decisions. Such a situation does, indeed, raise very serious questions concerning the possibility of effective democratic participation and control. In the final chapter of *Democracy and Its Critics*, Robert Dahl identifies the problem of the dominance in public policy-making of elite groups of specialists as 'even more formidable' than those raised by economic inequalities.[9] The virtual monopoly of detailed participation by what Dahl refers to as 'the public policy elites' is a function of the complexity of political decision-making and is itself the obverse side of the near impossibility, given time constraints and limitation of human cognitive faculties, of an ordinary citizen being able to process and appraise all the information relevant to all the important decisions made in the public realm.[10] There are, however, several important considerations that would suggest the inadvisability of attempting to solve this problem by drastically reducing the spheres of social life that we take collective responsibility for through political decision-making.

Firstly, though used only as illustrative examples, the areas Dahl cites when introducing his thesis are significant: defence, health, environmental control. At least the first and last of these will, almost of necessity, be thought of as falling within the public domain in any complex modern society. The general point is that though government involvement in the ensuring of access to resources for full participation will no doubt contribute to the scope of political decision-making, it is at least plausible to suggest that the main factors lying behind the size and complexity of modern governments are to be found in the size and complexity of modern societies. If this is so, the threat to the possibility of democratic control will always be with us, irrespective of whether or not ensuring the provision of democratic resources becomes part of the political agenda. As a consequence it becomes even more important that people have access to these resources, since decisions are being made daily with momentous consequences not only for the present but also for future generations as well. What emerges from the present argument, however, is that the possibility of popular control depends not only on individual people having the resources and motivation for participation but also on the possibility of our overcoming the virtual impenetrability of centralised bureaucratic decision-making and administrative structures. It is true that we have become so accustomed to decision-making and administration that is centralised, hierarchical and professional, so accustomed to seeing ordinary people as consumers whose only possible input into what affects them will depend upon freedom to choose between alternatives decided on externally, that even the modest proposals of a moderate such as Dahl are likely to strike most people as wildly utopian.

The elements of Dahl's proposed solution consist in the imaginative use of interactive telecommunication technology to ensure extensive dissemination of relevant information and possible feedback opportunities and the institution of a 'minipopulus' in major issue areas.[11] Each 'minipopulus' will be representative of the people as a whole by being randomly selected and for a limited period, say a year, will, with the assistance of scholars and specialists, debate and decide issues within its remit. If we react with incredulity, or perhaps horror, at the idea of major political decisions being made in this way, I would argue that this is indicative of either a deep distrust of democracy or at least the belief that any significant level of democracy is unrealisable in modern society; though I would admit that in this particular instance my conclusion is couched more in the language of rhetoric than in the pure terminology of rational analysis. Are Dahl's proposals wholly unrealistic?

Though analogies with ancient Athens must be used with great caution because of the very small-scale nature of the Athenian state compared to a twentieth-century state, it is still worth looking at how the principle of selection by lot was used in the filling of both governmental and, even more surprisingly, administrative positions. Selection by lot was used so extensively, as against even popular election, and the terms of office were so short that to all intents and purposes government and administration were run by 'amateurs', when not under the direct control of the Assembly of the People. As Hansen says, in Demosthenes' speech *Against Aristogeiton* 'we meet a fourfold division of the organs of state into the Council, the Assembly, the People's Court, and the boards of magistrates'.[12]

Apart from the Assembly, which all adult male citizens were entitled to attend, appointment to the other organs of state was almost exclusively by lot. The Council had 500 members, their function being to draw up the agenda for Assembly meetings. Individuals were appointed by lot for a yearly term, with the restriction of a maximum of two terms in office in a life-time. Judicial decisions of a civil, criminal or 'constitutional' nature were made by large popular juries. Juries of from 201 jurors upwards were selected by lot, on the day, for particular cases; the selection being made from a panel of 6,000 that was itself selected by lot out of the whole body of citizens on a yearly basis.[13] In the Aristotelian *Constitution of Athens* forty-six different magistrates or boards of magistrates are listed. A board of magistrates usually consisted of ten people and in the whole area of administration that was the responsibility of the magistrates the primary selection principle was the lot, the normal term of office was a year, the term of office was usually non-renewable and magistrates were required to give a rendering of accounts at the end of a term of office.[14] Throughout the whole period of Athenian democracy (508–322 BC) jurors and council members were paid, and in the earlier 'radical period', as Hansen calls it, magistrates were also paid.[15] Hansen estimates that in addition to the 500 council members there were about 700 magistrates selected each year with responsibilities covering such things as administration of the law courts, supervision of the docks, organisation of religious festivals and the management of various public funds, to mention but a few. Given both shortness of the terms of office and limitations on re-eligibility for the same office the resulting rapid turnover must have produced a level of popular involvement in administration that was, by any standards, extensive and impressive. As noted earlier, because of the relatively limited scale and complexity of decision-making and administration in ancient Athens compared to a modern state we should be extremely cautious in the conclusions we draw. What can be learned from the Athenian experience, however, is that far higher levels of popular involvement, such as would be required by such proposals as Dahl's, are not as literally utopian as might at first be expected.

Even if feasible, however, would such high levels of political involvement be desirable? Perhaps the result would be a 'frantic politicisation' of life that Giovanni Sartori claims was characteristic of Athenian democracy and led to both 'the complete subjection of the individual to the power of the whole'[16] and the self-destruction of ancient democracy 'in the class struggle between the rich and the poor, because it had produced only a political animal and not a Homo oeconomicus as well'.[17] Sartori's negative critique of Athenian democracy is only one in a long line stretching back to Laboulaye, Constant and Fustel de Coulanges,[18] as Sartori himself notes. The intent of Sartori's critique is to warn us not to be seduced into believing that ancient Athenian institutions carry a positive lesson for modern democracies. Rather, from the perspective of modern values:

> whoever continues to look forward to a society in which every citizen is actively and endlessly engaged in the management of public affairs, is clearly blind to the fact that actual participation in government – if it is real and not just talked about – demands that hypertrophic development of political activity which made Aristotle say that a man who has to work in order to live cannot be a citizen; a development that might well re-open the vicious circle of a growing penury in which the solution of the (economic) problem of prosperity is sought in the (political) redistribution of poverty.[19]

This is not the place to enter into a detailed discussion of the historical accuracy of this line of analysis of Athenian democracy, though it should be noted that many modern scholars support a radically alternative view.[20] The importance, in the present context, of the historical analysis is that it provides Sartori with the opportunity of articulating the essential contrast that lies at the core of the arguments concerning democracy as effective power and democracy as 'a juridical order, geared to a cluster of techniques of liberty'.[21] When, in commenting on the use of the word 'democracy' as applied to the Athenian government and to the ideals and actualities of the present, he states that there is merely 'an *arbitrary* uniformity of terminology' he is preparing the ground for an interpretation that *identifies* modern democracy with the liberal-constitutional state.[22] 'The so-called democratic state, if we go back to identifying it with its proper title, is the liberal-constitutional state; and this means that political democracy merges with liberalism and has been superseded by it.'[23] The essential contrast in question is between, to use Laboulaye's formulation of it, 'La liberté antique' and 'La liberté moderne',[24] the former consisting in participation in the exercise of power resulting in collectively binding decisions, while the latter is freedom from the directive constraint of the state. Both the distinction between the two and at least part of the rationale for ranking individual liberty higher are nicely captured in Sartori's statement:

> Participation in the exercise of power does not necessarily imply individual liberty. My liberty vis-à-vis political power cannot be derived from the infinitesimal portion of that power by means of which I concur with others in the creation of the rules to which I will be subject.[25]

It is precisely this contrast, and the valuing of individual liberty over the equal participation in collective decision-making, that constitute the third strand in Hayek's very similar approach to modern democracy. We arrive here at the very core of the liberal tradition's objection to the extending of the scope of authoritatively binding decisions, even if that extension can be achieved without adverse economic consequences and if the resulting decision-making process perfectly accords with the criteria of equal political effectiveness. The fundamental basis of this ideological orientation consists in the far higher value ascribed to action that issues from individual choice not subject to directive constraint by an external agency compared to action that is merely in accordance with a collectively binding rule. As Hayek puts it:

> morals . . . can exist only in the sphere in which the individual is free to decide for himself and called upon voluntarily to sacrifice personal advantage to the observance of a moral rule. Outside the sphere of individual responsibility there is neither goodness nor badness, neither opportunity for moral merit nor the choice of proving one's conviction by sacrificing one's desires to what one thinks right. . . . Freedom to order our own conduct in the sphere where material circumstances force a choice upon us, and responsibility for the arrangement of our own life according to our conscience, is the air in which alone moral sense grows and in which moral values are daily recreated in the free decision of the individual. Responsibility, not to a superior, but to one's conscience, the awareness of a duty not exacted by compulsion, the necessity to decide which of the things one values are to be sacrificed to others, and to bear the consequences of one's own decision, are the very essence of any morals which deserve the name.[26]

It is evident from this paragraph that the objection to the extension of authoritatively binding decisions is not just a pragmatic matter of the insufficiency of equal participation as a means for ensuring that such will not be wrong or disadvantageous to me or unduly restrictive of my liberties. The issue is that I cannot be acting as a fully moral being except in a sphere free from coercively imposed directive constraint.

There are within the liberal tradition several dimensions to this conception of the moral life. The one that lies on the surface of the passage just quoted consists in the claim that when there is the possibility of coercion backing the requirement to abide by a rule obedience is not fully moral, since the fully moral must be the wholly voluntary; we could add in a Kantian vein that the motivation to abide by the rule must be a recognition of the rule's intrinsic imperative force; it must not derive from anything extrinsic, such as, specifically, the possibility of coercion. The second dimension moves us on to the profounder plane of the assertion of the moral and intellectual autonomy of human beings. It is important to understand that the autonomy being referred to here is not the *de facto* autonomy of someone who is relatively independent both in the formation of values and beliefs and in the ability to act on them. Neither is such *de facto* autonomy being simply proposed as an ideal or goal to be striven for. Rather what is meant is that one cannot, in the case of moral autonomy, be morally bound except by a rule that one has autonomously, in the *de facto* sense, internalised, prescribed for oneself, seen for oneself the moral force of. A parallel claim concerning knowledge is what is at stake in the assertion of intellectual autonomy, famously formulated, for example, in Diderot's saying 'L'homme est né pour penser de lui-même'.[27] The Cartesian notion of rationality implies that not only is it not rational to believe something simply on the basis of an external authority, but also, more emphatically, I do not *know*, in the strict sense of that term, that which I am unable to prove to myself. The conditions of genuine knowledge must be internal to the individual mind. External authorities may have the power to force me to act, but as external they cannot constitute morally binding forces nor generate genuine knowledge. It follows that if the moral and cognitive dimensions of humanity are at its core, being under external directive constraint reduces a person to less than human status. A third dimension consists in what has come to be known as a 'plurality of the good and a monism of the right'. It is assumed that there will be certain very general rules of interpersonal interaction and sociopolitical organisations that are absolutely necessary to secure the continued existence of a society and the maintenance of a minimum standard of justice. These rules can be articulated and rationally defended. Beyond these, however, there will be a *de facto* multiplicity of richer and more substantive conceptions of the good life. One could be committed to a religious life, a rational epicureanism, a life of intellectual work, self-sacrificing humanistic altruism, a life devoted to ordinary decent family values, a bacchanalian existence or a life devoted to artistic creativity and so on, including combinations and syntheses of any of these. The argument is that there is no neutral perspective outside any of these conceptions of the good from which the definitive superiority of one over the others can be established. So in addition to the illegitimacy of the imposition of a morality and a world-view from the perspective of the moral and intellectual autonomy of the person, the thesis of the plurality of the good provides a further basis for the inadmissibility of subjecting people to any particular substantive conception of the good by authoritatively binding decisions. The first argument is negative; since no substantive conception is justifiable over others, there can be no justification for imposing any. More positively, it could be argued that the very profusion and multiplicity of conceptions of the good is itself valuable; it ensures the creativity and flexibility of the moral culture of humanity.

There is no doubt that some version of the moral and intellectual autonomy of human beings and a pluralist conception of the good have become, as Charles Taylor would put it, 'unavoidable frameworks' and, to some extent, constitutive of the 'modern self'.[28] Insofar as a person understands her- or himself through such a framework any political or social ideal that involved infringement of moral and intellectual autonomy by the extensive ordering of life through external directive constraint would be wholly unacceptable and without any possible justification. But would the kind of extension of authoritative decision-making envisaged in the ensuring of the resources required for full and equal political participation fall into this category?

The first obvious point that should be made is that though the envisaged expansion of the political agenda beyond the granting and enforcement of the juridico-legal rights of democratic citizenship is a substantive ideal it does not even begin to approach the coercive imposition of a single world-view and a unitary conception of the good. We can accept, as most of us do, that the moral and intellectual autonomy of the individual is of paramount importance and even that this importance is such that, no matter how democratic, authoritatively binding decision-making should respect, as a matter of right, this area of individual liberty. But it is not self-evident exactly where the boundary of this liberty should be drawn or what agency is, in practice, competent to draw it. Those who argue for the provision, by authoritative decision-making if need be, of the resources for democratic participation would claim that, whatever the intrinsic superiority of literal individual autonomy over what we could call that collective autonomy that results in equal participation in decision-making, the resources for such participation can be provided without the infringement of the values of moral and intellectual autonomy. Furthermore, the value of being able to participate in the making of decisions that are going to be collectively binding is so important that the relative diminution of the area of literal individual autonomy involved is justifiable. Only an extreme philosophical anarchist would argue that it is never justifiable to restrict in any way the area of literal individual autonomy. And just as even a liberal such as Hayek would accept that governmental action to secure the positive right to life is a justifiable limitation on unconditional individual liberty, so, it could be argued, is such action justifiable when the ability to be a fully active citizen, participating in making those decisions that shape the overall structure of the life of a community, is what is at stake. As was noted above, the absence of such an ability leaves the individual definitely under the directive constraint of an external agency, unable to influence the content of that constraint and even unable to ensure that the power of that constraint will not be used to further encroach upon the individual's liberty. If it is argued along with Sartori that such power is 'infinitesimal', it is worth pointing out that the infinitesimal is greater than zero, which is the measure of power in this regard for those without the resources required for participation, but also that Sartori's implied argument gains its persuasiveness from the improbable assumption that each individual is always going to find her- or himself in a literal minority of one. When we are talking about a group of people with similar interests and similar values, the power of such a group to protect the interests and liberties of its members through their effective participation in collective decision-making is not inconsiderable. The collective organisation of those resources required for effective participation in democratic decision-making, though it involves a more extensive scope for collective decision-making than that envisaged from the perspective of the juridico-legal conception of democracy, does not, then, involve the infringement of moral and intellectual autonomy by the coercive imposition of a unitary world-view and conception of the good.

But the participatory democrat is envisaging a greater, rather than a lesser, scope for collective decisions. How could we counter the argument that even if this greater scope did not infringe moral and intellectual autonomy, greater rather than less was always undesirable, since equal participation in collective autonomy is only a poor second best to literal individual autonomy? The aspect of the liberal conception of the moral life relevant here is that illustrated in the passage from Hayek quoted above, claiming that 'morals . . . can exist only in the sphere in which the individual is free to decide for himself'.[29] The central argument of that passage rests on the assertion that the coerced, not being voluntary, does not fall within the sphere of the moral; there is no virtue in doing that which is good, if one's reason for so acting is not the recognition of the value in question, but the mere fact that disobedience will be punished. The fundamental weakness of this position derives from an implicit assumption, necessary for the argument, but not defensible; namely, the assumption that if there is the possibility of coercive enforcement as a last resort, as is implied in a matter falling within the scope of authoritatively binding decision, it inevitably follows that a person's motivation will be, as it were, corrupted; so that no one will any longer do the good because it is good, but will obey simply because disobedience will be punished. Suppose we imagine a group of people coming to the realisation that in a certain sphere of their interaction serious problems are emerging, problems either of the efficiency of coordination of day-to-day action and/or problems arising from the fact that certain members of the group might be subject to such serious disadvantage or suffering that their position becomes a matter of moral concern. After debate and discussion of the issue, it is decided, according to the 'democratic' procedures of the group, to formulate certain rules of behaviour applicable in these circumstances. The content of the rules is determined by the belief that this specific way of organising matters will best meet the concerns that constituted the problem in the first place. The resulting decision is meant to be authoritatively binding; the matter is thought to be of such seriousness as to warrant enforcement in those cases when, perhaps, particular individuals might be tempted to disregard the rules. My contention is that it is completely indefensible to claim that the mere existence of coercive enforcement as a last resort will undermine completely the moral nature of conformity for the vast majority. The rules were formulated through participation and express what is thought to be the best or the right way of proceeding; that the rules are as they are depends upon at least a majority of people actually understanding the issues at stake and believing in the rightness of this particular way of behaving. Rather than being incompatible with moral insight into the intrinsic good being the primary motivational source of behaviour, such a procedure can be seen as the interactive generation and expression of that insight. Anyone familiar with Rousseau's reflections on the formation of the General Will in *The Social Contract*[30] will have recognised the

Rousseauian overtones in the above. While it is true that Rousseau's account of the nature of the General Will and its articulation in collective decision-making is often indeterminate, misleading and, even, redolent of the totalitarian subordination of the individual to the collective,[31] I would claim that there is an important and valid insight in Rousseau's work. If it is decided by the appropriate decision-making procedures in a community that a particular issue needs to be addressed by collective decision, equal and informed participation in the decision-making procedure at least has the potentiality for generating in each individual participant an understanding of the point and the rationale of the resultant decision by exposing participants to alternative perspectives and the possibly legitimate demands on the decision-making rooted in those perspectives. The point being made here is that not only is the ability to participate in collective decision-making *instrumentally* important for a person in that it enables a person to 'fight their own corner', it can be thought of also as the intrinsically worthwhile educative formation of an individual consisting of the internalisation of an informed respect for the interests and perspectives of others. None of this denies the paramount importance of moral and intellectual autonomy nor does it imply in any way the desirability of subjecting the individual to the power of the whole by the imposition of a single view of the good life requiring the regimentation of the totality of people's behaviour.

On the contrary, not only can it be argued that equal participation in those areas of collective decision-making can generate informed understanding of alternative perspectives and a willingness to tolerate and accommodate plural conceptions of the good, a strong case can be made for the claim that the very plurality of conceptions of the good itself generates the necessity for that understanding and accommodation that can be articulated in active decision-making.

There is an overly naive and simplistic understanding of the political implications of the pluralism of the good, monism of the right thesis. It consists in thinking that the theoretical acceptance of the plurality of conceptions of the good implies in a straightforward fashion, firstly, that, as I put it above, because no substantive conception of the good can non-circularly establish its superiority over others, there is no justification for the imposition by authoritative decisions of any of the conceptions of the good. It is then concluded that this implies an unproblematically identifiable minimal scope for legitimate collective decision-making informed only by an understanding of what this minimum requirement is and not informed by any of the alternative substantive conceptions of the good. The oversimplification of this view derives from the neglect of the possible serious tensions between different substantive conceptions of the good and between any of these substantive conceptions and the minimalist conception of the right. Such tensions are inevitable, particularly in a society in which there is not just a vague pluralism with respect to 'private' life-styles and values but which is also multi-denominational, multi-cultural and multi-racial.

A keen ornithologist, a dedicated Latinist and a committed philatelist could, presumably, pursue their chosen values with very little detrimental interaction and reciprocal constraint arising among them; even if they lived next door to each other. But if the fourth house in the road was occupied by a motor-cycle enthusiast who was also a devotee of 'heavy metal', whose life-style involved roaring up and down the roads in the company of gangs of leather-clad youths on motor-bikes, and dismantling and reassembling bikes in the front garden to the accompaniment of high decibel rock music, problems of compatibility would emerge. The compatibility problems in this case are purely practical and perhaps solvable by some form of compromise based on a mutual understanding of the respective value to each person of her or his chosen life-style, involving some principle of 'acceptable' and 'unacceptable' levels of mutual interference. But not all tensions are so easily tractable and subject to reciprocal accommodation on the basis of a minimal framework of general principles. Take, for example, the passionately debated issue of pornography and the symbolic degradation of women.

Look at the matter firstly from the perspective of the (male) hedonistic sensualist whose passion in life is the development of a heightened and sophisticated eroticism primarily through the consumption of literary and audio-visual erotic material. It is a perspective that might not command much explicit public sympathy; but the argument is on the basis of an acceptance of the pluralism of the good. From the point of view of certain radical feminists, the symbolic, though no less real for that, degradation of women is constitutive and hence inseparable from the using of images of women for the purposes of male erotic stimulation. One side would argue that this private pursuit of a particular version of 'the good' should be outside the sphere of the minimal framework of coercively imposed decisions; the opposite point of view would claim that, irrespective of any practical consequences on interpersonal behaviour, the mere availability publicly to 'consenting adults' of such degrading images of women constitutes a serious encroachment on women's well-being, and hence the whole matter does fall within the sphere of justifiable authoritative decision-making.

Before looking at the implications of the above kind of conflict, let us take another example that raises parallel problems and is, also, the site of current controversy. A supporter of a 'woman's right to choose' will argue that a pregnant woman's decision, at least in the early months of pregnancy, whether or not to allow the pregnancy to go to term or to have the foetus aborted is not an appropriate area for legislative control; it is an individual matter of a woman having control over her own body and destiny. An anti-abortionist, on the other hand, will argue that the individual pregnant woman's destiny is not all that is at stake; there is, in addition, the right to life of the 'unborn child'. This latter position is often grounded in a substantive world-view, part of which consists in the belief that by divine intention a real and separate human person begins to exist at the moment of conception. From this perspective, aborting a foetus is the killing of an innocent person and, hence, murder. As such, it should fall within the legitimate sphere of legally enforced rules just as much as the murder of an adult human being. If it is urged that specifically in the light of *de facto* moral pluralism all parties to the dispute should restrict their commitment in the area of legal enforcement to the absolute minimum acceptable to all, it is open to the anti-abortionists to claim that this particular element of their more substantive moral conception supersedes in importance the value of impartial, liberal accommodation; no one, it might be said, would or should impartially accommodate the rapist or the murderer.

The purpose of these examples is not merely to formulate one of the well-known problems with classical liberalism's distinction between the matters of private significance and matters of legitimate public concern, namely its excessive formalism. What I want to emphasise is that the problem of the determination of the boundary is not just a problem for liberal political theorists; it is itself a political problem. Furthermore, it is simply illusory to believe that the political problem can be solved in total abstraction from the substantive conceptions of the good. It is, consequently, of vital significance that all members of a community be both enabled and encouraged to participate in political decision-making. If it is argued that the politically significant tensions between substantive conceptions of the good and between such conceptions and some proposed boundary line between the public and the private are indeed real and important, but that their appropriate forum is the broader one of 'public debate', I would agree. But I would go on to insist that in the fuller conception of democratic decision-making that I am supporting, the forum of public debate is a constitutive element, and this only underlines the crucial importance of all citizens having the resources and abilities necessary to effectively participate both in the broader forum of debate and in the narrower, and inseparable, forum of formal decision-making.

We have been analysing in the above pages the case for and against the juridico-legal conception of democracy, or strictly limited liberal democracy, as a valuable and defensible ideal as against a broader more substantive ideal that would so emphasise the central importance of the effective powers of full and equal participation in the decision-making process as to justify including the provision of those resources necessary for such participation as a central item of the democratic commitment. Behind all the detailed arguments and counter-arguments, however, are, I would suggest, two conflicting assessments of the human condition and the nature of the individual human person. Despite frequent mutual misunderstandings there is also a great deal of common ground. Both traditions are committed to the moral and intellectual autonomy of the person, both traditions are fundamentally egalitarian, and both traditions accept the importance of each member of society achieving an independence and autonomy of mind that would enable each to be, as far as is possible for a human being, in control of her or his destiny and fate. The crucial divergence between the two traditions lies in a different estimate of the nature and impact on the individual of that plethora of 'external circumstances' that constitutes the inescapable context of human life. Though the liberal will accept the formative and constraining nature of those circumstances, there is the belief that so long as the formation and constraint is not intentionally directive there always remains open to the individual an escape route; one can maintain independence of mind and firmness of purpose, one can achieve the dignity of a self-acknowledged responsibility for oneself and perhaps be successful in minimising the effects of adverse circumstances on the positive ability to achieve one's life goals. The presence of a coercively backed intentional formation of the individual and intentional directive constraint is intrusive and ultimately inimical to independence of mind and human liberty.

Clearly, the basis for this different estimate lies in the differential interpretation of the nature of 'impersonal' constraint and intentionally directive constraint. At one stage of his argument Hayek is comparing what, from the point of view of the consequences, are two equally (perhaps identically) constraining sets of circumstances, one of which is the unintentional result of natural forces over the decisions of others, the second set of constraining circumstances being constituted by intentional human direction. The situation of intentional constraint is, he says, 'infinitely worse'.[32] Allowing for the poetic exaggeration in the reference to infinity, to really understand the liberal position we need to ask what could lie behind this radically different assessment of the significance of the two types of constraint. A critic of merely 'negative' liberty would argue, first, that what is important are the results of constraint on people's ability to satisfy their needs, realise their goals and live according to their values, the source of the constraint being of merely secondary significance. Secondly, though origin is secondary, constraints of an 'impersonal' nature are often viewed as of special significance; altering a whole complex of impersonal constraint is seen as a less tractable problem than changing a set of personal directives. Furthermore, when the impersonal constraints derive not from merely natural forces, but are the unintentional result of individual actions, the whole situation is viewed as one of 'alienation', where forces generated by human beings control them, as distinct from human beings being able to control themselves and the forces they generate. What is the basis of these contrary estimates of the relative significance of the impersonal and the intentional?

There is a whole complex of related factors involved, the first of which is the understandable human dislike of being told what to do. This dislike is itself readily explicable and justifiable. The explanation is what lies behind the commonly used phrase 'adding insult to injury'. A slap in the face from the branch of a tree blown by the wind is nothing, even if physically more damaging, compared to a slap in the face inflicted intentionally by another person. The latter is an insult, it is the public manifestation of a contemptuous estimate of the other person's worth. Now it is not plausible to interpret intentional constraint by governmental directive as a parallel manifestation of contempt. But it is possible to interpret it as a manifestation of an attitude, the demeaning paternalistic attitude both that one cannot be trusted and that someone knows better than you. Nothing of this low estimation of an individual's worth is carried in constraint by impersonal forces.

The second very closely related factor has already been

mentioned above, namely, the fact that impersonal circumstances offer one the opportunity for the development and exercise of moral virtue, whereas coercively backed directive constraint takes the whole area of life so ordered out of the sphere of individual responsibility. When directively constrained the person does not have to assess the context of action, attempt to understand the values at stake and responsibly choose the appropriate plan of action. The person is faced with a ready-made plan, with no possibility of 'virtue' in acting according to the plan because coercive sanctions have been attached to disobedience.

The third factor is more difficult to pin down with precision. A first approach can be made by saying that it consists, in part, in the thesis that in important ways impersonal constraints always remain external; they do not touch the inner self of the individual. If I find myself in a particular set of impersonally constraining circumstances, it is I, through my experience and knowledge, that determines the nature of these circumstances and the precise constraints they constitute. No definite response is predetermined by the circumstances; it is I myself that constructs the appropriate response. The constraining circumstances always remain external parameters to the decision-making process. In contrast, there is an essential moment in the situation of directive constraint in which I have to internalise in the organisation of my life the already planned structure of action. When intentionally directive power is exercised by one person over another, the person subject to the power is, at a crucial stage, implicated in its exercise, because this type of directive power is essentially communicative. Even a person who is being forcibly coerced, rather than being simply physically acted on, must understand what is being demanded and choose, so as to avoid the threatened consequences of non-compliance, to accede to, and so internalise, the demanded course of action. What starts off as external constraint to follow a particular course of action or rule can only be successful as constraint through the, albeit coerced, internalisation of the rule. This derives from the fact that directive constraint operates necessarily by means of communication of a pre-determined rule.

A fourth element in the complex emphasises the accidental nature of impersonal constraint. 'Accidental' here means not chaotic and unpredictable, but, precisely, not intentional. The very non-intentionality can lead to the orderliness and predictability and, consequently, can be seen as beneficial. The intentional, dependent as it is on human will, is arbitrarily variable and, hence, unpredictable. But the impersonal will, by and large, take on predictable form that can then constitute a stable environment in which the individual can plan with some level of security. Furthermore, though the impersonal can obviously be detrimental and constraining it is not designed to be so. It might become beneficial and facilitatory, rather than constraining. Even what is constraining may turn out to have hidden facilitatory features. Whereas directive constraint is meant to be constraint (though, not of course, meant necessarily to be detrimental) and will remain as constraint so long as the directing power wishes it.

The fifth dimension of this image of the impact on the individual of impersonal and intentionally directive forces goes even further than the fourth in claiming that, at least in certain areas of social organisation, the long-run consequences of the interplay of impersonal forces and individual response will be positively beneficial and liberating, in part precisely because of the absence of intentional directing control. The classic area for the application of this thesis is, of course, the economic market, where the operation of the invisible hand will result in an ever-present tendency towards overall efficiency, minimisation of costs, maximisation of standards of production and optimal and continuously flexible satisfaction of complex and changing demand functions. It might be thought that the invisible hand thesis depends on too specifically economic factors to have any applicability outside of its original domain. But this is not so. It has, it is claimed, great relevance to, for example, freedom of thought and the pursuit of truth and understanding. The crucial factor here is not some simplistic Darwinian thesis postulating a survival of the fittest, in this case the most true, among competing theories, it is rather the claim that intentional intervention resulting in the prescription of some theories, and the proscription of others will be, almost inevitably, detrimental. In the absence of imposed prescription/proscription, the possibility always remains open for views to emerge that challenge the current orthodoxy.

Complementing this fifth element is its obverse side, an almost Burkean pessimism concerning the possible beneficial consequences of the attempt to direct in the large by explicit reason and intelligence. Examining the specific area of freedom of thought we can identify the two central features of this negative assessment of the likely consequences of attempted intentional direction. At no time can any particular intelligence justifiably claim the competence either to prescribe what is true now or to predict the future course of human knowledge. But this limitation on individual intelligence is of much wider application. If we accept the indefinite plurality of the good and the inevitability of vastly differing complexes of interests and goals that, if left to themselves, people will develop, it becomes ludicrous to think that all of these could be understood and synthesised in a single directing intelligence, no matter how democratically constituted. The result will be not just the inevitable destruction of individual liberty but also the imposition of a deadening and mechanical uniformity which, at any given time, will satisfy nobody and in which there is no prospect at all of creativity and flexibility in the changing circumstances of the future. The appropriate mechanism here is not the supposedly all-seeing intelligence of authoritative direction but the slow accumulation in organic fashion of the wisdom and experience of generations of humankind as laid down in a continuously, though slowly, flexible tradition; using language that brings out the Burkean conservative element of this image.

It is easy to see why, from this perspective, one would wish to minimise the area of authoritative control; even if that area could be organised completely democratically, any extension of it is a diminution of the real area of human liberty, where people are left free to choose. Furthermore, any extension beyond the bare minimum of 'the Rule of Law' and the enforcement of the requisite juridico-legal structure of individual rights will in fact not successfully solve the social problems that it is directed at, but will result in the incompetent and usually arrogant meddling of supposed 'experts'.

The alternative perspective does not consist so much in a flat denial of the truth of these points as in the claim that they only tell part of the story. When the fuller picture of the relationship between individuals and impersonal and directive constraint is painted, it no longer seems obvious that individual freedom and autonomy is to be achieved primarily by instituting a juridical framework that will guarantee the maximum scope for individual choice free from the directive constraint of authoritative decisions.

The first element of the alternative view is a wholly different estimate of the extensiveness of constraint by impersonal forces and their impact on the individual. It is argued that the liberal claim that impersonal forces still leave the individual free to choose, remain in some sense 'external' to the individual, do not carry estimates of a person's worth and are likely in many areas to produce in a subtle and flexible way generally benign consequences is seriously wide of the mark.

Take, for example, the typical liberal claim that the absence of directive constraint leaves the person free. Like the word 'democracy' itself, the word 'freedom' carries a powerful evaluative charge, and, understandably, no one is willing to relinquish it to the opposing camp. The liberal side will accuse its opponents of illegitimately extending it so as to make it identical in meaning with 'power'; the opponents will argue that 'formal' liberty without effective empowerment is a travesty of human freedom. Though the debate sometimes does not get beyond persuasive rhetoric, some clarity can be achieved by paying close attention to the notion of 'freedom'.

Many of the problems in this area arise from the peculiar complexity of the concept or concepts of 'freedom'. It is best understood as a strictly contextual term, indicating the absence of some specific range of constraints, implicitly alluded to and identifiable by the precise context of use. If this sounds complicated a simple example will clarify matters. Consider the situation of a person who after a period of imprisonment is released; quite unproblematically, that person is now free. My contention is that what we mean by saying this is that a possible constraint, namely imprisonment, is now absent. Unless we were implicitly alluding to some specific possible constraint, which we do by the specific context of the utterance, we would be saying nothing definite or positive about the person. Furthermore, and this is crucial for the present argument, freedom as the absence of a specifically alluded to constraint implies nothing whatsoever about the presence or absence of other constraints.

A specific kind of freedom is that which consists in the absence of a coercively backed authoritative command or rule. This is a real and important type of freedom. But it does not and cannot constitute freedom *tout court*. This specific kind of freedom has no implications whatsoever for the presence or absence of other types of freedom. Secondly, we do use the concept of freedom quite as readily to refer to the absence of specific constraints other than the enforceable law constraint. It is simply misleading to claim that there is only one important kind of freedom, freedom from legal enforcement of a directive, such that if this freedom is present we are entitled to speak of a person in an unqualified fashion as free. Given the importance of the economy and the 'free market' to this whole debate, we should apply our analysis of freedom to this specific area. It is well-understood that the freedom of a free market consists in the relative absence of detailed governmental directives concerning who can produce what, what price goods should sell for, who can acquire what goods and in what quantities, who can work at what occupation, and so on. This is freedom from legally enforceable rules. However, the very system of private property exchanged through the medium of money is a complex network of constraint. This is not to deny that there is legal freedom; neither is it to deny that in many other respects the whole system is facilitatory and liberating. But it is to insist that monetary exchange operates through a system of constraint that even in ordinary discourse we conceptualise as freedom and unfreedom. Goods for which one has to pay are not 'free'. Of course, the level of constraint is less the more money one has. Providing that a person has a reasonable amount of money, the fact that the market economy is a set of constraints does not result in highly specific courses of action being pre-determined by objective forces. The people are free to choose how to dispose of their money; and this freedom is both legal and monetary; the monetary constraint is only relative. But the lesser one's financial assets the lesser one's freedom is in this regard. My point is that there is no illegitimate, persuasively rhetorical argument at play here. Though one's legal freedom to acquire is unaffected by the level of one's financial assets, one literally becomes less free the less money one has; constraint becomes more detailed and determinate.

It will be argued from the liberal perspective that true as this may be it totally neglects all of the other factors differentiating impersonal constraint from intentional direction. There may be a whole range of things that a person cannot buy because they do not have the money, but this, it is argued, is vastly different in its nature and implications from being forbidden by authority to acquire these things. The constraint is external, it does not carry the estimate of worth that intentional command carries, constraint though it is, the person still has freedom to choose, whereas the person constrained by authority has no choice. But how true are these claims?

Let us begin with the famous 'free to choose' thesis, the thesis, that is, that though people may be constrained by lack of financial resources in the matter of what they can acquire, if there is no legal restriction on them they are, in some sense, more free than what they would be if the situation were reversed, if, that is, they had financial resources but were subject to enforceable legal restrictions in their purchases. My contention is that simply from the perspective of 'freedom' there is no significant difference between the two types of situation. Confusion arises from the systematic ambiguity of the concept of 'freedom'. There are three types of freedom relevant to the analysis of such situations; freedom from financial constraint, freedom from legal constraint and freedom from certain general physical and psychological disabilities that would render a person unable to choose or to act in the relevant ways. It is this third type of freedom that a person still retains even when financially constrained. Suppose I have only a very limited amount of money, sufficient to buy the absolute necessities of life, which I cannot acquire in any other way. The two options I am considering are, firstly, to do the sensible thing and spend my money on the basic necessities of life, or, secondly, to squander it all at once on a good night out. There is no law forbidding the latter, but I am, of course, constrained in my choice and action. In what sense am I still free to choose? I am free in two senses; firstly, by definition, I am legally free, and secondly, I am free in that I am not lacking the resources, physical, psychological and financial, necessary for the implementation of either option; as we would say, I can squander all my money on a night out or I can spend it on the necessities of life, either course of action is a possibility for me. How, then, does the constraint in this situation operate, in what does it consist? It consists quite simply in the fact that one of the options, which in other circumstances I would find quite attractive, has attached to it negative consequences that will weigh heavily in my consideration of it. But this is exactly how enforceable law operates. When I am directed by law I can, in general, refuse so to act, but the negative consequences attached, in this case punishment if detected, weight the options. In both types of situation I am 'free to choose', but in each case I suffer from a level of unfreedom that consists in the negative weighting of one of the options, the obvious difference lying in the fact that in the case of legal constraint the negative weighting is the product of intentional design. If we wanted to compare freedoms we would have to look at the severity of the negative weightings and at the scope of 'feasible' action the negative weightings left open. For the sake of comparison of the 'pure types' we should, as logically we can, envisage negative weightings and correlative scope of feasible action as identical. In that case, the situations are identical, except for the source of the negative consequences.

It might be thought that in addition to the intrusiveness of the intentionality, which I will return to shortly, the situation of legal enforcement has another very significant factor present that is crucial for the type of freedom denied in such cases but absent in the case of constraint by impersonal forces. I have described legal enforcement as the negative weighting of one of the options, but doesn't it also imply the possibility of actual physical prevention? When a certain type of action is legally proscribed it might be removed outside of the sphere of human choice altogether by being physically prevented. This consideration does, in fact, lie deep in the liberal's conception of law as being, though sometimes necessary, in a very extreme way inimical to individual freedom. Though no extensive system of law could operate by physical prevention alone, the ever present possibility of such legal prevention removes a whole range of actions from the sphere of choice altogether, in a way that actions constrained by impersonal forces are not affected by. This, however, is an illusion. In the first place, almost all conformity to law is actually chosen, either because it is believed that the law is good and reasonable or because of a desire to avoid the negative sanctions. Secondly, the constraint associated with lack of financial resources is itself backed with legal constraint; I cannot have my night out and the basic necessities because if I spend my money now I will be legally prevented from acquiring the basic necessities if I try to do so without money. Thirdly, though in the case of monetary constraint there are some choices and actions not subject to physical restraint, constraint by impersonal forces generally often does involve removing a possible course of action outside the sphere of choice. Take the following example as a case in point. A family lives in a house on a quiet road, opposite a public park. The park is a great asset to the family; the children can use its facilities with relatively little supervision. They can be seen from the house and it takes only a few seconds, if necessary, to run across the road. Gradually, without any intentional plan, the road becomes more and more of a thoroughfare. The parents can still allow the children to use the park, though the option now has certain negative consequences; it takes a long time to cross the children over the busy road, the park is noisier and more polluted than before, it is more difficult to see the park from the house. Suppose, however, that the extreme is reached at which the traffic is literally continuous at the times the children would want to use the park. It is now physically impossible for them to cross the road. No individual driver speeding along the road intends this physical restraint. But their combined behaviour nonetheless produces it. The freedom to go to the park has been removed, and it has been removed not simply as a result of the option having negative consequences attached that are likely to weigh heavily against its being chosen. It has been removed by removing the option from the sphere of choice. But this has occurred indirectly and unintentionally. Hence, though there may be resentment at the lack of opportunity, this seems different from the situation of a law enforcement agency directly preventing someone from acting in a certain way. The negative nature of this latter situation stems, however, not from the mere fact of certain actions being removed from the sphere of choice, but from the directly intentional nature of the interference. What remains, then, in the contrast between the impersonal and the intentional constraint is, firstly, the claim that intentional interference with freedom adds an extra negative dimension to the constraint, and, secondly, that such intentional constraint becomes internalised, in a way in which impersonal constraint does not. What I am going to argue is that these contrasts are almost wholly specious, the difference being one of visibility and not of reality.

The evident visibility of the restriction of freedom by legal restraint arises partly from the personal directness of the application of the sanctions, but also from a curious interplay between the two types of constraint involved, leading to the perception of such constraint as peculiarly inimical to freedom, being both the removal of the relevant actions from the sphere of choice and, at the same time, having the character of an intrusion into the internal structure of choice. A law carries with it sanctions for breaking it. It also, as we have seen, legitimates physical prevention. Intentional physical prevention is a paradigm case of the lack of freedom; the specific type of restraint being also particularly 'inhuman' in that it acts, in the extreme, on the person as a body, not as a person. A Sabbath Observance law forbids me playing in the park, but I decide to defy the ban and I set off intending to enter the park. I am, however, apprehended and physically dragged away. My freedom to act is destroyed in a blatant way. Insofar as I am physically restrained I become, in that respect, not a person. I am not afforded the dignity of choosing or not choosing. I am acted upon. As noted above, however, no system of law could, in reality, be enforced wholly by physical prevention. Obeying the law when tempted to do otherwise is normally a matter of being deterred by the negative consequences of detection. The internalisation of these consequences produces a strange and paradoxical sense of constraint. The consequences occur only if the illegal action is detected by the law enforcement agency. If a person contemplating an illegal action gives any consideration at all to the possibility of such detection, the image of the law enforcement agency begins to play a central role in the calculation; we imagine being detected and apprehended. But the enforcement agency is also the agency of prevention, which might detect the law-breaker in *flagrante delicto* and physically prevent the crime. In the case of impersonal forces, the two types of constraint, physical prevention and negatively weighted consequences, operate independently. If the actions of some people render a course of action impossible for another, the impossibility is a *fait accompli*; whereas in the case of legal enforcement, precisely because I may not be physically prevented, the possibility of physical prevention and the possibility of the application of the negative sanctions become conflated in the imagination. The paradoxical consequence is that the internalisation of the police takes on the appearance of choice being restrained by physical prevention. The antithesis of freedom, physical external restraint, seems to become internal to the self; hence the peculiar feeling of an intrusive restriction on freedom. When impersonal forces remove a course of action from the sphere of choice, it is definitively removed and excluded as a possibility. In the case of legal prohibition, though physical prevention is a possibility, it is not a necessity. It is because the person bound by law is usually free to choose that the image of the possibility of physical prevention plays a role in the choice and the paradigmatic antithesis of freedom seems to become the structure of freedom itself.

As I stated above, however, the belief that intentional as distinct from impersonal constraint is more intrusive and becomes a more internal part of the self is largely a matter of phenomenological visibility. Impersonal forces can be just as much, if not more, intrusive; they can operate in a largely invisible and hence insidious way as formative of the self. This is especially true when such forces remove wide ranges of action from the sphere of choice in a continuous and systematic way. Habituation to restriction comes to structure, first, expectations and then values, and then constitutive images of the self. The point has been most persuasively argued with respect to structurally disadvantaged and oppressed groups such as women and racial and ethnic minorities. Even in the absence of the legal enforcement of subordination, subordination and disadvantage are constituted through the unintentional consequences of masses of individual actions, which, for members of such oppressed groups, render whole ranges of action impossible and attach to others such negative consequences as to make them unfeasible, unlikely to be chosen. A person unaccustomed to such constraints might, on first encountering them, perceive them as external, as parameters setting the external circumstances of choice. The normal situation, however, is that a person is born into and is formed by such circumstances as the inescapable matrix of life. As Anthony Giddens would argue, structure, and hence, structured disadvantage should be conceived of not as some non-personal, wholly external pre-determining parameter of action, but as produced and re-produced in the chosen actions of people.[33] Both as structuring choice and as forming the psyche, constraint is internal to the self. The deeper and more persistent the internalisation of constraint, the less visible it becomes, but not the less constraining for all that.

Of course, if such constraint is the unintentional result of a mass of individual actions, as unintentional, perhaps even unknown about, it does not carry the low estimation of worth that intentional direction and constraint can carry. But while unintentionality in origin might absolve of responsibility, known persistence does not. It is, in fact, quite common to hear disadvantaged groups complain of the low priority assigned to their well-known and well-publicised problems. Justifiably, this continued neglect is taken as an estimate of the unimportance of such groups. Persistent and extensive disadvantage and constraint, besides becoming an internalised and formative element of an oppressed and subordinate self often manifests itself in a self-consciousness of inferior status, adding a further dimension to the internalisation of constraint.

Extensive constraint by impersonal forces can be, I am arguing, just as inimical to individual freedom as constraint by intentional direction. It can also be just as intrusive, just as formative of the internal structure of the self and can carry a message of inferiority of status that itself becomes internalised and undermines self-worth in a manner that destroys all sense of power and responsibility for one's own destiny. To someone suffering such constraint, the extension of authoritative decision-making in which everyone is an equal and effective participant to the circumstances that generate the constraint will not constitute a diminution of individual freedom. If such circumstances are beneficially altered, the result will be an extension of the individual freedom of those previously disadvantaged and the transformation, in those areas where significant interpersonal constraint already exists, of a system of unintentional and unequal power and dominance into an area of collective decision-making organised on a basis of equality that will enhance, rather than detract from, a person's freedom. Equality of input does not, of course, guarantee that each individual will be literally ruling her- or himself. But it will provide equal effective opportunity for all to make their voice heard and to influence the outcome and it might even engender that informed respect for the interests and perspectives of others on which a genuine consensus can be based.

If it is argued that this respect and consensus is best left to the informal mechanisms of continuous accommodation and adjustment that result in the formation of tradition, it is worth pointing out that the reciprocity of mutual accommodation is no guarantee of its symmetry; accommodation between unequals perpetuates inequality. 'The strong will exact what they can and the weak will concede what they must.'[34] This is a recipe for the maintenance of the freedom of some at the expense of the constraint of others. Furthermore, though much of human knowledge will be tacit, unarticulated and experientially based, and though such tacit awareness can sometimes sediment into a wise and flexible tradition, such 'knowledge' and 'experience' is neither infallible nor incorrigible and there need be no sharp line between the tacit and the consciously articulate. Anyone who acknowledges the persistence of widespread structural disadvantage and oppression will be justified in asserting that though the traditional might be the embodiment of the collective wisdom and experience of humanity, it might also be that amalgam of unjustified prejudice, myth, stereotype and common nonsense that is often dignified with the title of 'conventional wisdom'. Though explicit attempts at rational ordering are just as fallible as the tacit accumulation of experience, in those spheres of society in which the conditions to which all are subject are going to be determined, willy-nilly, by human interaction and are likely to be determined in a manner detrimental to the interests of some, there is no cause for complete scepticism with regard to the possibility of sensible and rational organisation.

I have not been attempting to deal, in this chapter, with the question of how one would systematically justify the political ideology of democracy. Rather, I have been examining the arguments for and against a broader and narrower conception of what a commitment to democracy should involve. My conclusion is that both from the point of view of individual freedom and from the point of view of the benefits afforded by the ability to effectively participate in collective decision-making, for those currently so constrained by impersonal forces that they are incapable of effectively utilising their democratic rights, the juridico-legal conception of democracy is but a poor substitute for effective political equality. The arguments used in the attempt to demonstrate that the commitment to anything beyond juridico-legal democracy will lead to consequences inimical both to democracy and individual freedom are, I hope to have shown, ultimately unsuccessful.

Throughout the chapter I have been tangentially approaching, though not dealing explicitly with, one aspect of the relationship between democracy and individual liberty, in the precise sense of freedom from authoritative direction, that is central to the whole debate. I have emphasised during my argument that the commitment to a broader and more active democratic ideal is not inconsistent with giving a high value to individual freedom from collective control, it is not inconsistent with the claim to moral and intellectual autonomy. The crucial problem is where the boundary should be between individual liberty and democratic collective autonomy. There is a time-honoured solution to this problem that emerges in what I will call 'the liberal democratic synthesis'. Even if we give a high priority to effective political equality in the area of collective decision-making, the value of individual liberty from such decision-making is so great, the liberal democrat will argue, that the moral legitimacy of collective decision-making is dependent not just on its democratic procedure but on its respect for the inalienable right to individual liberty. It is to the analysis of this synthesis that I will turn in the next chapter.

6

Democracy, anarchism and the liberal democratic synthesis

I have been examining in the previous chapter the fundamental normative arguments underlying the juridico-legal conception of democracy. As I indicated at the end of that chapter, however, the boundary between individual freedom from government and the legitimate scope of collective control is, by many theorists, seen not as a matter to be decided on the basis of the general desirability or otherwise of a greater or lesser scope for collective decision-making, but as something fixed by fundamental individual rights whose infringement renders collective decision-making morally illegitimate no matter how socially desirable the results might be. There is a sphere in which the individual simply cannot be legitimately commanded by government, which implies that no matter how democratic the procedures may be, any governmental decision attempting to command in such a sphere of life is illegitimate. In such circumstances there can be no moral obligation on the citizen to obey. The extreme limiting case of such claims arises in the theory of 'philosophical anarchism', which argues that no government ever has the right to command obedience and hence, all governments are illegitimate in all of their actions. As an example of such a philosophical anarchist, let us look at the case of Henry David Thoreau.

In July 1846 Thoreau was imprisoned in Concord, Massachusetts, for refusing to pay his poll-tax. Despite the fact that his imprisonment lasted only one night, his case has become famous, for, as he explained in his essay – 'On the duty of civil disobedience':

> It is for no particular item in the tax-bill that I refuse to pay it. I simply wish to refuse allegiance to the State. . . . In fact, I quietly declare war with the State.[1]

A more forthright statement of the anarchist position could not be wished for. There are, of course, many different strands in the anarchist tradition, encompassing numerous types of argument attempting to show the radical undesirability of any form of organised government.[2] But right from the early days of Godwin's *Enquiry Concerning Political Justice*[3] one important persistent strain of anarchism has attacked not just the desirability but the moral legitimacy of government from the high ground of the inalienable moral autonomy of the individual. Even a democratic government, it is argued, has no presumptive, morally legitimate authority to command. For, as one commentator has put it:

> The nub of this position is that the individual's primary moral duty is always to maintain his moral autonomy, that is to say, never to subordinate his own judgement to that of another, and as the essence of political authority is that the state's imperative 'Do X' is itself a moral reason for doing X, moral autonomy and political obligation are necessarily incompatible.[4]

In the same Thoreau essay already referred to, we find an admirably clear statement of the basis of this position. 'The only obligation', Thoreau says, 'which I have a right to assume, is to do at any time what I think right.'[5] If any individual, that is to say *every* individual, has, at any time, the moral right to refuse obedience, and if it follows that government then has no right to coerce, it does begin to look as though government as the legitimate monopoliser of coercive power is completely undermined. Political obligation, political authority, the moral right to require obedience, legitimate coercion are all exposed as fictions. Citing Thoreau's case will, nowadays, confer a high degree of persuasiveness on this anarchist argument. For, though Thoreau couches his argument in terms of general principle, in fact his opposition to the government was also based on his refusal to be a party to certain specific policies, in particular, slavery and the Mexican war. Most modern readers would be inclined to applaud Thoreau's moral integrity, and his ringing declaration: 'Under a government which imprisons any unjustly, the true place for a just man is also a prison', is justly famous.[6]

But is there any substance to this 'philosophical anarchism'? Many commentators have believed so and have admitted that given the absolute moral autonomy of the individual, legitimate government, whatever its procedural form, is undermined. The most famous modern version of this argument is that formulated by Robert Paul Wolff in his work *In Defense of Anarchism*.[7] Wolff is absolutely clear that he is rejecting the legitimacy of even a direct consensus democracy. Even if there is a unanimity rule, ensuring that every governmental decision has my direct consent, and hence moral approval, the mere fact *that* I once consented cannot confer authority on that decision if, as is my right as a morally autonomous agent, I later decide that I was previously mistaken. If, at the time of compliance, I believe that what is required of me is, in terms of its content, my duty, that belief is the basis of my current obligation, not the fact that I had previously consented. If, at the time of compliance, I believe that what is required of me is morally wrong, no previous consent either to a procedure, or even directly to the current requirement, is of any force. My current obligation can only be to do that which I believe, now, is my obligation. How could it be the case that some previous judgement or consent can, of itself, oblige me to do that which I believe to be morally horrendous?

This is all very persuasive, but if we are to deal adequately with the contentions of philosophical anarchism we will need to identify the fundamental logical structure of the argument from moral autonomy to rejection of government legitimacy. There are three crucial features of the argument that should not be overlooked. Firstly, the basic premise of the argument does not purport to identify a general content of moral duty, either in terms of some general goal to be achieved or in terms of specific side-constraints on morally acceptable action. Rather it identifies the fundamental form of moral obligation for any moral agent. If certain requirements on the moral agent stem from this fundamental form of obligation, they will override all other considerations no matter how plausible. It is the neglect of this point that renders Keith Graham's treatment of Wolff's argument unsatisfactory.[8] Graham wants to argue that taking moral autonomy as the fundamental value to be achieved can actually provide an argument proving the legitimacy of democratic government based on consent. If we take a robust version of moral autonomy that includes 'freedom to' and not just 'freedom from', and if, as a theorist of moral autonomy must, we admit that everybody's moral autonomy is important, we can demonstrate that, assuming as a matter of fact that stable democratic government is a prerequisite of a stable social order that results in a maximisation of positive freedoms, a commitment to moral autonomy implies the acceptance of democratic government as legitimate. The philosophical anarchist will rightly protest that no matter how plausible such an argument might seem, it fails to take into account the anarchist's basic point that the fundamental form of moral obligation is to do that which one thinks right. Granted this, no matter how a government is constituted, no matter what its proclaimed goals are, no matter how much its putative legitimacy is supported by such arguments as Graham's, if what the government is requiring of me I believe to be wrong, I am obliged to disobey. Everybody, at all times, is obliged to follow what they believe is right, and that moral autonomy as the form of moral duty destroys the putative right of government to command.

This leads us to the second crucial point. In formulating the fundamental form of obligation the philosophical anarchist must make explicit reference to the role of individual conscience. Saying that it is my duty to do that which at the time it is my duty to do, is tautologically true, but is an unoperationalisable rule as it stands. What my duty is can be of no relevance or imperative force, unless I *know* it to be my duty. So the fundamental form is not the tautologous one, but the informative one used by Thoreau: 'The only obligation which I have a right to assume, is to do at any time what I *think* right.'

The final point needed to round out the picture derives from the distinction between procedure and content. When, at the time of compliance, the person is deciding what her or his duty is, the primary decision must be made with respect to the content of what is being required. If, with respect to content, I believe it my duty not to do this, external factors, such as the fact that the requirement is being made by a government to which others have consented or even to which I had previously consented, are overridden by what I now believe is my duty. It is the permanent possibility of my deciding in terms of the content of any requirement that it is my duty not to comply that destroys any putative claim to authority by anything or anybody external to me.

We have arrived, here, at the very heart of philosophical anarchism. It is always my duty to do that which I think right. I cannot, logically, alienate this autonomy. I cannot transfer ultimate authority, or sovereignty, to another person, institution or procedure. For whatever I actually do, it always remains true of me that I am obliged to do that which I believe right, and this fact conflicts with my having an alleged overriding obligation to obey another.

This is a powerful argument against the legitimacy of government, and it has been treated so by both defenders and opponents. Plausible as it may seem, however, I believe it to be fundamentally misguided as an attack on the moral legitimacy of, at least some forms of, state authority. Interestingly, I believe that both supporters and opponents of the argument overestimate its force because they share certain misconceptions concerning the nature of obligation and the preconditions of the stability of social institutions that depend upon the recognition of obligation by their participants. In particular, due recognition is not given to the distinction between the moral and the morally indifferent, and to the distinction between prima facie or conditional obligation and absolute or unconditional obligation. Further, it is assumed that an institution whose stability depends upon participants accepting reciprocal obligations will be viable only if those obligations are recognised as absolute. I will explain each of these three points briefly and then show their relevance to the anarchist argument.

Most systems of morality do not claim to classify every possible form of human action as either morally good or morally bad. In fact, the norm is for a huge range of human behaviour to be assigned to the category of the morally indifferent. Only in highly exceptional circumstances will my choice between marmalade and honey for breakfast be a *moral* choice, or determined, that is, by my specifically moral rules. In fact, except from an extremely implausible ultra-moralistic viewpoint, moral rules usually operate, even for very morally serious people, as setting the parameters of action, choices within those parameters being made by reference to non-moral considerations.

Secondly, the distinction between prima facie obligation and absolute obligation. Most moral systems claim to be reasonably specific guides to action by being able to classify general types of human action and morally assess them in abstraction from the actual concrete circumstances of individual choice. Thus, taking other people's property without their consent, lying to them, torturing them are, as general types of action, condemned. However, it is usually accepted that in the concrete circumstances of choice an abstract evaluation might have to be modified; there can be a conflict of duties, either because a concrete proposed action is, in the circumstances, seen to belong to two or more general categories with conflicting evaluations or because of very exceptional conditions that no general evaluation could have taken into account. Granted this possibility, when moral rules are formulated in abstraction from the actual circumstances of choice, they have to be thought of as implying a '*ceteris paribus*' clause, and consequently the obligation they carry has to be seen as only a prima facie obligation conditional upon the fulfilment of the '*ceteris paribus*' clause. Such a prima facie obligation is distinct from the unconditional, absolute obligation arising from an individual's full assessment of duty made in the concrete circumstances of choice by reference to all the relevant factors. It makes sense to talk of prima facie obligation, because the transformation of prima facie into absolute obligation is the norm; only in exceptional circumstances is it envisaged that the obligation deriving from the general pre-categorisation of action will be overturned in the concrete situation of choice.

Using this distinction, I can turn to my third point, which is that an institution that operates via recognition of obligation, generally only requires that obligation to be prima facie, not absolute. The precise relevance of these points can be demonstrated by the consideration of a social institution analogous to governmental legitimacy, namely, the practice of promising, and the consequent generation of obligation. It is generally accepted that a promise generates the obligation to fulfil. But this would be wholly incoherent unless the above considerations were taken into account. Firstly, unless some actions were considered morally indifferent, promising as generating a genuine obligation would be either unnecessary or impossible. If the promised action was already one's duty, the promise is irrelevant; if the action was one's definite duty to avoid, the promise would be morally illegitimate, the duty deriving from content overriding the alleged duty deriving from the external factor of promising. Only if, at the time of promising, the action is seen as morally indifferent does it make sense to think of the promise itself as generating the obligation to fulfil. Furthermore, a few moments' reflection will convince anyone that the obligation here referred to is a prima facie, conditional obligation. If between promise and time of compliance either one's moral beliefs change or new factual considerations come into operation such that what one previously believed to be morally indifferent is now perceived to be morally bad and one's duty to avoid, then it will be admitted that that subsequent conception of duty will override the duty deriving from the promise. But two crucial points have to be made. Firstly, it still makes perfect sense to talk about the promise as generating an obligation, which obligation, as a real duty, *might* be overridden at a later time. And, secondly, the bare possibility of the duty being overridden, rendering the obligation prima facie and conditional, does not undermine the stability of the institution of promising. This would only occur if people's moral beliefs were in constant flux or if factual circumstances were always so complex and variable that pre-categorisation of action was, for the most part, impossible. If, however, people's moral beliefs are relatively stable and what is thought now to be morally indifferent is usually thought to be so later, then it makes sense to say that promises generate obligations and prima facie obligations can ground the stability of institutions.

The relevance of all of this to the anarchist argument should, by now, be obvious. In fact, from the perspective of governmental legitimacy as being based on consent, the situation of promising is not just a simple analogy, but is rather the general rule of which consent to be bound by the results of a decision-making procedure is a particular case. Being a particular case, the general restrictions will apply. I can only bind myself, either in promising generally or in consent to a community decision-making procedure, to those things which I will not think it my overriding moral duty to avoid. It will follow that my obligation will not be absolute; it will be restricted both in scope, to the morally indifferent, and in force will be conditional upon my continuing to believe that what is required of me is, in content, morally indifferent. But the obligation will be a real obligation. Incumbents of government office might like to believe that their authority to command is absolute, but neither consent theory nor the general facts concerning the stability of institutions require this. Only by the neglect of these obvious points can it be thought that the moral autonomy of the individual is radically incompatible with any form of political obligation.

That government, in particular democratic government, can sometimes legitimately command obedience from its citizens does not, in itself, imply that it can command such obedience in any and every sphere of life. With the notable exception of Rousseau, it is undoubtedly true that most of the major mainstream thinkers that are, in retrospect, thought of as the founding fathers of the modern democratic tradition were, unambiguously, *liberal* democrats. When it came to the fundamental principles of legitimate procedures of authoritatively binding decisions, democracy might have been the overriding value, but equally important was the claim that no decisions, no matter how democratic their procedures, were legitimate if they trespassed on the domain of individual autonomy. In fact, although at first sight Rousseau, with his insistence on radical popular sovereignty, might appear the perfect democrat, ever since J. L. Talmon's work, *The Origins of Totalitarian Democracy*,[9] Rousseau has been viewed by many as something of an anomaly in the democratic tradition. This stems precisely from Rousseau's contention that the first precondition of the Social Contract had to be 'the total alienation of each of the associates, with all his rights, to the whole community'.[10] The result of such total alienation could only be the creation of a collective decision-making body that had unconditional, unlimited authority. The rights that individuals could legitimately claim depended upon, and had their origin in, collective decision-making, and thus could not act as an independent delimitation of the legitimacy of collective decisions. Such a conclusion, of course, runs completely against the very essence of liberal democracy.

Talmon traces the career of totalitarian democracy from Rousseau, through St. Just and Robespierre, to Babeuf and Blanqui and thence to Lenin and Russian Communism. It is, consequently, tempting to see the collapse in the late 1980s and early 1990s of the communist regimes in the Soviet Union and Eastern Europe as the final victory in practice of the liberal democratic synthesis.

Furthermore, there is no denying the appeal of that synthesis. No matter how unqualifiedly democratic we are, most of us would stridently reject the right of collective decisions to dictate to us in the areas of our religious (or non-religious, as the case may be) beliefs, our political opinions, our sexual mores, our choice of marital partners, our occupation, residence or general lifestyle, to mention at random just a few areas in which we value personal autonomy. I would, myself, endorse such a valuation and, consequently, it is not intended in this chapter to argue in favour of a totalitarian extension of the tentacles of government action into every sphere of social and personal life. What I do intend to argue, however, is that the traditional justification of limited government is seriously flawed. My thesis is that there is no logically consistent synthesis of liberal and democratic principles that does not either so subordinate democracy to liberal limitations that the democratic element is fundamentally undermined or so subordinates the liberal element to the principle of democratic decision-making that the position becomes indistinguishable from the Rousseauian stance that the demos can be the only democratic determinant and protector of the rights of citizens.

The argument will be organised in the following way. Firstly, I will set out the essential logical structure of any attempted liberal democratic synthesis that purports to preserve the independent and equal importance of both liberalism and democracy. Secondly, I will give an account of one specific version of this type of synthesis, namely that which bases liberal limitations on legitimate government and the unique legitimacy of democratic procedures on a set of Lockean-type natural rights. Thirdly, I will demonstrate the inconsistency of this proposed synthesis and suggest several reasons why this inconsistency has not been more widely recognised. Fourthly, I will argue that it is not the specifically Lockean features of such a theory of rights that renders the theory incapable of providing a consistent synthesis with the fundamental principles of democracy. I will argue that *any* theory of natural or human rights that grounds those rights on anything other than *actual* collective decision-making will prove to be fundamentally anti-democratic. Finally I will raise the question of what justifiable response there might be to the seemingly implied absolute rights of democratic government if these arguments are correct.

The basic outline of the liberal democratic synthesis is familiar; a distinction between two spheres is postulated, the two spheres usually being referred to as 'the public' and 'the private', with the clear implication that government action, as binding and legitimately calling on coercive implementation in the case of non-compliance, is itself valid and legitimate only in the public sphere. The private sphere is the domain of individual autonomy. The democratic element of the synthesis insists that even within its sphere of legitimacy, government action is only legitimate, in the fundamental sense, when it is thoroughly democratic. Talk about 'legitimacy' in any sense other than the purely positive implies a background normative framework which, if it is to successfully ground the liberal democratic synthesis, has to have a certain structure.

Firstly, the normative principles called upon must provide a criterion for a reasonably precise differentiation between the public and the private spheres. Secondly, the principles must justify the exclusion of government from the private sphere. Thirdly, the principles must justify, uniquely, democratic procedures within the proper sphere of government; and fourthly, absolutely crucial for the success of the synthesis, the first two aims must be achievable without any reference to the results of any actual concrete collective decision-making process. This is because the overall aim is to produce a double criterion of governmental legitimacy, with each part being independent, neither alone being sufficient, both together being necessary. It is perfectly obvious, for example, that if the criterion of differentiation between the public and the private was specified as being what had been decided as public and private by 'the people' democratically, then even if there was an independent proof of the principle of individual autonomy in the private sphere, no individual would have any fundamental protection from a possibly tyrannical democracy, since 'the people' could simply continuously redefine the boundaries of the public and the private, or, in the extreme case, define those boundaries so that the private was, in practice, an empty class. If individual autonomy is going to be protected against potentially tyrannical totalitarian democracy, the liberal principles must themselves be definable and justifiable independently of the democratic process.

It would seem that these conditions are relatively easily met within the context of a normative theory of liberal democracy, particularly if, as is normally the case, the justificatory principles of democracy form a logically integrated and interdependent set with the underlying principles of liberalism. I will expand a little on this, because even though we are still approaching the matter in a highly schematic way, the above observations can make the case for the liberal delimitation of democratic legitimacy seem logically inescapable.

If democratic procedures are going to claim normative legitimacy, this will have to be on the basis of a principle or principles that are logically prior to the claimed legitimacy, as democratic, of any particular decision or aggregate of decisions. Otherwise the argument would be viciously circular. But if the principles appealed to are such that they imply and are implied by the underlying principles of liberal restriction, the normative framework, as a logically integrated whole, will imply the limited legitimacy of democratic procedures. The very principles appealed to by the democrat to justify the political commitment to democracy will imply the existence of a realm in which government action, no matter how democratic, will be illegitimate. This, of course, is only the best possible scenario for the liberal democratic synthesis. The synthesis would be justifiable without the logical interdependence of underlying principles, needing, as a minimal condition, the bare consistency of the justificatory principles and the claim of equal evaluative importance or status.

Again, meeting such conditions in the construction of a political theory would seem to be unproblematic. By definition, a normative political theorist is looking for principles logically prior to the acceptance of specific institutional structures as legitimate. There would seem to be no logical difficulty in the supposition that a set of, at least consistent, at best interdependent, general principles might be found which would, first, establish a realm of the private in which the value of personal autonomy must be preserved, and second, the condition that when individual actions become the legitimate subject of authoritatively binding collective decisions, all individuals subject to such decisions should have equal rights of participation in their formulation. To examine in more concrete fashion the issues raised here I will move on to an exposition of what was, and to a large extent still is, the traditional justification of the liberal democratic synthesis, namely that rooted in the theory of natural rights.

Though John Locke was not known for a commitment, either in theory or in practice, to democratic forms of government, except in the very limited case of those property-holders who were enfranchised in regard to governmental decisions concerning the taxation of their property, his theory of natural rights is seen as providing a fairly lucid, and historically influential, basis for the liberal limitations on legitimate government.[11] And in the hands of such thinkers as Paine and Jefferson,[12] the same basic theory of natural rights was interpreted as providing a foundation for democracy, albeit a democracy restricted by liberal limitations. We have here, then, an almost perfect concrete instance of the abstract schema of a normative framework justifying the liberal democratic synthesis sketched in the previous section.

Locke begins his account of legitimate political authority by formulating the structure of fundamental human rights enjoyed equally by all members of the human species. I will not give an account of the explicitly religious foundation that Locke provides for his theory of natural rights. Presumably, those not convinced by Locke's, or anyone else's, natural theology but still basing moral and political theory on a schema of natural rights will believe that they have some alternative philosophical foundation for the set of natural rights postulated. I am concerned here only with the political implications of the schedule of rights postulated.

The fundamental right in that schedule as outlined by Locke is the right to freedom, the natural 'state of liberty'. He then adds the right to life and bodily integrity, and finally, in Chapter V, the right to the acquisition of private property, providing the acquisition meets the well-known Lockean criteria.[13] Locke was insistent, of course, that the state of liberty was not a state of licence, the right to freedom is not the right to do whatever one wishes. It is the right to do as one chooses, providing that one's actions are in accordance with the natural moral law, and, of course, do not infringe the natural rights of others. This restriction is essential for self-consistency. A right is a claim against others, and I can only have a claim against others if they have specific obligations to me, at the very minimum, not to interfere with me in the pursuit of that to which I have a right. But if everyone is said to have a right to do as they please, no one has any obligations to anyone else and so no one will be in a position to claim any rights against others' potential actions. The only consistent sense that can be given to the assertion that everyone has the right to do whatever they please is by interpreting that claim to mean that the language of right and reciprocal obligation has no place in the determination of interpersonal relations.

For Locke, these rights are the fundamental determinants of legitimate interpersonal interaction and are inalienable. With the exception of specific property rights, not, of course, the right to acquire property, which is inalienable, which Locke is willing to subordinate to democratic decision-making, his conception of the fundamental rights is a conception of them as logically inalienable; one cannot morally legitimately enslave oneself or cede to others the right to one's life. The resulting situation is one in which all human beings have the absolutely indefeasible rights to act as they choose within the understood limits. What can be ceded by consent to an agreed agent is the power to exercise the secondary rights of prevention and punishment of those acting in infringement of the fundamental rights of others.[14] As has often been noted, this theory places very severe restrictions on the legitimacy of control of a person's behaviour by any external agent in general and by government in particular. I am not specifically concerned here with the extent of the autonomy postulated. It is enough that the theory defines a sphere of absolute personal autonomy within which no government interference, no matter how legitimate its form or procedures, would ever be valid.

As noted above, Locke did not draw particularly democratic conclusions from these premises. Only in the case of proposed expropriation through taxation did he think explicit, substantive consent, albeit through a very weakly justified majority rule procedure, was required. And he, notoriously, gave a very weak interpretation to the required[15] general consent to government as well.[16] However, it is not difficult to imagine how on the basis of such a theory of natural rights, especially the right to freedom, given a strong interpretation of the stated egalitarian principles and a suitably robust interpretation of the necessity of consent if government is to be legitimate at all, a strong democratic conclusion could be, and was, drawn. If legitimate government is, as consented-to-agent, accountable to the people, not just ultimately, but continuously, all that is lacking as a justificatory base of democracy is the specification of the appropriate institutions of continuous accountability. But such a democratic government will necessarily be a liberal democratic government. It will have a highly and absolutely restricted scope of action. The very structure of natural rights appealed to in the grounding of its legitimacy constitutes the basis for its limited scope of legitimate action. The case for the liberal democratic synthesis, with the two necessary and independent criteria of legitimacy, seems logically watertight and inescapable.

Far from being logically watertight, the case for a liberal democratic synthesis is radically flawed by an internal inconsistency at its very core. This can be easily demonstrated by considering the following simple example.

Imagine a political theorist who has just formulated some such theory of rights as outlined above and has gone on to specify a set of constitutional provisions grounded in the theory. Leaving her or his study he or she descends into the world of real-life politics in an actual community. Though delighted to find that the procedures of rule perfectly conform with democratic principles, our political theorist is horrified to discover that the scope of power actually claimed by the democratic process pays scant respect to the theorist's liberal principles. What response can the theorist make? He or she could, of course, express disapproval, proclaim the illegitimacy of even democratic government in areas prescribed by the theory of natural rights, publicly proclaim the constitutional limitations that would respect the schedule of natural rights. But how would our theorist envisage such constitutional limitations being implemented, ratified, interpreted and enforced? By what agency? This is the simple, but crucial question for the consistency of the liberal democratic synthesis. Constitutional provisions restricting democratic legitimacy cannot, even in theory, materialise out of thin air. A theorist not adverting to this fact is being fatally disingenuous. If we commend the delimitation of democratic power, we must indicate the agency that will be given the power to specify these limits, interpret them and enforce them. I am not denying the desirability, both in theory and in practice, of limited state power. What I am claiming is that in practice this limitation is exercised either by an agency that is subordinate to the democratic process and so cannot be the foundation, in theory, of external limits on the scope of democratic legitimacy, or by an agency independent of the process of democratic decision-making, a situation that is fundamentally non-democratic. Someone may so value the preservation of natural rights against democratic sovereignty that democratic sovereignty is assigned a lower priority than the preservation of such rights. This is a perfectly consistent position, but not one that can claim to be fundamentally democratic.

The best possible scenario for such a liberal theory is to imagine, firstly, that there is a unique, known, a priori and objective set of natural rights with clear and unambiguous weightings that would determine their relative priorities and thus would provide an unambiguous delimitation of the scope of democratic legitimacy. Secondly, one must postulate the existence of an agency with the power, superior to the democratic decision-making process, to ensure that democratic decisions remain within their prescribed sphere of legitimacy. The imagined agency, we will assume, is infallible in the determination of the schedule of natural rights and its interpretation, and wholly incorruptible. Such a structure of political power would not be democratic, but we would have the consolation of knowing that the people are denied the right of self-determination by the superior power only when they would be illegitimately using that power to infringe the rights of some or all members of the community.

Such a scenario is, evidently, wholly unrealistic and could not be proposed by any serious political theorist. Not even Plato was prepared to claim that, in practice, one could guarantee the existence of such an infallible and incorruptible agency.[17] In reality instituting an agency with superior supervisory power over democratic self-rule is equivalent to giving unlimited power to a minority to dictate to a people as whole when it can rule itself. Let us not imagine that the power of such an agency can be itself theoretically limited by constitutional provisions; such provisions would need an agency to specify, ratify, implement and enforce them. If the limitations are to have their source in the decisions of the minority agency, they cannot, logically, constitute an independent check on the power of that agency. It is worth emphasising again that I am not questioning the desirability in practice of a democratic community setting up constitutional limitations on its own power and numerous checks and balances to limit the probability of hasty and unwise decisions. What I am questioning is the democratic consistency of justifying such practical measures by identifying a source, independent of collective decision-making, which will specify those limitations and enforce them.

The case for the liberal democratic synthesis is worse than presently stated. I have so far been arguing on the basis of an acceptance of the existence of a clearly defined set of natural rights that would provide the basis for an unambiguous delimitation of democratic legitimacy. It is time to question the plausibility of such an assumption as part of an operationalisable political theory. So far, the only problem for the consistent liberal anti-democrat has been the practical problem of ensuring the infallibility and incorruptibility in practice of the minority agency limiting democratic power. There has not been any notable consensus, even within the tradition of liberal political theorists, concerning an exact specification of natural rights, their basis and, of crucial importance, the delimitation of the scope of governmental legitimacy. It would take an extraordinarily self-deluded theorist to envisage the institution of a non-democratic agency to limit government to a sphere of legitimacy the extent of which has been a constant matter of dispute. It is not my intention here to attack the philosophical foundations of the claim that there is some uniquely specifiable set of objective human rights. I merely want to highlight the total implausibility of thinking that the question of limiting government legitimacy, whether this be thought of as democratic self-limiting or undemocratic limiting by a minority agency, can be unproblematically solved by referring the matter, as it were, to some set of fundamental natural rights when, in fact, there is radical dispute in democratic communities concerning the existence and/or specific structure of such a set of rights. Rousseau, I believe, was correct; there is no democratically legitimate way of identifying, independently of the process of democratic decision-making, a basis for the limitation of democratic legitimacy.

The general failure to identify this radical inconsistency in the liberal democratic synthesis has several sources. The first lies in the failure to think through the implications of the lack of consensus concerning natural rights. If we imagined the objective existence of a unique set of natural rights and a universal consensus in a community concerning both the schedule of rights and the desirability of limiting governmental action by reference to them, then we could be excused for confusing a non-democratic delimitation of power with democratic self-limitation, because of the universal moral approval of the non-democratic agency. But even the universal moral approval of a non-democratic power-structure does not render that structure democratic. The universal belief in the correctness of the doctrine of the divine right of kings would not transform monarchy into democratic self-rule.

The second source of the general failure to recognise the inconsistency is the regrettable failure, noted by Machiavelli,[18] of political theorists to raise questions concerning the actual structures of political power that would be required in any real, concrete context, to implement the theoretically postulated values.

The argument of the last section was aimed explicitly at a liberal democratic theory based on a Lockean-type theory of natural rights grounded on an acceptance of a universal, objective natural law. I want to argue now that the weakness of the synthesis does not specifically derive from the Lockean-type theory of rights. My argument would be just as valid directed at any other theory of rights just as long as the process of the specification of the rights was theoretically independent of the results of any actual democratic decision-making process. There have been two notable trends in contemporary political theory, communitarianism and neo-contractarian theory, particularly as based on Habermasian influenced theories of the 'ideal speech' situation, that purport to provide a justifiable basis to normative debate and, in that context, to a theory of rights. The latter theory is couched in overtly radical democratic terminology. Communitarians argue that though from an abstract consideration of human beings no universal moral imperatives are logically derivable, real and relatively rational moral debate can, and must, be carried out against the background of the embedded values of a culture and common life, without which that culture and common life are unintelligible. Neo-contractarians argue that a theoretical specification of basic moral values is possible on the basis of a reflection on what would be the outcome of collective decisions in some 'ideal' situation, such as behind a Rawlsian 'veil of ignorance' or in a Habermasian 'ideal speech situation' in which the dialogue is between equal and unoppressed participants.[19] It is not my intention to provide expositions and critiques of such theories. My specific arguments against the consistency of the liberal democratic synthesis would remain valid even if one or other of these attempts to provide a foundation for a theory of rights proved to be completely acceptable. No matter how theoretically valid, if such a schedule of rights conflicts with the schedule of rights specified by an actual self-governing people, in practice there are only two options open; the acceptance of the validity of democratic self-determination or the institution of a non-democratic agency with the power to impose its will on the people, hopefully in accordance with the validly grounded schedule of human rights.

In Chapters 12 and 13 of his recent book *Democracy and Its Critics*, Robert Dahl arrives at conclusions somewhat similar to my own. At the end of Chapter 12, however, he adds:

> The supposed failure of the democratic process to guarantee desirable substantive outcomes is in important respects spurious. We need to reject . . . the familiar contrast between substance and process. For integral to the democratic process are substantive rights, goods and interests that are often mistakenly thought to be threatened by it.[20]

In the following chapter, against the claim that some 'substantive outcomes should have priority over the democratic process',[21] he goes on to assert that '(it) seems to me highly reasonable to argue that *no* interests should be inviolable beyond these integral and essential to the democratic process'.[22]

It looks as though what might be being suggested here is something of a compromise between the liberal non-democratic external control over the democratic process and the, in principle, unlimited power of democracy. For if democracy consists of a set of substantive rights that are integral to the democratic process and depends upon an even wider set of such rights, we seem to have (a) a very robust set of rights that (b) as integral to the democratic process cannot be self-consistently rejected by the democrat and, consequently, (c) ought, by the democrat, to be considered inviolable. This alleged compromise is, however, premature, misleading and incoherently grounded.

The ambiguity of Dahl's position derives from the problem of how we are to take his claim that the integral rights 'should be inviolable'. Does this mean that because these rights are integral to democracy then a democrat must be so committed, precisely as a democrat, to the protection of these rights that he or she must accede to the legitimacy of a non-democratic institution with a power superior to the power of the democratic process to protect democracy from itself, if need be? This is certainly not what Dahl envisages. He is just as adamant as I have been that any institution or agency with power superior to the democratic process is both undemocratic in principle and likely to be even more undemocratic in practice.

What, then, is the intended force of 'should be inviolable'? This is a moral 'should', that Dahl thinks a self-consistent democrat ought to abide by and might be well-advised to implement through democratic self-delimitation. So, in the first place, there is no compromise. And in the second place, the basis Dahl gives for singling out these particular rights is seen to be flawed. I have argued against, as undemocratic, an institutionalised control over the democratic process as whole that is supposed to protect basic rights. But someone can believe in the existence of basic rights, including those that are not integral to the democratic process, and believe that those rights should, in Dahl's sense, be inviolable, that is, that the democratic process should be, with respect to those rights, self-limiting. The integral nature of Dahl's democratic rights is not really relevant to democratic self-limitation. The only thing that can be said about integral rights is that if someone proclaims themselves a democrat, the argument for self-limitation with respect to integral rights is easily provable. But not even Dahl is *only* a democrat. This can be shown quite easily. Dahl's fundamental justification for democracy rests on the evaluative premise of the supreme importance of 'personal autonomy'.[23] If his justification of democracy is going to be anything more than the uninformative tautology that if people have the right to equal participation in collective self-rule, then they have the right to equal participation in collective self-rule, Dahl has to interpret the fundamental value of personal autonomy in more than a restrictedly political sense. What is ultimately valuable is the maximisation of control over oneself, in the individual sense of self-control. The function of 'maximisation' is to signal the likelihood that no real life situation will allow for total actual autonomy for all individuals in all circumstances. Because of significant interaction between the consequences of individual decisions, the maintenance of equal maximisation of autonomy will involve some areas of human life being organised by collective, and binding, decisions, taken in accordance with the principles of effective political equality. Dahl is not, in practice, a totalitarian, and would seem to be committed to the inviolability of pre-political personal autonomy, providing that this inviolability is not interpreted as implying the justification of a power superior to the demos to enforce it. As Dahl puts it, we must, as democrats, presuppose that 'the demos is qualified to decide which matters do or do not require binding decisions'.[24] Personal autonomy outside of the sphere of collective decision-making is not something that is integral to the process of democratic decision-making. But there is no inconsistency in a democrat proclaiming that such personal autonomy 'should be inviolable', provided that this is interpreted, as Dahl interprets the inviolability of integral rights, as a reason for democratic self-limitation. Dahl's emphasis on the uniqueness of integral rights is misleading and misplaced. The appearance of compromise was illusory; in the final analysis, no matter what rights one believes to be morally inviolable, whether integral to the democratic process or not, the only options are between non-democratic sovereignty over the process of democracy or democratic sovereignty, hopefully of a self-limiting demos that would preserve a whole range of freedoms, including those integral to democratic self-rule.

The main aim of my argument has been to demonstrate the inconsistency of any attempt to synthesise liberalism and democracy that purports to preserve the equal and independent weight of both principles. I have not argued explicitly that the tension ought to be resolved in favour of the democratic principle, though the general drift of my analysis would indicate that, like Dahl, I believe that giving institutional superiority to the liberal principle is not only, by definition, undemocratic in theory, but also in practice so replete with the dangers of minority despotism as to be objectionable. But a liberalism that openly accepts only the conditional sovereignty of the demos and the restricted legitimacy of the democratic process is self-consistent. If there were reasons for thinking that the democratic process might in fact not only infringe non-integral rights but undermine itself by destroying integral rights, such a liberalism might claim to be the only consistent democratic ideology. Admittedly, the democratic principle would be secondary, but at least limited democracy could be consistently protected, if need be, against itself.

This raises the final issue that I want to discuss in this chapter, namely, the paradox of popular sovereignty. In the liberal resolution of the tension the paradox does not arise, the situation that produces the paradox can be consistently dealt with from the perspective of liberal theory. The paradox can only arise within the context of 'pure' democracy, and if it is genuine and destroys the consistency of the democratic resolution of the tension, that solution is proven to be internally incoherent.

The paradox is generated on the basis of the following two premises:

1. there is only one fundamental criterion of governmental legitimacy, conformity of the process of decision-making with democratic principles;
2. some particular government is assumed to perfectly conform to those principles in the structure of its decision-making procedures.

From these premises it can be concluded that the results of the decision-making process in such a polity are legitimate, legitimately enforceable and, of course, command the obedience of anyone accepting the first premise of democratic legitimacy. But what would be the position of someone accepting the two premises and their implied conclusion if one of the decisions consists in the total abrogation of the rights integral to democracy and the democratic institution of a system of minority rule? Since the only principle of legitimacy is democratic procedure, the result must be accepted as legitimate. But the result is profoundly undemocratic and must be opposed. A classic instance of an inescapable logical paradox. If genuine, the paradox would indeed demonstrate the internal incoherence of the 'pure' democratic principle as the unique determinant of legitimacy. But its real purpose, I think, is its intended demonstration that nobody really accepts the pure principle. Any real democrat, it is being suggested, would know exactly what it was right to do, namely, to reject the legitimacy of the undemocratic regime. And this would demonstrate operationally that there was at least one principle that was superior to the legitimacy of the process, that was concerned with the nature of the result, and that limited the legitimacy of the process. So the supposedly pure democrat is exposed as a covert 'liberal'.

But the paradox is not genuine. It is made to appear genuine by an invalid interpretation of the principle of legitimacy that confuses absolute with conditional legitimacy and further confuses the acceptance of only the conditional legitimacy of democracy with the acceptance of the legitimacy of non-democratic power-structures. Earlier in this chapter I formulated the distinction between prima facie and absolute obligation, and the corresponding distinction between conditional legitimacy and unconditional legitimacy. I also showed that conditional legitimacy is a perfectly serviceable basis in practice for any institution whose stability depends upon the acceptance of its legitimacy. To accept the legitimacy of democratic procedures is not to accept their unconditional legitimacy. But crucially, to accept the conditional legitimacy, conditional, in particular, on the results of the procedure not abrogating the rights integral to its preservation, is not equivalent to the acceptance of the legitimacy of the institutionalisation of non-democratic procedures to protect democracy from itself. It is, simply but importantly, to reserve the right of individual moral dissent. To accept the legitimacy of individual moral dissent when, from the perspective of any particular person, there is a serious conflict between fundamental values and what is being required by compliance with the results of the democratic process is not to accept the anarchist argument that democracy has no legitimacy. Such a conclusion would be justified only if there were, in practice, a complete and permanent conflict between fundamental individual values and the results of democratic decision-making. Neither is it to accept that there should be some agency wholly external to the democratic decision-making process that had the power to ensure that democratic decision-making stayed within morally legitimate bounds. Such a conclusion could only be justified in theory on the assumption that these morally legitimate bounds were unproblematically identifiable and, in both theory and practice, would imply a complete subordination of the legitimacy of democracy to a non-democratic authority. The undesirability of this latter situation is, of course, dependent on the demonstration that in the matter of collectively binding authoritative decisions the democratic process is uniquely justifiable. The justification of democracy is the subject of the next chapter.

7

Justifying democracy

The whole *raison d'être* of democratic theory ought to be the demonstration of the superiority of democracy as a form of political organisation. Given the unquestioned status of democracy in the pantheon of political values one would be entitled to expect that the literature of justificatory democratic theory would be rich and extensive, exploring in depth the values and virtues of democracy. One of the great puzzles of contemporary political thought, however, is the utter poverty of the normative analyses of democracy. W. N. Nelson's *Justifying Democracy* is, to my knowledge, the only work in English published in the last 20 years or so devoted solely to the normative theory of democracy.[1] Yet it consists almost entirely of a dismal catalogue of alleged mistakes, fallacies and unproven assumptions that Nelson detected in the usually implicit justifications of democracy that he has managed to unearth. When it comes to positive justification, democracy as Nelson defends it is little more than a mechanism that ensures, at most, that political decisions will not stray too far outside the boundaries of the necessarily indeterminate 'moral opinion' of the day. It is hard to find fault with John Dunn's conclusion that contemporary theories of democracy are either hopelessly utopian or, when realistic, wholly dull and uninspiring.[2]

Part of the problem lies, of course, in the very fact that democracy is perceived as the only politically correct form of government. Its unquestioned status means that it does not have to justify its existence, and the consequent lack of any serious political challenge has left the normative theory of democracy in such a weakened state that it hardly exists at all. In addition, democratic theory has been a victim of that general demise of substantive normative philosophy that was the heritage of logical positivism's fact/value dichotomy thesis. At the very time that democracy was emerging as the supreme ideal of modern society, philosophers, particularly in the Anglo-Saxon tradition, were turning away from substantive evaluative questions on the basis that such issues were completely unamenable to rational analysis and argumentation. The recent renaissance of normative theory in general has not yet had a major impact in the field of democratic theory.

I set out in Chapter 1 what I think are the defensible forms of rational argumentation concerning evaluative questions. There is, however, a preliminary issue that must be dealt with before we can begin to explore directly the possible justificatory arguments for democracy. This is the question of what dimensions or aspects of a democratic political system are important for the purpose of normative assessment. In a famous, perhaps notorious, passage of his book *Capitalism, Socialism and Democracy*, Joseph Schumpeter laid down how he thought the question of the evaluation of democracy should be approached. This consisted in conceiving of democracy as 'a political method, that is to say, a certain type of institutional arrangement for arriving at political–legislative and administrative decisions'.[3] This is, of course, uncontentious. Schumpeter's point, however, is to claim that that which is method, an instrument, can only have 'instrumental value', it is 'incapable of being an end in itself'.[4] If democracy is to be justified this must be done by showing that, as a method for arriving at political decisions, it is superior to any possible alternative. And this amounts to demonstrating that the decisions arrived at will be better decisions than those produced by alternative political arrangements. Schumpeter is obviously correct in thinking that this is a crucial dimension of democracy. His mistake lies in his belief that it is the only dimension of the democratic process that is normatively significant. It is instructive to compare Schumpeter's approach to the evaluation of democracy with that exemplified in Thucydides' reconstruction of Pericles' praise of Athenian democracy in the funeral oration that he delivered to honour those Athenians who had been killed in the first year of the Peloponnesian war.[5] Some of what Pericles has to say in defence of democracy is concerned with the quality of the decisions arrived at by the democratic process. He implies that because of popular involvement in the political process the outcomes of that process are likely to be just and wise, partly because the lack of barriers to participation ensure that no one of real ability will be excluded and partly because the mode of decision-making involves proper debate of all proposals. Most of what Pericles has to say, however, is aimed not at the direct consequences in terms of the outcome decisions, but at the whole way of life that Pericles believed to be inseparable from a democratically organised political system. He talks about the spirit of pluralistic tolerance in the day-to-day lives of citizens, obedience to those whom we put in positions of authority and obedience to both written and unwritten laws. He refers with pride to the high level of political knowledge even among 'those who are mostly occupied with their own business' and the general attitude that involvement in politics is an integral part of the citizen's life. He emphasises the readiness with which citizens will defend the democracy and the famous 'happy versatility' of the Athenian citizen who can look after his own business, participate in political life and be as good a soldier as the Spartan whose whole life is devoted to military training.[6] The inadequacy of Schumpeter's conception of the possible value of democracy lying only in the nature of the specific decisions arrived at is clearly demonstrated by this passage. Schumpeter drastically oversimplifies the process of evaluation by neglecting the fact that something that has a direct instrumental purpose may, at the same time, have many other instrumentally valuable consequences and may even have constitutive features that are intrinsically valuable. If I set out on a fine summer's day to visit a friend, walking a few miles through beautiful countryside, I am engaging in an activity that has a direct instrumental purpose; but in addition to achieving the desired purpose of arriving at my destination, my walk will have the further beneficial consequences of the contribution made to my general health and fitness and may, at the same time, be something that I consider intrinsically worthwhile.

The robust conception of democracy as effective political equality grounded in an informed understanding of public affairs will have to be evaluated as a political ideal from three perspectives. Firstly, as Schumpeter says, it is a method for arriving at political decisions; it will be, in this regard, justifiable if we can show that, by whatever criteria we evaluate decisions in terms of their content, democratic procedures are more likely to produce better decisions than any alternative political arrangement. Secondly, however, we need to take into account the more general impact that the operation of democratic procedures might be expected to have on the quality of life of people living in a community of political equals. Thirdly, we need to take seriously the possibility that the complex of human actions and institutions that constitutes democracy in action have constitutive features that are intrinsically worthwhile, independent of any consequences whether direct or indirect.

Apart from the obvious empirical problems that are likely to be encountered in any attempt to demonstrate that democracy is likely to generate certain consequences, directly or indirectly, there are two major normative questions that the justification of democracy must answer. The first question concerns what we can call the basic substantive values by reference to which we are going to construct the evaluative assessment. Many democratic theorists have attempted to argue, for example, that one value of democracy lies in the fact that compared to some system of minority rule there is a much higher probability under democratic rule that political decisions will conform at least to the perceived interests of citizens. This is itself, of course, an empirical claim that requires supportive arguments and I will be returning to that question later. Even if the empirical claim was established beyond doubt, however, that would constitute a justification of democracy only on the assumption that correspondence between authoritative decision and perceived interest is a good thing. This, evidently, is a normative claim requiring demonstration. There is one way of construing the claim that renders it evaluatively unproblematic; this is to see it as an assertion about the non-moral good from the perspective of some particular individual. There are several simple and quite plausible arguments that could be formulated to support this assertion. We could argue, for example, that even when perceived interest did not necessarily coincide with real interest, it would be a bad thing (not a morally bad thing, but simply an undesirable state of affairs), for people to be subject to a rule or an arrangement that they perceived as contrary to their interests. We might want to go further and argue that because it is reasonably probable that an informed person will tend to correctly perceive her or his interests, the correspondence between decision and perceived interest is likely also to be a correspondence between decision and real interest. By definition, a state of affairs that is in a person's interest is a good one. To make the argument more specific we would have to begin to identify what things were likely to be in some particular person's interest. Again, for a large range of things this would not constitute a serious problem. For almost anyone it is going to be in their interest to have access to a sufficiency of material resources, the possibility of forming affective relationships, the opportunity for education and useful, interesting work, health, leisure and physical security, a degree of individual autonomy and freedom, and so on. These basic substantive values for a given individual could then be used in the justification of democracy if the above referred-to chain of connections could be established; again, probability of correspondence between perception and interest, and higher probability of correspondence between perceived interest and political outcome when the person has an effective voice in determining the outcomes as compared to a system of simple subjection to the monopoly power of minority rule. Another substantive value that democratic theorists have appealed to is what we could call that *de facto* operational autonomy that consists in the exercise of one's capacities of understanding and decision-making. Again, it can be plausibly argued that such operational autonomy is, for both instrumental and intrinsic reasons, a valuable state of affairs. Here we would be arguing that a political system that guaranteed effective political equality afforded to any particular person as one of its constitutive features the opportunity to exercise such operational autonomy. The first evaluative task in the justification of democracy, then, would be the establishment of the range of substantive human values that we were going to appeal to in our arguments, whether those arguments were framed in terms of direct consequences, indirect consequences or constitutive features.

There is, however, a second and far more difficult evaluative task that faces the democratic theorist; this is the task of establishing the egalitarian underpinnings of democratic theory. That such egalitarian underpinnings are essential for the justification of democracy is evident. No matter how successful the type of arguments we have just been discussing, what they prove is that for any person taken at random, and hence for everyone, democracy is better than subjection to the rule of others. What this does not demonstrate is that democracy is the uniquely best system of rule. A better system for any particular individual, it could be argued, would be one in which that individual had a monopoly of power; there would then be an even greater probability that that individual could ensure the satisfaction of her or his interests and such a person would have plenty of opportunity for the exercise of autonomy and the realisation of whatever other substantive values we might postulate. We would only have demonstrated the value of democracy to any particular person if we could show that having an equal share of political power was better than having power over others. The justification of democracy is simply a special case of the general justification of egalitarianism.

Even more so than the democratic ideal, the normative principle of equality has been rarely attacked directly. Human history, of course, has been little else than a succession of inegalitarian systems of power, hierarchy and privilege. Such systems have been usually justified, however, not by renouncing the principle of equality, but by arguing that that very principle, when properly understood, justifies differential treatment of people who are relevantly different. It has been a standard part of the philosophical repertoire at least since the time of Plato and Aristotle to distinguish between a simplistic misconception of equality as identical treatment from a proper understanding of it as requiring proportionality; the relevantly similar are to be treated similarly, the different differently. Plato complained that what was wrong with Athenian democracy was that it treated unequals equally. Even more notoriously, Aristotle argued that slavery was perfectly justified and in accordance with the principles of equality and justice in the case of 'natural slaves', those human beings who were simply incapable of becoming autonomous persons by forming conceptions of themselves and their life goals. Consequently, attacks on systems of different and unequal treatment have usually had to deal not with a principle that rejected the relevance of equality, but with non-normative theories through which relevant differences were allegedly detected.

What can be said, though, in favour of the principle of equality itself, how have theorists attempted to justify the basic values of egalitarianism? This is not the place to attempt a comprehensive account of the history of the principle of equality, but the principle is so obviously at the very hub of normative democratic theory that we must briefly outline and evaluate the main approaches. Robert Dahl is perfectly aware of the centrality of equality in democratic theory. In fact, in his work *Democracy and Its Critics*, he puts forward the thesis that two distinct beliefs about equality underlie democracy both in the sense that they are required in the justification of democracy and in the sense that the emergence of democracy in any society depends upon the widespread acceptance of the beliefs in question. He refers to these beliefs as 'the Idea of Intrinsic Equality' and 'the Strong Principle of Equality'. The latter is not a directly normative principle; it consists in the empirical assumption 'that all members of the association are adequately qualified to participate on an equal footing with the others in the process of governing the association'.[7] The idea of intrinsic equality is the normative principle that Dahl interprets as implying the equal intrinsic worth of human beings, interpreting this as meaning that 'the good or interests of each person must be given equal consideration'.[8] When it comes to a justification of the principle, however, Dahl simply notes that for many people it has its basis in religious faith, that it is so deeply entrenched in all Western cultures that we cannot reject it without denying our cultural heritage and that its reasonableness lies largely in the fact it is difficult to imagine a justification for any alternative.[9] It is, in fact, that last suggestion that I will develop into what I think is the best polemical defence of equality. At the moment I merely want to point out that Dahl's brief remarks are an example of what I referred to earlier as a non-foundational justification. Dahl's purpose is to argue for the acceptance of democracy as an ideal, as the best form of political organisation. He does this, in part, by citing the principle of equal intrinsic worth, without, however, attempting to provide any foundations for that principle, contenting himself with remarking on its deep entrenchment in Western culture. The problem that I find with such justifications, however, is that they are far from enlightening and provide no bulwark against arguments from alternative traditions and cultures. Particularly when the principle is interpreted as Locke interprets it, the attempted justification becomes almost literally tautological. For Locke, the natural equality of man means 'that equal Right that every Man hath, to his Natural Freedom, without being subjected to the Will or Authority of any other Man'.[10] But this is about as useful as defending democracy by laying down the value of political equality as an axiom and then arguing that democracy is the uniquely justified political system because it best accords with the principle of political equality. Since we have defined democracy as political equality, this amounts to the true but unenlightening statement that democracy is the most justifiable political system, because it is the most democratic. Let us see if we cannot go slightly deeper than this by returning to the question of how we could justify the principle of equal intrinsic worth.

There are several lines of approach to this question and while none issues in a logically water-tight justification, they do take us some way in understanding the basis of the commitment to equality. The least satisfactory is the classic utilitarian approach. In his argument in favour of his version of the principle of equality, that each should count for one and no one for more than one, Bentham's thesis is that, looked at from an impersonal perspective, one person's happiness or well-being is simply neither more nor less important than another's.[11] Using the utilitarian 'happiness' as the measure of individual good, we could say that though some specific individual will be inclined to ascribe superior importance to her or his own happiness and perhaps to the happiness of those that happen to be near and dear, this superior importance is obviously not, as it were, a general objective fact; rather it depends in its entirety on the particular perspective of that specific individual. It is true only in a relative and personally perspectival sense. According to Bentham, if we adopt, not the biased and partisan limited perspective of some specific individual, but the perspective of the 'impartial observer', it will become evident that no one person's happiness is more important than any other person's, and hence each person's happiness should be given the same weight both in formulating the rules for personal behaviour and in designing the principles of legislation.

This sounds quite persuasive, but it suffers from three basic weaknesses. Firstly, Bentham provides no argument at all as to why anyone should adopt the perspective of the 'impartial observer'. Secondly, even if we did adopt this perspective, how could we show that a subsequent arbitrary favouritism would be wrong? The claim that this would imply an unjustified neglect of the good or happiness of those not favoured, far from supporting Bentham's argument, reveals its fundamental weakness. Impartiality in itself does not imply positive concern; I am impartial to flies by swatting them all indiscriminately. The perspective of the impartial observer would only lead to a policy of equal consideration if the impartial observer took the interests of everyone equally to heart. So, in addition to being purely hypothetical, reference to the impartial observer turns out to be, as a justification for the principle of equality, wholly tautological as well; it consists in the claim that if we took everyone's interests equally to heart this would imply a policy of equal consideration; which is true, but uninformative.

One of the major aims of John Rawls' *A Theory of Justice* is to demonstrate the inadequacy of the utilitarian 'Greatest Happiness' principle as a political, social ideal and as an articulation of our intuitive conception of justice and fairness.[12] Its basic weakness, according to Rawls, consists in the fact that it legitimates the sacrifice of the interests and rights of some if this is 'justified' by the resultant contribution to an increase in net aggregate happiness. This would not be condoned by our intuitive sense of fairness. Justice as fairness, Rawls argues, implies a far more robust set of principles of equality; the absolute equality of every member of the community with regard to what he calls 'primary goods', certain fundamental rights and access to basic material resources, and equality with respect to all other benefits and burdens, except when inequality in this regard would lead to a betterment of the condition of the least well-off. Although Rawls' primary purpose is to argue for these principles as implied by our already existing conception of justice, his neo-contractarian method involves an argument to the effect that justice and hence the equality principle it implies is, for any given human being, the most rational mode of sociopolitical organisation, quite independent of any commitment the person might have to the good of others. This promises, then, to be quite a strong justification for the principle of equality. This aspect of Rawls' analysis is not an attempt to prove that justice is a moral value that ought, morally, to structure the lives of people. It falls, rather, in the third category of justificatory argument that I identified in Chapter 1.[13] It is an attempt to demonstrate that from the perspective of any given person's individual good, justice is the best and most rational policy, despite the fact that at first blush alternative policies that granted the person in question privileged status might appear more preferable. Rawls sets out to prove this by attempting to determine what basic rules of social organisation a rational person, who was then going to be subject to those rules, would choose. He asks us to imagine a group of people, ourselves perhaps, gathered as members of a 'constituent assembly' whose purpose is the design of the fundamental principles that will structure the life of the community. What principles would suggest themselves to a person as the most rational? To answer this question Rawls makes two further, specific, assumptions. Firstly, while rational persons will want to maximise the positive good that might accrue to them, they will also want to minimise the probability that they might suffer severe disadvantage. Each person will do this by ensuring that the rules of social organisation under which they are going to live are such that the position of the least advantaged would in fact be quite tolerable in case, for any given person, the least advantaged turned out to be that person. This is the famous 'minimax regret rule' of parametric rationality (minimising the maximum regret one might suffer) giving rise to the maximin rule of social organisation, the rule that maximises the position of the least well-off. The objection that the minimax regret rule would not result in a rational person choosing the maximin principle if the rational person could be certain that he or she would not end up occupying the worst-off position is met by Rawls with the famous 'veil of ignorance' requirement, which is the second specific postulate. It might be understandable if specific persons were biased in their deliberations concerning the principles of justice that were to organise their society by giving a special privileged position to the interest of the group to which they knew they were going to belong. To prevent the entrance of such morally irrelevant considerations in to the deliberations of his rational choosers, Rawls requires them to make their decisions in ignorance of what specific groups or categories of people they will end up belonging to. Rational agents who do not know who they are going to be and what specific position they are likely to occupy in the society that they are designing will, according to Rawls, choose the maximin rule, which will be seen to be equivalent by further argument to the two principles of equality enunciated above. Hence, the rational person will choose equality.[14]

The difficulties with this aspect of Rawls' argument have been well-rehearsed in the literature.[15] Firstly, and least importantly, it cannot be conclusively established that extreme adherence to the minimax regret rule is a self-evident part of rational choice. It seems perfectly sensible to take certain risks if they lead to a reasonable probability of relatively high returns. Even if I was completely ignorant of the position I was going to occupy in society, it could be rational for me to prefer some form of hierarchical society, so long as there was a good possibility of me occupying a position of relative advantage and, perhaps, so long as the worst off position was not wholly intolerable. This, of course, is far from a principle of equality.

The second difficulty with the argument is far more substantial and centres on the use of the veil of ignorance requirement. Suppose that we could successfully demonstrate that from behind the veil of ignorance it would be rational to choose the Rawlsian principles of equality, of what relevance is this hypothetical conclusion to people not behind a veil of ignorance? The conditions under which the argument of the rationality of equality might be valid are so far from the conditions of real life as to render the conclusion wholly irrelevant and inapplicable. If it is countered that the purpose of the ignorance requirement is to enable us to outline a condition of ideal rationality, it has to be noted that we are including in our concept of rationality the premise of moral impartiality; we are demonstrating the rationality of the principles of equality by making their acceptance a condition of rationality itself. The argument ends up just as circular as Bentham's, though both arguments are of some value in highlighting the centrality of impartiality to any justification of equality as a sociopolitical ideal.

That element of Rawls' theory of justice that consists in the claim that prudential rationality would lead to a ratification of the principle of justice and equality is not the only, or most important, dimension of his thought. Rawls himself traces another aspect of his thought back to Immanuel Kant's conception of the person as a morally autonomous agent and, as such, having a dignity that requires the recognition of the person as an end in her- or himself.[16]

This can be the basis for an approach to the justification of equality that is particularly relevant to democratic theory, for the equal respect involved here is not simply the equal consideration of some amorphous interest of each person; it is implicit that an integral part of this interest lies in the opportunity to act in a morally autonomous way, in a manner, that is, such that one's life and the actions and projects that constitute it are the product of one's conception of the good. And this itself can be taken to imply the maximisation of literal individual autonomy and the equal and full participation in the process of collective decision-making.

The movement from the analysis of what it is to be a person, to the assertion of the moral dignity of the person, to the claim that recognition of this dignity requires a respect for the person as such, and hence a respect for all persons, a respect that consists, in particular, in the maximisation of autonomy in all its dimensions, can be viewed as an example of what I referred to in Chapter 1 as deep non-foundationalism. There is, as I argued earlier, an ordinary type of non-foundational evaluative argument that consists simply in either postulating certain values or principles as axioms or establishing that as a matter of fact certain groups of people actually hold such values or principles, and then producing lower-order justifications whose validity is seen, quite explicitly, as being conditional on the acceptance of the axiomatic values. The more profound type of non-foundationalism attempts to explain and explicate our adherence to certain values by demonstrating that such adherence is inextricably bound up with ways of conceiving of ourselves and the world in which we live which are themselves 'unavoidable', to borrow the terminology of Charles Taylor.[17] Such arguments go some way towards overcoming the paralysis of rational evaluation induced by the fact/value dichotomy thesis. Some concepts and categories, it can be admitted, are purely descriptive; and no series of true statements with such concepts as their predicates can logically imply an evaluative conclusion. This does not mean, however, that basic principles and values are purely arbitrary and optional postulates unconnected with our conception of what the world and ourselves are. The three fundamental theses underlying this position are as follows. Firstly, that some concepts and categories are, at one and the same time, both descriptive and evaluative; for example, pain, suffering, sorrow, brutality, to cite cases where the evaluative dimension is negative. Secondly, the descriptive and the evaluative dimensions of such concepts are logically inextricable in that, for example, the factual categorisation of bodily sensations as 'pains' involves a judgement of the goodness/badness of the sensations. There is no wholly non-evaluative way in which sensations can be categorised as pleasures and pains. The third thesis claims that there are whole ranges of such concepts that a human being unavoidably uses in the process of being-in-the-world, although it is admitted that there is not a single determinate range necessarily common to all human beings or that any particular range of such concepts would issue in, if they were explicitly articulated, a complete and consistent set of evaluative principles.

In Charles Taylor's argument one particular complex of concepts that is central to the possibility of being a person in the world is the conception of ourselves as choosing, responsible agents situated in a field of evaluatively discriminated possibilities.[18] I will not be motivated to act unless my imaginative construction of future possibilities presents me with some that are desirable above others and unless I conceive of myself as being able to choose and implement appropriate courses of action. Put more simply, action is motivated by desire and the belief that we can do something to satisfy the desire. The profound dimension of this consists in the claim that the recognition of desire and belief in the possibility of choice and action cannot be seen as, in some sense, external to the self, as something that the core self simply adopts. Rather, they are constitutive of the core self. The self that I am is the, at least tacitly, self-conscious complex of orientations in a field of possible choices and actions, structured by my perceptions of the good.

The connection between this and the Kantian notion of autonomy as implying a special dignity of the person can be explained by laying bare the ancient Stoic roots of the theory. The Stoics were the first philosophers to make central to their theory of the good a precise distinction between the moral and the morally indifferent.[19] There are numerous realms or orders of value, but one realm has to be clearly differentiated from all others, this is the realm of the moral and its distinctness consists in two things. Firstly, its precise locus is the choosing, rational agent. Second, not only is the moral a distinctively human value, it is of inestimably more importance than other realms of value. Other things, such as health, beauty, talent, riches, intellectual or artistic achievement, may be goods, and some of them may be thought to be far superior to others, but all of them have to be radically distinguished from the value, the moral value, that is realised when a person chooses the good, and, of course, chooses the good for the right reasons. It is a good that consists in a specific state of the self as choosing agent; it is even independent of the actual consequences of the choice and action, which consequences simply as *de facto* conditions of the world may be good or bad, but not morally so. As Kant himself put it, the only unconditional good in the world is the good will.[20] This is what lies behind the common belief that someone who perhaps is not successful, who is not capable of great intellectual or artistic achievement, who does not have the benefits of health or beauty and so on, can still be 'a good person' and being a good person is, in fact, the most important thing. Being a good person consists, fundamentally, in the ordering of one's life in accordance with one's conception of the good. Once someone is simply recognised as a person, it is automatically conceded that this distinctive and important value can be achieved by them. The value in question is not a utilitarian, pragmatic, individually perspectival value; it is something that has to be recognised as a value by anyone who recognises what it is to be a person. Recognition of others as persons, as beings capable of rational agency, coincides with the recognition of them as having the rights necessary to its achievement and the rights to the resources necessary for the exercise of those rights. Central to this complex of rights, given what the value consists in, is autonomy in all its dimensions.

All that seems to remain to convert these reflections into a fully fledged justification of equality in general and democratic political equality in particular is the seemingly unproblematic empirical premise that we cannot justifiably, epistemologically, conceive of ordinary adult human beings except as personal selves. We might accept that, for example, very young children (under the age of two, perhaps) were not fully-developed selves; they lack a constitutive conception of themselves as continuous self-identical responsible agents situated in a relatively extensive and stable set of evaluatively discriminated possibilities. But it is hardly conceivable that a human being could live without being constituted as a personal self. And whatever else a personal self is capable of, it is capable of the ordering of life in terms of its conception of the good; it is capable of that supreme value that entitles it, equally along with other persons, to the rights and resources required at least to live as a person.

Do we have, here, a conceptual and non-religious justification of equality in primary goods and political, including, democratic, rights? There are serious weaknesses to be seen in the argument that undermine its general validity, even if we accept the connection between being a person, the value of the ordering life in accordance with a conception of the good, the presumptive entitlement that the possibility of this value provides with respect to the means necessary for its realisation and the fact that all ordinary human beings are persons in the required sense. To illustrate the weaknesses before analytically identifying them, I will refer to an often remarked upon technique of military training.

Rendering combat-troops capable of ruthlessly and brutally killing the enemy is often said to involve, among other things, the inducing in them of the belief that the enemy is sub-human. This might be thought to be, as it were, a demonstration in practice of the validity of the above argument. Only if I believe the enemy to be sub-human will I be capable of denying them personal rights, or of conceiving of them as fit to be tortured, mutilated, slaughtered. If 'sub-human' is meant to mean, here, literally not persons, the above argument seems to me to involve a complete misconception. If it is hardly conceivable that an ordinary adult human being could live and survive long in the world without being a person in the relevant sense, it is hardly conceivable that one could overlook this obvious fact in the case of enemies. The mechanisms of hatred are different. They do not rely on literally conceiving of the other as a non-person; the other, rather, is portrayed as a 'barbarian', 'scum', 'irredeemably wicked and evil'.

This enables us to see the first weakness in the whole argument. The possibility of ordering one's life in accordance with one's conception of the good, cannot be confused with the inevitability of a life being so ordered. The possibility of what, following Kant, we will call 'the good will' involves the possibility of the bad or evil will. And it is not at all evident that someone who believes of another person that that person's life is or continues to be the expression of an evil will would conclude that because of the bare logical possibility of the realisation of the value of a good will, the evil person is entitled to the whole panoply of equal respect and rights of autonomy.

It is here that the central weakness of the argument becomes manifest; this lies in the assumption that the good will is the supreme value, completely independently of the substantive conception of the good that a particular will orders its life by. There is no unavoidable framework of values implying the necessity of this conclusion. Most people do not, as a matter of fact, accept it. Rather than taking the example of one group that believes of another that the substantive conception of the good according to which it orders its life is totally abhorrent, take instead the less difficult case of children. Very young children might be what we could call episodic selves, but 12 or 13 year olds are undoubtedly persons. Yet most people are happy not to accord them the full rights of autonomy and democratic participation. But such persons do have a constitutive conception of their self-identical continuity situated in a field of evaluative possibilities; they could order their lives according to their conception of the good and hence realise the value of the good will. On what basis is it thought that we are not denying the equal intrinsic worth of children by denying them full autonomy? The answer is that though we conceive them as persons, we conceive of them as, temporarily, a different type of person; as, fairly obviously, immature persons. This means that though they have a conception of the good by which they could order their lives individually and participate in the ordering of the life of their community via collective decision-making, we believe that their conception of the good, not solidly grounded as it is in sufficient experience, would likely be such that its realisation would be dangerous and disadvantageous to themselves and others.

The first conclusion that this leads me to is, somewhat unsurprisingly, that in addition to conceiving of someone as a person, before we would be required to extend to them equality in autonomy and democratic rights we would have to establish the truth concerning them of Dahl's strong principle of equality, the empirical principle of equal qualification. More generally, as the example of our treatment of children indicates, the bare fact of accepting other human beings as persons in the relevant sense is not inconsistent with the belief that there might be relevantly different types of person. This becomes acutely problematic in the situations that we have so far side-stepped; the situations, that is, in which one group believes of another group that their substantive conception of the good is abhorrent. It is important to point out that there is no easy Lockean solution to this problem. The Lockean solution I am referring to is that discussed earlier in the context of the limitation of democratic legitimacy by inalienable individual rights. It will be recalled that Locke claimed that asserting the natural right to freedom of every human being was consistent with the legitimacy of sometimes denying some particular person the freedom to act as he or she had chosen. Liberty is not licence, and if what a person has chosen is in contravention of the rights of others he or she can be justifiably restrained. In such a situation, it might be claimed, we do not fundamentally deny the value of the person whose concept of 'a good life' in fact infringes other people's rights, we simply legitimately restrain them. In which circumstances this is a legitimate course of action is determined by the set of basic human rights. The reason for the unavailability of the Lockean solution is the same as in the earlier context, the possibility of disagreement concerning basic rights. The group whose substantive conception of the good I find so abhorrent that its realisation would be disastrous and in flat contravention of fundamental values and rights will almost certainly believe the same about my conception of the good. At best, they will believe about me that I am, precisely because I am constituted by my unavoidable framework, a criminal and an undesirable, and, hence, can be justifiably deprived of my liberty and the entitlement to have my conception of the good play any role in the determining of collective decisions. At worst, I will be seen as a sacrilegious blot on the face of the earth fit only for justifiable annihilation, despite the fact that it cannot be denied, of course, that I am a person. My conclusion has to be that the bare fact that we unavoidably recognise others as persons provides no basis whatsoever for the belief that we are, as a consequence, inevitably required to extend to them anything like what they would consider full recognition of equal rights or worth in practice.

It is sometimes thought that an aspect of the Hegelian analysis of the master–slave relationship can provide the missing argument as to why it is imperative for one person not simply to recognise the other as a person but also to extend to the other recognition of equal worth and status.[21] The basic assumption of the argument is that a rational self-consciousness needs and desires as a condition of its existence recognition of its existence and worth by another. The attempt to ensure such recognition by the subordination of the other and the commandeering of the other's recognition, which is what Hegel takes to be a central element of the master–slave relationship, is doomed to dialectical self-defeat. The problem is that it is not any kind of recognition from any source that is desired. The recognition must be voluntary and from a source that is itself worthy of respect; and it is precisely these factors that are destroyed by the subordination of the other and the conceiving of the other as inferior. The recognition of worth that the self craves can only exist as the reciprocal recognition of worth in a community of equals. Such craving has its basis in self-interest but can realise itself only by its own transcendence through the creation of this community of equals that is in fact constituted by relations of reciprocal recognition of equal worth. And this is for Hegel, as it was for Kant and Rousseau, the very possibility and form of morality.

What this argument demonstrates conclusively, however, is not the necessity of a community of equals that open-endedly includes all rational persons, but the self-defeating nature of a literal solipsistic autocracy in which one individual self subordinates the rest of the human race through a conception of their utter worthlessness and inferiority. A community of equals that afforded to all its members equal recognition of worth can quite feasibly exist as a part of a highly hierarchic community in which those excluded from privileged status are conceived of by the privileged as worthless.[22] There is no inevitable mechanism of dialectical transcendence at work leading to the breakdown of the exclusivity of privilege. The argument is still important, however, in that it highlights the value of public recognition of worth and it identifies a mechanism whereby exclusive self-interest can be transcended. Furthermore, though I have just argued that once dialectical logic has led to the transcendence of solipsistic self-interest it loses its imperative force, it is worth investigating whether there might not be, as it were, substitutes that might have the power to extend the limited transcendence of self-interest that might already have occurred in the constitution of an exclusive community of equals. Are there any considerations that might tend to show to the privileged that the value of recognition of worth by respected others would be greater in a non-exclusive community of equals?

We can appreciate better the value of recognition if we see it as involving not just a once and for all reciprocal recognition, but as being continuously reproduced in the day-to-day dealings of equals with each other. The continuous re-affirmation of worth generates a security in the sense of worth that gives a particular character to the day-to-day dealings of equals with equals. Considering equal and being considered equal are the warp and woof of the continuously woven fabric of life. How does this contrast with the fabric of life in a community in which only the members of a privileged group consider each other equally worthy of respect? I am asking this question not about the impact on the lives of the outcasts, which is obvious, but with respect to the self-conceptions of the privileged. A hierarchic society of advantage and privilege will almost inevitably generate resentment, fear, mistrust and hatred between the differentially privileged strata. The privileged strata of such societies have always had mechanisms, repressive and ideological, for dealing with these phenomena. In particular, the privileged can seek to neutralise within their own consciousness the knowledge that they are despised by those they exclude by a mechanism that is the complementary opposite of the Hegelian mechanism of mutual recognition of worth. Being despised by those whom one despises is as insignificant as being respected by them is worthless. The result is not just an absence of reciprocal recognition of worth but a positive system of mutual loathing that is the sinister shadow inevitably cast by the very exclusiveness of recognition of equal worth. And it is not only the excluded who live in this shadow. Of course, the dark dialectic of mutual disrespect does to a certain extent fulfil its neutralising function and it has its own mechanisms of self-reinforcement. But the neutralisation of disrespect and loathing cannot entirely obliterate them from consciousness nor remove the effects that manifest themselves in the distrustful daily encounters of unequals. And the stability of the system as neutralising is purchased at the cost of a heavy investment in myth and falsehood that renders the whole system permanently vulnerable. There is, in addition, the heavy investment, in the literal sense, in the instruments and institutions of repression. The Spartan 'Equals' maintained their hegemony over the Helots by transforming their society into an armed camp.[23] A society of non-exclusive equality of respect has an altogether different type of stability, openness and light.

I do not pretend that these considerations will inevitably arise in a hierarchical society, nor that if they did they would ineluctably lead to the dismantling of privilege by the privileged, though a hypothesis cautiously formulated by Jon Elster is relevant here.[24] When such considerations and demands have their origin in the underclass, it becomes peculiarly difficult for the privileged to continue to justify their position, particularly to those who constitute the challenge. The entering into debate can be seen as an operational concession of the very point debated, for the acceptance of others as worth debating with constitutes a large and important element of accepting their general worth as equals.

This brings me to the final and, in a way, one of the strongest arguments for a basic principle of equality. This is the argument from impartiality. We have seen how, particularly in Bentham's and Rawls' arguments, the notion of impartiality plays a central role. Rather than assuming impartiality as a premise, the present argument attempts to show that only a rule or principle of social organisation that was based on an assumption of fundamental equality of consideration would be impartial. Secondly, impartiality is understood procedurally, in the sense that the impartial is defined as that which would be accepted by all as demanding no more from anyone in particular than was demanded from anyone else and giving to no one an unjustifiable advantage over anyone else. It might seem tautologically true that only a principle of equality would be impartial, but this is to forget the procedural definition. This, in fact, is one of the difficulties of the argument. A rule or principle is, as we have said, impartial if it would be accepted by all to whom it is to apply as being no more unjustifiably advantageous to one than to another. If we are going to operationalise this procedural definition, we are obliged to give some specific characteristics to the imagined people who are going to be subject to the rule and whom we are imagining as deciding on its acceptability. It is not at all obvious that, say, some hierarchic principle of privilege and disadvantage would not be found acceptable to all to whom it was going to apply. For even those who were certain to be disadvantaged by the principle might have internalised its legitimacy. Suppose, for example, we imagined a rigid caste system, with the lower castes being thought of as inferior to the upper castes and being treated extremely unequally in terms of the distributions of benefits and burdens. This might, though, be thought of as acceptable even to those who were to be disadvantaged, because they themselves have already accepted their own inferiority and consequently view their disadvantaged position as justified. We could, of course, avoid this conclusion by postulating that all those we imagine deciding on the acceptability of something believe in their equal worth. But this would clearly make the whole argument circular from the very start. We can get a little further than this by postulating at least that belief in either of the contrary positions is suspended; that is, that for the purposes of the argument no one begins either with the principle of equal worth or with the principle of unequal worth. And this would seem entirely logical considering that it is precisely these principles whose impartiality we are testing. It then does seem to follow that no one would accept as justifiable any rule or principle that gave them an inferior status. The only rule that would be acceptable to all as demanding no more from one than was demanded from another would be the rule of equal worth or consideration. Hence, only such a rule could be deemed impartial.

But how does this constitute a justification? As I argued in Chapter 1, the best way of understanding arguments from impartiality is to view them not as direct demonstrations of justifiability, but as indirect proofs that no contradictory alternatives could be found that were justifiable. As I pointed out then, if a rule is accepted as impartial, any contradictory alternative will favour the partisan interest of some at the expense of others, and will, consequently be incapable of being given a justification acceptable to all. Such an argument has a strong polemical force. The whole point of entering into debate concerning the justifiability of a rule of social organisation is to convince one's opponents of its acceptability. Whatever one's own normative standards are, there is an operational commitment in entering into debate to the production of a more than partisan justification. Arguments from impartiality attempt to unmask opposed positions as partisan and, hence, not acceptable to all parties to the debate. It is this fact that lies behind Dahl's passing remark concerning the difficulty in imagining a successful justification of anything other than a principle of equal worth.[25] The depth of its entrenchment in modern civilisation lies partly in the centrality of at least a public commitment, operationally involved, as we have noted, to proof in public debate, to the production of justifications that will convince and be acceptable to all. Impartiality then becomes a necessary criterion of justifiability; and unless we imagine parties to a debate already starting with substantive assumptions of unequal worth, basic equality of worth will be established as impartial and, so, as the only generally justifiable rule.

Polemically strong as the argument is, however, it has its difficulties and it is not of inevitable categorical force. As indicated above, the difficulties arise from the procedural nature of the definition. This evidently results in the impossibility of a theorist establishing the impartial independently of what the subject of theorisation would accept as impartial. If the imagined members of a community had no substantive values and/or no criteria of reasonableness, we would be simply unable to theorise about what would be accepted by them as impartial. But as soon as we begin postulating specific sets of values and norms of reasonableness we are in danger of building the desired conclusions into the premises. Before arguments from impartiality can be thought of as having any relevance or force, or even being possible, some basic overlapping or complementarity of values has to be postulated. In a community in which different groups were committed to radically different values, it may simply not be possible to imagine a general agreement on what is impartial; one group might believe that another was being wholly irrational in refusing to accept that no more was being required of them than of others. In their own eyes, but not in the eyes of others, it might seem that major sacrifices of an unequal nature were being demanded. Furthermore, even if impartiality could be established, substantive values may be held to be far more important than the value of impartial compromise. As we noted earlier, an extreme anti-abortionist may believe that abortion is murder and the violation of the rights of the most vulnerable. It would be wicked to compromise on such an issue. Even if it was argued that compromise was essential to the very survival of society, it would still be logical for the anti-abortionists to prefer social collapse. It is, of course, precisely in such morally extreme cases that, as noted in Chapter 6, we must expect to meet the limits not just of the imperative force of impartiality and compromise but of democratic legitimacy itself.

I have argued in this chapter that whatever substantive values are likely to accrue to people from the operation of some particular system of rule, we are only going to be able to justify the democratic organisation of such a system through the principles of political equality if we can first argue that everyone should have equal access to those substantive values the system is thought to afford. I have spent a lot of time looking at how such a basic egalitarian principle might be justified, concluding that the impartiality of the egalitarian principle is a polemically very strong argument in its favour and, also, that a positive value, equality of respect by equals, requires, as is evident, a system of equal reciprocal respect, though for that value to be achieved for specific individuals, the system of reciprocity does not have to be open-ended and universal. There are, however, quite persuasive arguments that the value can be achieved in a more secure, stable and undiluted manner, and with far less investment in repression and myth, if the system of reciprocity is universal. What we must look at now is how we can move from the general egalitarian principle to a justification of effective political equality in terms of its direct and indirect consequences and its constitutive features.

Let us begin by looking, as Schumpeter would have us, at democracy as a method, as a way of producing binding outputs. Such outputs are likely to have a major impact on the achievement of value in individuals' lives and the major argument in favour of democracy from this perspective has to be the greater likelihood of egalitarian consequences from egalitarian entitlement to an effective say in determining the outcomes. It might be thought that to begin this process of justification the theorist would have to attempt to specify the types of values that citizens are likely to look for as outcomes of the decision-making process. But on this level of democracy that would be a mistake. Of course, it is likely that it would be in any person's interest to have secure access to a sufficiency of material resources, to have, particularly in a democracy, opportunities for educational and cultural development; it might even be probable that most citizens will believe that governmental outcomes should satisfy certain moral criteria such as justice. The basic justification of democracy as method, however, consists in the claim that there is to each individual citizen an instrumental value in having a share in determining the outcomes. Whatever the specific values and goals of a particular citizen, having a say in whether outcomes tend to realise these values and goals is more instrumentally valuable than being simply subject to others. There is an operational contradiction in a theorist attempting to justify democracy in terms of its greater likelihood of producing certain types of consequences that the theorist finds valuable. For what is being justified is the entitlement of citizens to decide for themselves the criteria of value they will use to assess possible outcomes. And it can be argued that the strongest justification for democracy, even in terms of outcomes, is not that there will be some specific correlation between outcomes, desires for certain outcomes and successful achievement of certain values, but rather that there is a generic correlation, by definition, between outcomes and maximum autonomy, both individual and collective, in the production of outcomes.

What is being argued, here, is that the possible mistakes that decision-makers may make in discerning their interests and values and connecting these with policy options may be of less importance than the fact that decision-makers will be assured of living under decisions that, both in terms of scope and content, are the outcome of equal maximum autonomy. I argued in Chapter 6 that though there was no democratic manner of externally restricting the scope of democratic decision-making, it did not follow that it was not desirable for decision-making to internally limit the extent of collective decision-making through the democratic procedure itself. In circumstances of real effective political equality, then, each person will exercise the maximum amount of autonomy that is compatible with the equal autonomy of others in deciding how far collective decision-making should extend and what its content should be. In such a situation even non-participants have exercised that autonomy by deciding not to participate. This generic feature of the complex of outputs is a strong justification for democracy, if we give any value at all to personal autonomy.

There are weaknesses to the argument, however, which show not that the argument is invalid, but that there may be other values that need to be balanced alongside autonomy. The other values may not be completely independent, they may even consist in the securing of individual autonomy and equal participation in the future. Decision-makers may arrive at foolish or mistaken conclusions; they may be so unwise as to decide democratically on something that destroys individual liberty and democracy itself, such as handing over power to an unscrupulous despot. Episodically, the outcome will have been the product of an exercise of autonomy, but only someone who gave an absolute and unconditional value to episodic autonomy would think that the generic connection between output and equal autonomy would, in such a case, outweigh the dis-value of the permanent slavery produced. Other values, such as the avoidance of massive suffering and death, for example, could play the same role. So, is the likelihood of producing good, wise and desirable outcomes of overriding importance? And do we have to conclusively demonstrate that democracy will always be instrumental in producing such outcomes?

The first point that needs to be made is that it is completely misleading to think in terms of absolutes and extremes. At several points in the whole argument I have been at pains to emphasise that believing that democracy is the only justifiable system of rule is not equivalent to granting to democracy and democratic procedure an unconditional legitimacy. In the present context we need to note that accepting that episodic autonomy is not an unconditional value is not a question of giving it no value at all; accepting that the nature of the content of the likely outcomes is important is not equivalent to the claim that the nature of the outcomes is the only thing of significance. The balancing of these two values has to be reciprocal. Consequently, we do not have to prove that democracy will always produce the best outcomes or even that it will produce better outcomes than some alternative system. Some sacrifice in the area of the specific content of outcomes is a rational cost to pay for autonomy.

Secondly, as many theorists have argued, the kind of assessment of the likely nature of outcomes produced by extensive participation that characterises Schumpeter's theory of democracy may not only be overly pessimistic in terms of its claims concerning the competence of ordinary citizens; it takes no account of the possible educative consequences of higher rates of effective and more extensive participation. This is a point I will be returning to when discussing the indirect consequences of democracy.

But supposing that it is argued that some alternative system would function in such a significantly better way that the cost in terms of loss of autonomy would be justified. Dahl has formulated clearly and accurately the fatal weaknesses in such a supposition.[26] Firstly, we would have to give a very low value to autonomy indeed to think its sacrifice would be desirable. Secondly, the alternative to democracy, which Dahl refers to, following Plato, as Guardianship would only begin to look justifiable if two crucial assumptions could be proven; firstly, that we could identify a group of potential rulers as having superior knowledge, and secondly, that the same group could be guaranteed to have the incorruptible virtue necessary as a bulwark against abuse of power. The knowledge required would be of two kinds; knowledge of what constituted good outcomes and knowledge of the technical means needed to achieve the good outcomes in practice. The difficulty of establishing the likelihood of the first type of knowledge, particularly in the modern world, is threefold. In the first place, the values of moral and intellectual autonomy are so central to our conception of the self that no substantive theory of the good would be credible that denied those values. But if our supposed guardians accepted such a theory of the good there would be an operational contradiction in attempting to implement it through a permanent system of tutelage. Secondly, even the most sanguine revivalists of moral theory do not pretend that a complete theory of the good is a matter of provable knowledge, which could even conceivably be the special domain of the minority of guardians. The pluralism of the good, though it creates problems for democracy in practice, is as fundamental to the anti-paternalism of democracy as it is to its liberal variant. Finally, any conceivable theory of good government will have to give a large role to governing in the interest of subjects. When it comes to the diverse interests of diverse people, though we may expect something less than infallibility in self-understanding, there can be no presumption at all that some external authority will understand the interests of a mass of diverse people better than they will understand themselves.

Technical knowledge of means–ends relationships might look like a better terrain for the claims of expertise. The problem here is that any decision on means is always likely to involve not just cause–effect relationships and efficiency, but a balancing of values, and the balancing of values is not a technical decision. Consequently, even if there existed a consensus on goals, technical experts could never claim on the basis of their expertise the right to decide on means. Secondly, the technical experts are part of the citizen-body, and the results of their expertise can be made publicly available. Finally, as Dahl delights in pointing out, there is in the realm of the impact of decisions on society a huge, unavoidable uncertainty as to whether supposed technically sophisticated experts prove as competent or as incompetent in dealing with such matters as ordinary people.[27]

The case for the guaranteed virtue of the guardians is, if anything, even weaker. The issue is not if the guardians were incorruptibly virtuous, but what is the likelihood of being able to permanently guarantee that virtue? All historical experience would counsel against the wisdom of trusting in the benevolence of despots. On this whole matter of whether, in terms of interests of subjects or in terms of some other criterion of good outcomes, any system of government other than democracy is likely to perform better, I would concur with J. S. Mill, whom Dahl quotes in this context:

> The rights and interests of every or any person are only secure from being disregarded when the person interested is himself able, and habitually disposed, to stand up for them. . . . Human beings are only secure from evil at the hands of others in proportion as they have the power of being, and are, self-*protecting*.[28]

There are four major types of indirect consequence that democratic theorists have cited as general values that the operation of democracy and the informed involvement of people in the process of decision-making are likely to produce. Consideration of these general consequences both supplements and reinforces the arguments concerning direct outcomes, for apart from identifying additional possible values realised through the operation of democratic structures, all of these values are likely to have a positive impact on the process of decision-making itself, increasing the likelihood of informed and sensible decision-making, and the production of outcomes in accordance with the interests of citizens.

An integral part of the robust conception of democracy defended in these pages consists in political equality in the first two moments of decision-making and this itself was seen to require the maximum availability of relevant information through multiple channels of communication and free and open debate in the determination of the agenda and in the evaluation of options. The first argument is that this is likely to produce open government and a spirit of critical opposition. Governmental decisions are not seen as dictates issuing from some sacred and mysterious source, rather they are viewed for what they are, the fallible product of human deliberation always open to criticism and revision, based on arguments and information that are in the public sphere. Of course, all of the arguments from indirect consequences deal in probabilities and are also conditional in the sense that the suggested value is being postulated as a value by the theorist. But it is plausible to suggest, firstly, that people are likely to want open and flexible government and rules whose rationale is openly available for inspection. It is also plausible to suggest that benefits will accrue to people in terms of the impact of specific decisions on their lives as a consequence of the atmosphere of openness and the possibility and legitimacy of critical opposition. An important aspect of this argument is that *these* indirect consequential values are not directly dependent on some specific person actually participating in decision-making in an extensive way. The general beneficial effects of openness of government accrue to every member of the community and are dependent only on the number of people actively involved being sufficient to maintain the general availability of relevant knowledge and the spirit of critical debate. The other three types of indirect consequence are, however, dependent in their availability to any particular person on that person's active participation. They are closely interrelated and though they can be seen to have instrumental value in that they can be expected to have a positive impact on people's ability to realise other values in their lives, a full appreciation of their appeal as intrinsic values depends upon an understanding of their connection with an Aristotelian-like activist theory of the good. The values in question consist in the postulated consequences of active participation in political life on the cognitive and moral education of people and in the fact that such active involvement simply is the exercise of the distinctive capacities of human beings to be autonomous and responsible for themselves.

C. B. Macpherson is noted among modern democratic theorists for his promotion of an activist conception of human good and well-being, the roots of which he finds in Aristotle's ethical and political philosophy.[29] Macpherson argues that two images of the human person and human well-being have dominated modern (and, perhaps, ancient) political thought: the utilitarian image of the person as a bundle of desires seeking satisfaction whose well-being consists in the maximisation of the subjective feeling of happiness and the Aristotelian image of the person as a set of distinctive potentialities oriented towards development and actualisation whose well-being will consist precisely in that development and realisation. For the use that I wish to make of it, Aristotle's theory of human well-being is based on four assumptions which, so long as they are not erected into metaphysical absolutes and so long as it is not thought that a comprehensive theory of categorical moral rules can be based upon them, are eminently sensible.[30] The first assumption is that human beings are living systems and like all other living systems are constituted by a set of developing capacities to engage in those processes and activities that themselves constitute living. Secondly, though many of the life-processes and their underlying capacities are common to human beings and other life systems, human beings have certain distinctive capacities, the important ones in this context being the capacities for developing complex affective relationships, the capacities for knowledge and understanding and the capacities to organise life in a relatively deliberative fashion as distinct from all activity being an unthinking response to an immediate impulse. Thirdly, Aristotle assumes that, episodically, a living system will be living well when it is exercising its life-capacities in an undistorted manner and will achieve overall, stable well-being when it is living in such a way as to develop harmoniously its life capacities and exercise those life-capacities in practice. As part of this assumption, it was Aristotle's belief that for living systems with consciousness, and particularly for human self-conscious beings a feeling of well-being, pleasure and contentment was an inseparable dimension and natural accompaniment to living well. Finally, Aristotle claimed that human beings were social creatures, partly because of pragmatic interdependence in the satisfaction of desires but partly also because some of their distinctive capacities, particularly those for complex affective relationships, can only be exercised and developed as part of a shared life. It is because of this sociality that the deliberative capacities have both an individual and a collective dimension. One of the most important and valuable expressions of this sociality and the capacity for affective relationships was, for Aristotle, a Hegelian-like recognition of another self as one's equal, as, in fact, one's other self in friendship, although he also saw the less affective recognition of equality that constitutes equal citizen status as an important, if somewhat diluted, form of such friendship.

The relevance of such a conception of human well-being to the justification of democracy is evident. However, even if we accept as important values, cognitive development, due recognition of the good of others and the exercise of deliberative capacities, we do have to concede Nelson's point that as indirect consequences of the operation of democratic procedures they are still contingent consequences and, hence, do not follow with logical inevitability from the mere existence of democracy, even as effective political equality.[31] To begin with, a person may have all the entitlements and resources needed for full participation and still, for one reason or another, not utilise them. Secondly, even if people were to wholeheartedly participate, they might still begin as ignorant, narrow-minded, impulsive and self-interested and end up that way as well. But capacities can only be developed and exercised through practice, and democracy is the only system of rule that provides the opportunities for such practice in an egalitarian way. Secondly, it is the only form of rule that has equal respect for others inscribed in its structures and so affords a particular opportunity, as Rousseau argued, for that habituation to the respect for others that can result in a transcendence of narrow self-interest. Finally, for anyone who does avail of the opportunities afforded, even in the absence of further beneficial consequences, it can be truly said of them that they are living a life organised by the exercise of their deliberative capacities, irrespective of whether any further valuable consequences occur as a result.

The final argument I want to put forward in favour of democracy, the argument that concentrates on certain constitutive features of democracy, is in many ways the strongest. The constitutive features in question are the public recognition of equal status and the extension to everyone of the rights to be equal participants in political decision-making. They are constitutive features in the precise sense that irrespective of any further consequences, regardless of whether rights are utilised, the public recognition of equal status and the definition of each member of the community as the possessor of equal political rights are simply integral to and inseparable from the existence of democracy. Furthermore, these very things are in themselves not only intrinsically valuable to people, but of fundamental importance. We do not need Hegelian dialectic to convince ourselves of the importance of such recognition of worth to us; all we need do is to imagine the contrary situation, imagine ourselves, that is, as publicly proclaimed inferiors, unfit for the responsibility of self-government. It is sometimes said that people vote in mass representative democracies not in the belief that there is a significant probability of an individual vote being effective in influencing ultimate outcomes but as a manifestation of party loyalty or as an expression of belief in the legitimacy of democratic structures. It is, I would argue, equally plausible to see the exercise of democratic rights as itself a public profession of one's equal status, an episodic ritual ratification of the equality of status in which democratic citizenship consists.

The strength of this particular justification of democracy has a threefold basis. Firstly, because equality of citizenship status is a constitutive feature of democracy, because it is definitory of democracy, the proof of its existence in a democracy is unproblematic, untroubled by empirical doubts as to whether the alleged valuable consequences of democracy will actually occur. Secondly, for related reasons, it is largely independent of how closely democratic polities approach in reality the ideal of democracy. It is not only a constitutive feature, it is basic. Providing that democracy in its quantitative dimension as universal suffrage has been achieved, public recognition of equality of status is guaranteed. Finally, as noted above, it is of fundamental importance to people; it is not only an intrinsic value in itself but it has vast repercussions on the quality of a person's life as a whole, being, as it is, the legal and public expression of one's full membership of a community of equals that constitutes a matrix in which the achievement of value in life might be possible.

The argument of this chapter has been complex, and at times difficult, so it is worth concluding with a summary of the argument and my tentative conclusions. I began by claiming that there were three dimensions of the democratic process that were relevant to its evaluative appraisal: the direct consequences, consisting in the binding decisions arrived at; the indirect consequences on the lives of citizens that resulted from the existence and operation of democratic procedures in society; and the constitutive features of democratic procedures. The argument then turned to an examination of what a normative framework that might justify democracy would look like. Here I claimed that we would need to establish firstly, a range of substantive values that people would be likely to want realised in their society and, secondly, a basic normative egalitarian premise. It was to this latter task that I then turned, examining four major types of argument that could be used in the attempt to justify some principle of basic equality of worth and respect. I rejected the classic utilitarian and neo-contractarian arguments as being wholly hypothetical and as smuggling the assumption of equal worth into their premises. I went on to consider a third type of argument, the argument based on the contention that to recognise another as a person, as someone capable of making responsible choices, was *ipso facto*, to recognise a specific type of worth that consisted in the person's ability to be what I referred to as 'a good person'. The recognition of this worth was itself a recognition that, as such, any and every person merited equal respect, extending even to an equal respect for the autonomy of the person. The weakness that I found in this argument lay, I claimed, in the fact that it seems possible to recognise another as a person in the minimal sense of someone who can make choices but, at the same time, quite consistently to believe that there are relevantly different categories of person, with the implication that some categories of person do not merit the extension to their members of that equality of respect and autonomy that we are concerned with. Was there to be found in the Hegelian analysis of the master–slave relationship a remedy to the defect in this argument? Did the craving of the self for recognition of its worth by others, whose recognition was valued because they were valued, provide a mechanism for the self-transcendence of egoism and its transformation into egalitarian recognition of equal worth? Along with Plamenatz I argued that this transcendence of egoism was, as an ineluctable imperative, of limited scope. It required not the recognition of the equal worth of others in general, but only the recognition of the worth of *some* others. I went on to argue, however, that a plausible case could be made for the thesis that recognition of self-worth grounded in an open-ended recognition of the worth of others could be enjoyed with greater security and stability. The final argument for a basic egalitarian principle that I considered was the argument from impartiality. What I attempted to establish here was that unless people had already accepted an inegalitarian principle, only an egalitarian principle would be equally justifiable to all who were to be subject to it, and, hence, only an egalitarian principle would be impartial. Secondly, however, I claimed that the strength of this argument lay in its polemical force. Once it is accepted that a principle of social organisation requires, not a frankly partisan justification, but one that will be generally accepted, then impartiality becomes a necessary condition for such a justification. Only fundamentally egalitarian principles will be so justifiable.

On the basis of these conclusions I moved on to examine possible justifications of democracy along the three dimensions previously identified. With regard to direct outcomes I argued that, independently of whether direct outcomes maximally accorded with fundamental interests, there was a generic feature of such outcomes, namely, that they were the outcomes actually preferred, that was, in itself, a valuable state of affairs, other things being equal. People would be living under rules that, for the participants in the decision-making process, maximally conformed to each person's preference, insofar as this was compatible with equally conforming to the preference of others. Could it be argued, though, that this would result in conformity of outcomes to fundamental interests? At this point I accepted Dahl's argument that to justify democracy above alternatives what needed to be established was only whether any of the possible alternatives held out any hope at all of generating outcomes that would conform, in an egalitarian manner, to fundamental interests to a higher degree than those produced by democratic procedures. I contented myself with summarising Dahl's arguments to the effect that, in both theory and practice, the case for the only feasible alternatives was totally unconvincing.

With regard to indirect consequences, though I outlined a plausible argument for the thesis that the democratic process would produce a generally valuable openness in government that would be valuable even to those who did not actively participate, I concentrated on those alleged consequences that depend upon participation: cognitive and moral development and the affording of opportunities for the exercise of the human capacity for responsibility and autonomy. I concentrated first on outlining the assumptions behind an Aristotelian conception of human well-being as consisting in the development and exercise of human capacities. While accepting Nelson's point that these alleged developmental consequences were contingent, I did argue that no system of rule other than democracy offered the permanent channels for the exercise and development of the capacities in question. I ended by claiming that there was one important constitutive feature of democracy that was itself a significant value, both intrinsically and instrumentally. The feature in question was the public proclamation of equality of status. Though I would argue that this public recognition of equal worth is of vital significance, particularly with regard to its impact on the whole quality of a person's life and interaction with others, the possibilities for the development and exercise of autonomy in the living of one's life are, I would claim, the central values that democratic rule affords. The next chapter will deal with the issues of autonomy and subordination in both the political and non-political spheres of life.

8

Democracy, power and domination

At the end of the previous chapter I argued that the public ratification of equal citizenship status was a constitutive feature of democracy and an important intrinsic value, irrespective of any further consequences. This could be interpreted as an endorsement of that merely alienated equality and universality that Marx criticised in his early work 'On the Jewish question' where he argued that political emancipation that leaves the structures of inequality of 'civil society' unchanged results only in man becoming an 'imaginary participant in an imaginary sovereignty'.[1] This would be to forget, however, that I have argued all along that democracy should be interpreted as effective political equality; such equality depends upon far more than legal recognition of equal citizen status. As I emphasised in Chapters 3 and 4, effective political equality in all four moments of political decision-making requires real access to an extensive range of non-procedural resources. The procedures are important, and so is the recognition of equal status carried by entitlement to participate in the procedures, but they do not themselves constitute democracy, nor, so I have argued, could a consistent democrat be committed simply to the achievement of political equality as a constitutional form. Stressing the necessity of access to the background resources required for full equal participation, while important, is in no way an adequate account of the non-procedural conditions for the realisation of democracy. Simple lack of access to such resources would lead to what we could call a negative deviation from full democracy that consisted in the non-uptake of democratic rights in practice. Another major problem for the realisation of democracy, however, consists in the undermining of the potential for equality inscribed in the democratic procedures by the existence of extra-political power relations. The existence of non-political power relations, and even the fact that such power relations can inhibit the realisation of democracy in the political sphere, are relatively uncontentious, perhaps obvious, points. Take, for instance, the not wholly unrealistic example of organised crime. A local community decides on its own local affairs in an exemplary democratic manner. One of the issues might be the number of liquor licenses and who should get them. The decisions arrived at, however, are never implemented as intended. The local branch of the 'Mafia' has its own ideas on the number of licences and so on. By armed force, financial inducement, general harassment and making offers that cannot be refused, the democratic process fails in the final moment of implementation. A wholly other set of power relations and resources determines the implemented outcome in a non-democratic fashion. This non-democratic power can, of course, undermine political equality at any of the four moments of decision-making. Conspicuously armed representatives of the mob might attend the town-meetings and by making it plain what final decision they would find acceptable predetermine the decision. It is even uncontentious to claim that such power can operate in a much more covert and tacit manner, achieving the desired effects without any visible or outward signs of intentional intervention. The common knowledge that certain decisions would be unacceptable to the local 'godfather' is sufficient to remove whole ranges of potential options from the agenda of the town-meeting entirely. Furthermore, once the possibility and varied mechanisms of such power are conceded, it is evident that well-placed, well-organised and well-financed groups other than organised criminals might be able to wield, whether by legal or illegal means, such a disproportionate influence over the determination of political outcomes that the potential for political equality is seriously undermined. And very few people would contest the proposition that differential levels of wealth and income play a pivotal role in the determination of which groups will be more likely to be well placed, well organised and well financed.

There have been three main issues of contention among modern democratic theorists, revolving around claims concerning the precise extent to which modern polities have, despite democratic constitutional forms, failed to achieve significant levels of political equality because of the existence of countervailing power structures having their loci outside the institutional political sphere. The first issue concerns the identification of the most important of these alleged countervailing powers, the main contenders being capitalistically organised economies, male-dominated culture and racial bias, the contention being that, in the first instance, capitalist owners, in the second, men in general, and in the third, privileged races have a vastly disproportionate, and hence undemocratic, share of power. The second area of debate concerns the mechanisms by which such alleged countervailing power is wielded. As I noted above, no one doubts that there can and do exist many instances of the intentional exercise of power based on unequal resources leading to disproportionate influence. Many theorists have argued, however, that such overt instances of unequal power are merely the tip of an iceberg, insignificant when compared to the impersonal structural bias that, without any intentional intervention, distorts decision-making in supposedly democratic states by rigidly fixing the parameters of feasible options such that preferential priority is given to the interests of a privileged sub-group, resulting in the effectiveness of democratic equality being swamped by a sea of institutional inertia that favours the already advantaged.

The final area of debate, with which we can actually deal now rather than simply introducing, concerns the different ways in which unequal power might be inconsistent with democracy. When political theorists refer to democracy they do so usually in the context of what we might call the strictly political, the sphere that has as its core the institutional formulation of authoritatively binding decisions applicable to the community, whether national or local, as a whole. The kind of impact on the achievement of democracy flowing from unequal power resources that we have been considering so far consists in the possible subversion of strictly political equality stemming from disproportionate influence on institutionalised political decision-making. Disparity of power might, however, be thought to be incompatible with democracy independently of its impact on strictly political democracy. Disparities of power in the non-political, in the economic relationships between private individuals, for example, or in the day-to-day interactions of men and women, might be alleged to be 'undemocratic' in their own right.

Take, for example, the forceful argument formulated by C. B. Macpherson in his work *Democratic Theory: Essays in Retrieval*, that democracy and capitalism are radically incompatible. Macpherson offers no evidence whatsoever concerning the possible disproportionate influence of capitalist interests on governmental decision-making. The strictly political sphere is hardly mentioned at all. Rather, Macpherson concentrates on how, according to his interpretation, capitalist enterprises generate profits, by means of 'the net transfer of human powers'. The relevance of this to democracy consists in the fact that democracy's goal, as interpreted by Macpherson, should be the equal maximisation of human powers.[2] Since capitalism is alleged to function necessarily by the net transfer of such powers or capacities, leading to their concentration in the hands of capitalist owners, Macpherson concludes that there is a fundamental and ineradicable tension between capitalism and democracy. The logical basis of the argument is that one of the central normative principles underlying the justification of democracy in the strictly political sense has much wider implications and, in particular, these implications are incompatible with the structure of economic enterprises organised along capitalistic lines. Although using quite different arguments, and certainly quite different terminology, Dahl's conclusion that corporate capitalism is incompatible with democracy, as argued for in his *A Preface to Economic Democracy*, is based on the same structure of argument. He sets out the general assumptions underlying the justification of democracy in the normal political sphere and then concludes that these same assumptions imply the right to democratic self-government in the organisation of economic enterprises, quite apart from any impact such organisation might have on democracy in the state. As he puts it:

> Although political theorists who favour worker participation have often emphasised its potentialities for democratic character and its beneficial effects on democracy in the government of the state, a stronger justification, one with a more Kantian flavour, seems to me to rest on a different argument: If democracy is justified in governing the state, then it must also be justified in governing economic enterprises; . . .[3]

The structure of the argument is the same: a reasoned commitment to democracy involves acceptance of certain assumptions and normative principles, in particular, for Dahl, the value of equal maximum personal autonomy. These principles, it can then be argued, imply not just the justification of political equality in the governing of the state but the justification of equality in decision-making power in all relevantly similar associations, where people are bound by decisions and subject to rules.

It seems to me that this extension of the concerns of democratic theory to disparities of power wherever they might emerge in human relations is logically unavoidable. A commitment to the maximisation of personal autonomy has implications ranging over the whole spectrum of the power structures that characterise human interaction.

But should democratic theory be also concerned, not just with the multiple sites of power outside of the strictly political, but also with the multiple dimensions of power, in particular with the covert dimensions of power that never manifest themselves in explicit and intentional decisions? Are there such covert dimensions of power? The debate concerning the possibility and extent of hidden dimensions of power was sparked off in contemporary democratic theory by the critical assessment of a relatively early work of Robert Dahl's, *Who Governs?: Democracy and Power in an American City*. One of the main aims of Dahl's work was to empirically test various 'elitist' theories that had become popular among American political scientists and sociologists. The central theory that Dahl set out to test, as he puts it himself, 'asserts that beneath the façade of democratic politics a social and economic elite will usually be found actually running things'.[4] Not only do such hypotheses require systematic empirical investigation but also the methodology of research must take into account two crucial conceptual points concerning the nature of power. Firstly, there is a radical distinction between having access to a political resource and successfully wielding that resource in the determination of a particular outcome. There can be numerous reasons why a potential for influencing an outcome is not in fact converted into an actual influence.[5] The methodological implication of this obvious point is that if we are attempting to establish who in reality wields actual power, the simple categorisation of people in terms of their access to potential political resources is wholly inadequate. We must try to decipher the actual lines of influence by identifying who was in favour of which alternative, which alternative was finally implemented and what the participants in the conflict actually did in the attempt to get their preferences realised. Secondly, the identification of conflictual opposition is critical. The importance of this second point is readily established by a simple example. Imagine a small group of people who regularly have to make certain decisions. One member of the group is a particularly prominent initiator, always getting in first with 'What I would like to see done is . . .'. Furthermore, with no demurral from the rest, the eventual outcome is always in accordance with the initiator's preference. We might be forgiven for thinking that we have identified, fairly unproblematically, the real power in the group, irrespective of what formal decision-making procedures are in operation. This is, however, far from obvious. The evidence as so far presented is consistent with several other incompatible hypotheses. For example, to take the extreme case, the initiator may have no significant power to determine outcomes at all and the coincidence between the outcomes and the initiator's preferences is itself explained by a coincidence between the initiator's preferences and those of other members of the group who are the real holders of power. The impotence of the initiator would only become manifest if there was a conflict of preferences. In general, to establish that one group has more power than another we need, firstly, evidence of contrary preference and, secondly, evidence of which participant is successful in determining the outcome against opposition. The concept of power at the basis of these distinctions is formulated by Dahl as follows: 'A has power over B to the extent that he can get B to do something that he would not otherwise do'.[6] The methodology designed by Dahl to answer the central question of *Who Governs?* led to an impressive research programme into the decision-making process in the government of New Haven, Connecticut. Having identified certain key issue areas, Dahl went on to establish 'all the decisions that the participants regarded as the most important'[7] in these areas over a period of about seven years, and then subjected each of these decisions to detailed scrutiny 'by means of interviews with participants, the presence of an observer, records, documents and newspapers'.[8] Dahl's aim was to identify who supported what against which opposition and to log successes in getting preferred alternatives implemented against opposition so as to establish precisely the actual lines of power in the decision-making process. Although Dahl was somewhat cautious in stating his conclusions and wary about overgeneralisation, he did commit himself to certain definite hypotheses concerning the loci of power, at least in New Haven. Firstly, the standard elite theory which asserted 'covert integration by Economic Notables' was, he concluded 'safe to reject'.[9] Furthermore, though he emphasises the unequal distribution of political resources, he concluded that: 'Individuals best off in their access to one kind of resource are often badly off with respect to many other resources. . . . Virtually no one, and certainly no group of more than a few individuals, is entirely lacking in some influence resources.'[10] The general conclusion was that the non-cumulative nature of inequalities in resources led to a pluralistic structure of power in which no one group dominated political decision-making and that provided multiple channels whereby almost all legitimate interests could make their voice heard and have an influence in determining political outcomes.

The critical assessment of Dahl's work that led to the controversy concerning dimensions of power concentrated not on the reliability of Dahl's empirical evidence nor on his interpretation of that evidence at the level at which he chose to deal with it, but on the very concept of power on which his methodology was based. It was not denied that power as Dahl conceptualised it was a reality; what writers such as Peter Bachrach and Morton Baratz claimed, however, was that Dahl's conception of power was too narrow.[11] There was, in Bachrach and Baratz's words, a second face of power, whose operation would remain almost entirely undetected by a methodology such as Dahl's, no matter how systematic and exhaustive the research programme. The attack depends upon a rejection of what Dahl implicitly assumes would count as evidence of opposition. Dahl's sources, as quoted above, included direct observation of decision-making, interviews with participants, records of meetings, documents and newspaper reports, all used in the attempt to identify, to simplify matters, proposers and opposers. But what if there were opposers to some range of proposals whose opposition, though real and felt, never emerged in the public forum? There would be, by Dahl's methods, no detectable decision constituting the success of the actual outcome over that opposition. But if the opponents were ineffective in their opposition, as by definition they were, then those supporting the outcomes would be exercising, even by Dahl's general definition, greater power than the ineffective opposition. The invisibility of the power is a function of the invisibility of the opposition. The invisibility of the opposition, the fact that the opposition never gets voiced in the public forum, has many possible causes. It may derive from the opposition's belief in its own impotence; because it is believed that intervention would be pointless, no intervention is contemplated and the opposition remains mute. Or there may be an attempt at intervention that simply fails to register in the public forum because of a lack of the necessary resources. As the title of one of their works, *Poverty and Power; Theory and Practice*[12] indicates, Bachrach and Baratz were less sanguine than *Who Governs?* concerning the pluralistic dispersion of political resources. The poor, it is true, may have access to *some* political resources, but their poverty can be such a critical handicap in their ability to utilise those resources that not only are they ultimately ineffective but also they never even get to the stage of making their demands heard. In addition, the hiddenness of opposition may be deliberately engineered. According to this analysis there are numerous techniques available to powerful vested interests that enable them to organise certain issues out of politics, thus removing the necessity of having to make explicit decisions in the areas in question:

> Power is exercised when A devotes his energies to creating or reinforcing social and political values and institutional practices that

> limit the scope of the political process to public consideration of only those issues which are comparatively innocuous to A.[13]

This 'non-decision-making' whereby the covert opposition is kept covert constitutes the core of what Bachrach and Baratz call 'the second face of power'. The clear implication is that any democratic theory seeking to delineate the structure of power in a community that concentrates only on success and failure visible within the conventional sphere of political decision-making will fail completely to detect a vast undercurrent of domination and powerlessness in which the impotence of the oppressed is so severe that it issues only in a silence that could, perhaps, be wrongly taken as an index of satisfaction. By the early 1970s even Dahl was beginning to talk about 'crucial inequalities in political resources'[14] and connecting such inequalities with race and 'gross disparities of income'.[15]

Of course, the claim that there is or might be a vast network of oppression hardly detectable by 'superficial' research methods constitutes a radical challenge to the pretension of democratic states to have achieved an approximation to political equality by the twin methods of universal franchise and the non-cumulative fragmentation of political resources. The challenge became even more self-consciously radical in the short work *Power: A Radical View*, published by Steven Lukes in 1974. Lukes accepted that 'the second face of power' theory was an advance on Dahl's concept of power, but argued that this two-dimensional concept of power was still too narrow to capture the full range of power and subordination. The focus again was on the role of opposition and conflict in the definition of power. For Lukes, the inadequacy of the two-dimensional theory derived from the fact that it shared in common with Dahl's theory an overly behaviourist conception of opposition and conflict. Establishing the existence of power depended upon establishing the existence of conflict and opposition; but though the two-dimensional view extended the range of relevant evidence of opposition, the evidence still had to be behavioural. But, Lukes asks, 'is it not the supreme exercise of power to get another or others to have the desires you want them to have – that is, to secure compliance by controlling their thoughts and desires?'.[16] But if one group exercises power over another by so fashioning the consciousness of the subordinate group that its members unquestioningly accept their subordinate role because of their manipulated misconception of their interests and their real situation in society there will be no behavioural evidence of opposition. This, according to Lukes, is the most insidious and effective use of power, the use of power that, through the fashioning the perception of interests, prevents conflict from arising in the first place; it can hide its existence behind a real, though produced, consensus.

That Lukes can introduce this third dimension of power by means of a rhetorical question is in itself evidence of the intuitive appeal of the claim that power can be exercised through the fashioning of a subservient consciousness. There is even an intuitive appeal to the thesis that such manipulated consensus and consent is widespread in allegedly democratic societies, undermining their self-conception as democracies and enabling the privileged to maintain their position of dominance. The appeal of the theory is easy to understand. We assume that if people are in a radically disadvantaged position they will, other things being equal, attempt to remedy the situation. Secondly, we accept that modern democratic societies have made great advances towards procedural political equality. We note, however, that there are certain persistent structures of disadvantage. And so we conclude that procedural equality is in itself an insufficient means to remedy these disadvantages. Though with Bachrach and Baratz we can postulate that political resources are not as non-cumulative as Dahl claimed in *Who Governs?* there does seem to be some truth in the claim that most groups do in fact have access to some level of such resources. Why, then, are there not vigorous attempts to utilise those resources in the effort to counter the persistent disadvantage? It is tempting to see the answer to this question in 'false consciousness' and to further assume that such false consciousness, such a misconception of interest and possibilities, is not the natural state of things and could only occur systematically as a result of some third-dimensional manufacturing of consciousness. Lukes' extension of the concept of power into this third dimension, particularly when the concept is intended as a tool for the explanation of structures of persistent disadvantage, raises certain philosophical problems, however, that must be dealt with if whatever is valid in this perspective is to be saved.

The first set of problems derive from the fact that, for obvious reasons, Lukes can no longer appeal to conflict of preferences as a necessary condition of the existence of disparities of power. In the case of third-dimensional power in particular, the effect of the exercise of power is, by definition, the ensuring that such oppositional conflict of preferences does not occur. So there is power but no conflict of preferences. This involves Lukes not just in the extension of the concept of power into the third dimension but also in the revision of the general concept itself. In this revision the role of conflict of preferences is taken over by conflict of interest. 'A exercises power over B when A affects B in a manner contrary to B's interests'.[17] This seemingly simple revision, necessary if the concept is to be extended into the third dimension, produces major problems.

The first problem has not been much commented on in the literature; it consists in the fact that a radical re-categorisation of the alleged phenomena of power in the first and second dimensions becomes necessary. Furthermore, the re-categorisation is wholly counter-intuitive and contrary to nearly all standard uses of the language of power. Imagine two people, A and B, who know exactly what they want and know that what each wants is incompatible with the other's preference. They engage in a bitter struggle in which A is successful; A's preference is realised and, in this instance, B is subjected to A's will. We have a clear case of disparity of power; A is more powerful than B and exercises power *over* B. According to Lukes' revised concept, however, we ought not to have arrived at this conclusion, because, as yet, we have not considered any evidence concerning the real interests of A and B. It is insufficient to claim that we do not need evidence of specific substantive interest since it is always contrary to a person's interest to be subject to the power of another. This would render the application of the concept completely circular: we would have to establish *that* a person was subject to the power of another before we could decide whether anything contrary to that person's interests had occurred, but we can only determine whether a particular interaction was an instance of power by knowing whether or not a person's interests had been infringed. This seems to me almost incontrovertible evidence that the revised definition radically misconstrues the general concept of power.

The second major problem, and one that Lukes himself acknowledges, centres on the notion of 'interest'. It is generally recognised that the concept of 'interest' is philosophically complex. The use that Lukes wants to make of this concept in his theory of third-dimensional power renders it even more problematic. Third-dimensional power as Lukes defines it depends critically upon the distinction between a person's real interests and the manipulated subjective consciousness that leads the person to act contrary to real interests and, presumably, in accordance with the interests of the powerful. Evidently, this requires us to be able to identify a person's interests not just independently of some particular preference but independently of the person's entire subjective consciousness. This is because Lukes is claiming that a person's consciousness could have been manipulated on a fundamental level. Lukes' solution to this problem consists in the argument that from the postulation of a general theory of human nature we will be able to extrapolate, firstly, an account of real interest and, secondly, an account of how a true conception of interest would emerge in the absence of external, distorting, factors. This solution suffers from two major weaknesses. Firstly, a theory of human nature robust enough to ground a substantive conception of interests will necessarily be implicitly normative and hence will not be open to straightforward proof and disproof. There can be, and are, rival theories of human nature leading to incompatible conceptions of real interest and the human good. Lukes acknowledges this point and goes on to argue that the implication is that the concept of power becomes 'essentially contestable'; different conceptions of interest lead to radically incompatible judgements concerning the structure of power within a community. And since no conception of interest can establish finally its unique superiority over alternatives, debate concerning specific conceptions of power and judgements about the loci of power in any community is itself irresolvable. The whole concept becomes irretrievably embedded in an epistemological relativism.

The second weakness is even more fatal. Any conceivably defensible theory of human nature will inevitably have to have an evidential basis grounded in human experience. But this will render any attempt to construct a third-dimensional power theory on such a conception of human nature viciously circular. If we base our theory of human nature on distorted experience we will be unable to detect third-dimensional power; but we will only be able to determine which experiences and forms of consciousness are the products of distortion after we have formulated a defensible theory of human nature. As a simple example will illustrate, however, the problem lies not with the thesis that there can be a form of power that operates through the moulding of consciousness, but with certain specific features of Lukes' account of such power.

Take the example of two acquaintances, A and B. A wishes to lodge money into her or his bank account but has forgotten the identification number. Remembering that B had kept a copy of the number, A asks B for it. B is a rather unscrupulous character and sees an opportunity to make a bit of money by misinforming A, giving A, in fact, B's account number. Compliantly and unquestioningly, at least until informed otherwise, A continues to lodge money, unknowingly, in B's account. There is, for the time being at least, no consciousness on A's part of a conflict of preferences. B has exercised power over A through a very modest piece of misinformation, getting A to do willingly what otherwise A would probably not have chosen to do. The example is deliberately schematic and simple so as to establish the basic conceptual point: we do have a coherent notion of a type of power that results in misinformed, willing compliance and we can apply this notion fairly unproblematically. The political importance of this possibility, illustrated, for example, in campaigns of disinformation, hardly needs stressing. What features of Lukes' account do we need to revise if we are to rescue the concept of third-dimensional power?

Two fairly substantial changes are needed. Firstly, we have to abandon the claim that we can, independently of the whole of a person's consciousness, preferences and values, establish an objective set of real interests. This does not lead to the complete collapse of the notion of interest into specific *de facto* preference. A person's preference and value structures will be organised both hierarchically and in accordance with principles of importance and priority, possibly in a manner not immediately open to self-conscious introspection. This, and the possibility of inadequate and false understanding of the world, allows plenty of room for the possible incompatibility between the fulfilment of specific preferences and that which is in a person's interest. The concept of interest that is being applied here is the notion of that which is maximally in accordance with the whole range of a person's more fundamental preferences and values. Though we disclaim the possibility of establishing the real interest of people independently of their subjective consciousness as a whole, we are still left with a possibly powerful tool for the critique of forms of consciousness as contrary to their fundamental interests. In an extreme case it could even be empirically established that the totality of a person's *substantive* values and preferences were contrary to fundamental interests. For this to be possible two things would have to be established; firstly, that the person in question had a second-level value lying in the general goal of living a life that would be experienced as fulfilling, enriching and productive of happiness and contentment. And secondly, that the complete achievement of the first-level substantive goals and preferences would not, in fact, bring about the desired fulfilment and contentment. Whatever about the likelihood of encountering such extreme cases, my main contention is that the suggested revision rescues the coherence and applicability of the notion of third-dimensional power operating contrary to a person's interests. In the light of the second suggested revision, however, this will be seen as necessary not for the rescue of the concept of third-dimensional power as such, but for the rescue of the distinction between power contrary to a person's interests and power not contrary to a person's interests.

The second revision consists in dropping any reference in the general definition of power to conflict of interest or conflict of preference. But did not Dahl establish that evidence of conflict of preference was, at least with respect to first-dimensional power, critical for the positive proof of the existence of power? My argument is that though in some instances conflict of preference is a sufficient condition of having conclusive evidence for power, it is not, in all instances, a necessary condition. Consider the following possible scenario in the kind of issue area Dahl was actually investigating. A general scheme for major urban renewal is proposed and a committee of advisers and planners is suggested. A relatively open-ended invitation to become a member of this committee is extended to whoever might want to join it. Imagine that not many members of the general public are interested in active membership and the committee comes to consist of a small group of like-minded interested politicians and business people. Supposing that on some particular issue, say the pedestrianisation of a certain area, there is genuine consensus in the committee and no opposition from outside interests. The committee sets about preparing a detailed plan, explaining the plan and its benefits to the various agencies that are going to be involved. Everything goes smoothly, everyone is convinced of the benefits, decisions are made, the plan is implemented, work begins, the physical face of the city is transformed and there are consequent effects on the life of the citizens. If we wanted to identify the intentional agency that had the resources and used them to bring about this whole chain of effects, it seems to me that the evidence points incontrovertibly to the members of the planning committee. If Dahl were to reply that in the absence of actual opposition we would be uncertain as to whether there might not be a potential coalition of interests which, had they been opposed, might have had the resources necessary to scotch the plan, he would be guilty of that confusion that he himself warns against, the confusion between potential power and actually exercised successful power. In the absence of opposition we cannot, to be sure, measure the degree of power possessed by the planning committee in comparison with the possible power of a potential opposing coalition. But we can still definitively establish, on the basis of direct evidence of active agency, where in this instance power resided.

To convince ourselves that this is not a peculiarity of power in the political sphere, consider briefly the following two cases. A young, seriously religious and responsible person puts herself or himself under the spiritual guidance of another, much older and more experienced person. The guidance is gentle and benevolent, though detailed and directively interventionist. The novice is subjected to minute regulation in diurnal organisation of life, a regimen of spiritual exercises, prescribed reading, detailed advice and exhortation, all leading to profound changes not just in the overt pattern of daily activity but, more profoundly, in the whole structure of the person's outlook on life. Again, it seems incontrovertible that the spiritual director is the major intentional agency of these effects, though presumably with the willing compliance of the novice. The point is that we can establish all of this without any reference to conflict of preferences or action contrary to interests. Just as we could, for example, in the case of two close friends, one of whom was innovative, forceful, dynamic and active, the other being passive and impressionable. As was argued above, it is insufficient to reply that the very fact of coming under the power of others, even if in terms of substantive interests no ill effect occurs and no dissatisfaction is actually felt, has the consequences of diminution of autonomy, which is contrary to a person's interests. Even if it is accepted that such diminution of autonomy is contrary to interest, the conceptual independence of the notion of power from negative impact on interest is conceded, for to determine whether such a negative impact has occurred we need first to establish whether a person's autonomy has been diminished and, hence, whether asymmetric power is being exercised over the person. I conclude, then, that power does have first-, second- and third-dimensional manifestations and that if our interest in disparities of power is motivated by a desire to achieve an egalitarian maximisation of autonomy then our diagnostic analysis must be aware of the multiple dimensions of power. My final critique of Lukes, however, will suggest that the diagnostic analysis needs to be even broader in scope.

This final criticism concerns not the concept of third-dimensional power as Lukes understands it, but the use to which he wishes to put it. As I indicated above, one of the main motivations for the extension of the concept of power into the second and third dimensions is the belief that the persistence of systematic disadvantage is plausible evidence for disparities of power, despite the procedural equality of rights of democratic participation. In particular, it is plausible to assume that a miscontrual of interests, a misunderstanding of what would be required to achieve interest satisfaction, a general 'false consciousness' concerning one's situation, are major factors in the persistence of oppression and disadvantage. But is it plausible to assume that such 'false consciousness', if it occurs at all, is the product of third-dimensional power? I have accepted that there are likely to be instances, perhaps widespread, of intentional disinformation and the manufacturing of consent. What I am questioning is the plausibility of interpreting all 'false consciousness' as the product of such intentional manipulation. Suppose we accept that the millennial persistence of the disadvantaged position of women in the subordination of women's interests to those of men is, in part, to be explained by a subordination of consciousness without oppositional consciousness of subordination. My contention would be that to explain the generation of such consciousness by means of third-dimensional power would be to adopt a wildly implausible conspiracy theory. The reason for this is that despite Lukes' professed intention of taking into account 'systematic or organisational effects', 'the bias of a system', 'institutional inertia' and the 'the unconscious effects of socially structured and culturally patterned behaviour of groups' the element of intentionality, of individual responsibility, is central to the general concept of power that Lukes defends.[18] Consequently, third-dimensional power as a sub-species of power must itself be intentional. If all 'false consciousness' is the product of third-dimensional power, all such consciousness must be the effect of persistent and widespread intentional action. I would argue, however, that though such intentional action can and does occur, a major factor in the persistence of systematic oppression and disadvantage is what is best understood as structural dominance and subordination, which, though related in multiple ways to disparities in intentional power, is quite distinct from such power and of more fundamental explanatory importance.

The distinction between what I am calling intentional power and structural dominance can be readily illustrated. Imagine a city in which there are two residential areas, a desirable area and a slum area. The city is also racially divided, the privileged ethnic group living in the desirable area, the disadvantaged group in the slum. Many members of the disadvantaged group would in fact like to live in the desirable area, but, though there are no apartheid laws and houses in the desirable area frequently change hands, the initial pattern of residential settlement is reproduced over the years. Now, consider two different ways in which this might have occurred. According to the first scenario, it is a frequent occurrence that members of the disadvantaged group initiate proceedings to buy a house in the desirable area. The ethnic group living in the desirable area, however, are not only privileged but also racist; street demonstrations are organised, threats are made to burn out the new potential residents and so forth. As a result, every putative purchaser from the 'wrong' ethnic group eventually withdraws; and thus, the residential separation of the ethnic groups continues. Evidently, the mechanism at work here is intentional power; in fact, it is intentional power in the face of explicit and overt opposition. Suppose, however, that the vast majority of the privileged ethnic group are extremely liberal and non-racist; they would, let us say, positively welcome multi-racial settlement. There is in the society as a whole, though, a systematic disparity of wealth, and the houses in the desirable area are sold by auction to the highest bidder. Everyone finds the area desirable, there is keen competitive bidding for any house and, inevitably, members of the privileged ethnic group always succeed in making the ultimately accepted bids. The same pattern of residential settlement is reproduced over the years. There is nothing mysterious about the mechanism of reproduction at work here. Given the rules that people follow in the buying and selling of property and given high demand from members of each ethnic group, the critical factor leading to the reproduction of the residential pattern is the disparity of financial resources. Whenever a house comes up for sale there is at least one member of the privileged group wanting to buy and with more money available than any potential purchaser from the disadvantaged group. As we have described the situation, there is no intention on the part of the successful purchasers, either individually or collectively, to prevent, in any specific instance, purchase by a member of the other ethnic group, nor is there any intention to reproduce the pattern of residential separation. Given that bids are made privately, not at public auction, there could be complete ignorance on the part of a successful purchaser concerning who was being prevented from buying.

The crucial factor, then, in my distinction between power and dominance, is the presence or absence of intentionality. The reason why I refer to the type of dominance exemplified above as structural dominance is that there is a predictable pattern of dominance deriving from a patterned distribution of the relevant resources. The distribution is itself likely to have been the product of another cycle of structural dominance in which members of the privileged group dominate in the competition for higher paid jobs and do so dominate on the basis of a patterned distribution of other resources such as educational opportunity and achievement, family background and connections and, perhaps, place of residence. The kind of structural dominance illustrated in this example is not, of course, a parallel in the sphere of dominance of third-dimensional power. The dominance parallel in that sphere would have to be concerned with consciousness formation. The parallels in our examples are with first- and second-dimensional power. It is worth drawing out these parallels in detail before moving on to the dimension of consciousness formation.

In outlining the first scenario I pointed out that the mechanism at work there was quite clearly overt, conflictual power. Extending the scenario in quite a plausible fashion we could illustrate a transition from first-dimensional power to a specific type of second-dimensional power. The extension would consist in postulating a growing infrequency of attempts by members of the disadvantaged group to move into the desirable area in the light of a growing realisation of the ultimate futility of such attempts. At the point at which this becomes total cessation we pass definitively to second-dimensional power. Though there is still, we assume, a general desire to move into the area, this does not issue in any overt attempts to purchase a house, nor are there any overt decisions leading to overt actions to prevent any such purchases. There are exact parallels in the sphere of dominance. Suppose, in contradiction to what we originally postulated, that auctions were public. The successful bidder would be aware of the existence and identity of any unsuccessful bidders. It still does not follow, of course, that the successful bidder has the intention of preventing a member of the disadvantaged group from moving into the area, just as if I, as a man, am a successful candidate for a job against competing candidates, some of whom I know to be women, my success is not evidence of my intention to exclude women from such positions. We can postulate an exactly parallel transition to second-dimensional dominance if we imagine the unsuccessful bidders from the disadvantaged group realising that demand will always push prices beyond their means and consequently withdrawing completely from the market. The importance of highlighting the ease of transition into what I am calling second-dimensional dominance lies in the fact that the very covertness of such structures of dominance might make a crucial contribution to their perpetuation, their hidden ubiquity being their undesigned protective camouflage.

I introduced the concept of structural dominance as probably a more important factor in the explanation of systems of persistent disadvantage than the phenomenon of intentional third-dimensional power. We have yet to look, however, at the possibility of dominance in the process of the formation of beliefs, attitudes, preferences and values. The idea of such dominance, and, as I will be emphasising, it is more usually a matter of dominance rather than intentional power, is often appealed to in theories of cultural imperialism, hegemonic class relations and the oppression of women in and by a male-dominated culture. The concept, however, needs careful analysis, particularly in respect of what it is in such postulated asymmetry that constitutes the negative dimensions of dominance, an issue that will bring us back again to the meaning and value of autonomy, the egalitarian maximisation of which as central to the normative basis of democracy, is the major reason for our interest in the theories of power and domination.

In my revision of Lukes' theory of third-dimensional power, I argued that we could, in fact, make sense of the thesis that a certain range of a person's beliefs, preferences and values could be contrary to that person's interest, provided that we could establish a contradiction rooted in a more fundamental dimension of the person's consciousness. My claim would be, however, that when we talk of a person's consciousness being so distorted and dominated we could be referring to two distinct, though often causally interrelated, factors: the external nature of the source of the consciousness formation and the specific content of the beliefs, preferences and values. I want to begin by looking at the latter, the specific content of consciousness independently, for the time being, of its source. Let us take an example from the area of gender relations. Imagine a woman whose conception of herself and her goal in life accorded with what, until relatively recently, was the stereotype of the perfect woman. She believed that 'a woman's place was in the home', this being the proper sphere for the achievement of appropriately feminine values as home-maker, bearer and rearer of children, provider of practical and emotional support for her husband, as well as an appropriate amount of sexual satisfaction, and all this to the virtual exclusion of activity in other spheres, except perhaps a modest and secondary involvement in voluntary 'caring' work, itself appropriate to the emotional and nurturing nature of women. We could take the example further by assuming that the woman believed not only that such would constitute a genuinely valuable life but also that it was particularly appropriate to her capacities as a woman, and, as a woman, she simply did not have either the capacities for or the motivational orientation towards achievement in the male spheres of career, politics, culture and public life generally. One thing we could mean by referring to such a self-image as a dominated and subordinate self-image relates, on the basis of the content of the self-image, to the consequential negative impact on the life of the person. We could see such negative impact as lying primarily in three spheres; firstly, the sheer limitation in opportunities for achievement, secondly, the subservience of the roles, in the strict sense that the valued behaviour is almost exclusively defined in terms of serving the interests of others, and finally in the inevitable disparity of access to resources, as compared to men, which itself is likely to result in men being dominant over such a woman across a whole range of diurnal interactions, and may even result, if the men in question are unscrupulous, in the woman becoming a victim of negative intentional power. Such a self-image is likely, then, not only to have some general kind of negative impact but also in particular, to lead to an on-going, continuously reinforced, subordination to the dominance and power of men. The first point that I want to make here is that this subordination to dominance and power is likely to occur in every one of the three dimensions; the disparity of resources will lead to overt subordination in achievement, subordination that is covert because of a tacit self-limitation and, most importantly in this context, subordination in the sphere of the determination of the perspectives and values that will constitute the general culture of the society. So far, however, even when the subordination is in the sphere of belief and value formation it is as a *result* of the particular form of consciousness, we have not explicitly established that the form of consciousness is itself the effect of third-dimensional domination. If we made the unlikely assumption that the form of consciousness originally emerged spontaneously, without any external influence, in the psyche of a particular woman, the resulting negative consequences would be the same. I want to ask two questions about the source rather than the content of such a self-image. Firstly, what mechanisms of self-image generation would have to be operating if we were to justifiably conclude that the process of generation of the self-image was itself the result of third-dimensional dominance? Secondly, how valid was our original assertion that the very externality of the source of consciousness formation would itself be a seriously negative factor?

The two questions are rendered more problematic than at first sight they may appear to be in the light of a general assumption of theories of socialisation, namely that socialisation is the major determinant factor in the fashioning and moulding of the specific forms of consciousness of all human beings. What additional factors might be being claimed in the case of a dominated consciousness? And are the additional factors when identified something to do specifically with the external nature of the determinant factor?

There are two aspects of the process of socialisation that can help to differentiate what we could call two modes of externality. The first aspect consists in the precise nature of the dominant external agency, rather than in there mere fact of its externality to the individual as such. The agency is doubly external if the dominant individuals who are the major determinants of the content of socialisation belong to a group different from that to which the socialised individual belongs; in the case of gender, men as distinct from women. An understanding of the operation of socialisation from this perspective is dependent on distinguishing the proximate agencies of socialisation from the fundamental determinants of the content of the socialisation process. Even if it is other individual women that are the proximate, direct agents in the socialisation of a specific female, if male influence is the dominant factor in determining the content of beliefs, attitudes, preferences and values into which the woman is socialised, the source is still external in this additional sense. The specific nature of the content is crucial here, because the externality of the dominant group has to be grounded in the social reality of the group; men have to be not just not women in some arbitrary logical classification, but, perhaps primarily in terms of social organisation, *different* in a manner relevant to a whole range of actions and practical implications. The importance of this lies in the assumption that if two groups of people are so differentiated and members of one group are the dominant agencies in the determination of those dimensions of the general culture into which the others are socialised, the forms of such culture will be partisan, the different interests and perspectives of the dominant group will shape the forms in a manner contrary to the interests of the subordinate group. This is the unstated assumption behind Marx's famous claim that the ruling ideas of any age will be the ideas of the ruling class. That a group's interests will inevitably shape both the cognitive and attitudinal dimensions of cultural forms in a manner that is favourable to those interests and contrary to the interests of others may not be a logical truth,[19] but one of the most important tasks of feminist theory, theories of race relations and theories of cultural imperialism generally, has been to spell out the details of the partisan nature of the cultural forms generated by the dominance of particular groups.[20] All that needs to be established on the level of general theory is that if the members of a socially differentiated group are the dominant agencies in the formulation and determination of cultural forms that are in fact partisan, the socialisation of individuals from other groups will be external in a sense additional to the externality of all socialisation. I would emphasise, however, that seeing as this additional externality is crucially dependent on the negative impact of the content of socialisation, once again it is not the mere external nature of the source that is at issue; the source is only judged to be external, in this added sense, if the content is partisan. This can be illustrated by a simple example. Suppose that a woman who had become identified with the subservient self-image described above encountered a non-sexist, liberated and liberal man who so transformed her consciousness that not only did she come to reject the myths of the female stereotype but she also became critically independent of the details of her mentor's perspective. The externality, in both senses, of the original source would be irrelevant to our assessment of the dominated or independent state of her current consciousness.

This brings me to the second aspect of the process of socialisation that allows us to differentiate the two modes of externality, namely, the manner of assimilation of external influence. The process of socialisation should not be thought of as the analogue of a once-off programming of a computer. It is ongoing, interactive and multi-dimensional, many of the dimensions having little to do with explicitly intentional formation. Though I stated above that the externality of the source of consciousness formation is conceptually distinguishable from the negative impact of a form of consciousness on the realisation of interests, there is a causal link between these factors, particularly in the case of the kind of subservient consciousness described above. In the ongoing process of belief and attitude formation there is both an internal and an external factor leading to subordination in consciousness formation. The external factor we have already referred to; members of the 'other' group are dominant in the field of achievement and in the field of directly shaping and articulating cultural forms. The internal factor consists in the predisposition of such a subservient consciousness to give disproportionate weight to the beliefs and attitudes of the dominant group. To get at the essential nature of this internal factor I will describe the two opposing extremes. Take the example of two people who, whether intentionally or not, are, as part of their general socialisation, socialised into two different sets of principles concerning the assimilation of influence and experience. The first set of principles emphasises the importance of continuous reflective criticism on beliefs, attitudes and values, the necessity of constant monitoring of the effects of these on one's life, the value of seeking out not just as wide a range of knowledge as possible but also multiple alternative perspectives that one should approach both sympathetically *and* sceptically. As part of this whole process the person is introduced, both theoretically and operationally, to techniques of logical analysis and criticism of a formal and informal nature. The person is taught to identify the typical sources and forms of fallacy and self-deception and is pointed towards bodies of work the reflection on which is likely to heighten the powers of reflective criticism. Lying behind all of this there is an emphasis on the general value and worth of the self and in particular the ability of the person to develop a confidence, though a self-critical one, in her or his own abilities. The contrary set of principles, on the other hand, emphasises the person's general worthlessness and her or his inability to properly understand the truth; the person is taught to think of her or his capacities as weak, inadequate and inevitably distortive; he or she is taught to be simply suspicious of desires and beliefs that seem spontaneously generated by experience. Furthermore, a particular limited range of 'sources' are identified as authoritative, and such sources prescribe in detail the beliefs and values that one should have. My claim is that in comparing the results of the successful socialisation into these two very different sets of principles we would be justified in claiming a radical difference in degree in the external nature of on-going consciousness formation. The difference is so radical that we would be justified in referring to the first type of person as having achieved an essential ingredient of autonomy. It is important to emphasise two points here; firstly that autonomy as so understood consists in a lasting disposition, in particular the disposition of reflective criticism, and, secondly, that autonomy consists in precisely this form of consciousness and capacity and is independent of the original source of the disposition. My argument, then, is that it is the lack of such autonomy that constitutes the possibility of subordination both to third-dimensional power and, more importantly, to third-dimensional dominance. Third-dimensional dominance and subordination are misconceived if they are thought of as deriving from the mere externality of the original source of influence or socialisation. Lack of autonomy in this regard, like autonomy itself, is an on-going disposition; it consists, in fact, in the uncritical assimilation of influence.

It is at this point that we need to return, as I indicated above, to the meaning of autonomy and its value. I noted in the previous chapter the central role given, particular by writers such as Dahl, to autonomy in the normative basis of democracy. Dahl is aware of the complexities surrounding the notion of autonomy and recognises, in particular, the distinction between that individual autonomy in making individual decisions that consists, in part, precisely in the person not being subject to collective authority in such areas and the kind of autonomy, in fact political equality, achievable in the making of collective decisions.[21] As I have emphasised throughout, the proper boundary between the two is extremely problematic and the drawing of this boundary will, to a large extent, depend upon how precisely we conceive of the fundamental value of autonomy itself, what autonomy consists in and in what ways valued autonomy is diminished. It is, then, obviously essential that we be clear on this issue of the meaning and value of autonomy.

The actual usages of the term 'autonomy' should be thought of, as I argued in the case of 'democracy' itself, as constituting a set of family resemblances. Our problem is to identify, perhaps construct, an interpretation that can be the basis for the evaluative importance of autonomy. In one sense of the word, a person whose operative principle of choice is to obey someone else, to serve another's needs and desires, is not autonomous. But what if we discovered that such a person had, as we might say, 'freely chosen' a life of service to others, would we be still justified in judging such a person lacking in autonomy? So, perhaps the relevant interpretation of autonomy should be that whatever our principles and beliefs may be they should be 'our own'. This, however, is clearly inadequate, since, in a quite defensible sense whatever beliefs and values we happen to have will be, tautologically, our own. If we try to remedy the situation by identifying autonomy with the situation of having, in a principled way, chosen our beliefs and principles of choice we would have, as a moment's reflection will show, articulated a self-contradictory ideal. Furthermore, whatever the status and nature of our beliefs and values, a valuably autonomous life has certain conditions. A person can be forced to hand over money to an armed robber; the choice to comply with the robber's demands might be quite rational and based on beliefs and values that were appropriately 'autonomous'; but a life that consisted entirely in actions chosen in this way could hardly be considered an autonomous life. Is the problem here that though the person *chose* what to do the choice was not made in circumstances that were themselves chosen? But rarely, if ever, are choices so made.

We can approach the question of the appropriate interpretation of autonomy by making the following three points. Firstly, autonomy will always be a matter of degree and the concept of 'total autonomy' is simply incoherent. What autonomy is a degree of depends upon points two and three. The second point is that there is an internal condition of autonomy that consists in the degree to which the process of belief and value formation is, in a continuous manner, reflectively critical. As Gerald Dworkin defines it:

> . . . autonomy is conceived of as a second-order capacity of persons to reflect critically upon their first-order preferences, desires, wishes and so forth and the capacity to accept or attempt to change these in the light of higher order preferences and values.[22]

A person's capacity so to act is, as a matter of both inevitable fact and logic, limited. Procedures of criticism are themselves subject to critical revision and procedures without accepted substantive content are inoperative formulae. In the critical reflection on life, just as in the pure theory of knowledge, if we start from a position of absolute scepticism, that is as far as we will get. In the image used by Quine, the process is more like the rebuilding of a raft while still afloat and hence while still relying uncritically at any given moment on substantial parts of it, than it is like standing in a supposedly neutral nowhere from which the boat is constructed *ex nihilo*.[23] Before leaving this point, we should note that though when contrasting subordinate lack of autonomy with independence above the second-order critical reflection was focused on influences deriving from other people, Dworkin's definition as just quoted is meant to apply to all of a person's substantive values and preferences, whatever their source. This is what lies behind the ancient idea of freedom as necessitating independence from our passions. The fact that an addict's addition is either self-induced or, perhaps, the result of physiologically 'internal' circumstances is irrelevant to its impact on autonomy. What is crucial is the ability to engage in second-order critical reflection, evaluation and change.

The third point concerns what I called above the external conditions of choice. I may choose my actions on the basis of values that are the product of critical reflection, but if the circumstances of my choice are always characterised by the type of coercion mentioned previously, I can hardly be considered to be living an autonomous life. To identify the precise relationship between circumstances and choice that favour autonomy is, however, a difficult matter. As I said earlier, to say that the circumstances must be of my own choosing would be to identify autonomy with, quite literally, continuously creative omnipotence. Neither is it true that the diminution of autonomy derives from the fact that the weighting of the options facing me are the product of intentional human agency. Imagine a person having to choose between rented accommodation and buying a house opting for the former because it was cheaper, involved less expense and responsibility in maintenance, and afforded greater flexibility in respect of mobility and change. The government, however, wanting to encourage home ownership offer such substantive tax relief on mortgage repayments that buying becomes much cheaper than renting, provides generous grants for maintenance so that the burden is all but abolished, and establishes an intervention system for buying houses so that anyone wishing to move house can be guaranteed an immediate sale. A sensible person might then choose to buy; the options the person is now facing are differently weighted as a result of intentional intervention. But is the person's autonomy diminished?

What is actually at issue here is what I would call the desirability or otherwise of the point of intersection between the two axes of importance that structure a person's values and preferences. If a person was asked to specify the most important things in life, the question could be justifiably interpreted in two ways. On the one hand, a person might cite happiness, success, self-development and so forth. On the other hand, one could say the most important things were getting enough food, being able to stay alive and so on. In the latter case one would be answering the question from what I call the perspective of immediate pragmatic necessity; in the former case, the perspective would be that of intrinsic worth. The most desirable intersection between these two axes is that in which a person can meet the requirements of immediate pragmatic necessity in a manner that is perfectly compatible with the full realisation of the intrinsically worthwhile values. This is, of course, an impossible ideal. Any agency that moves the point of intersection in that direction enables a person to 'live as they would choose', which we can now interpret not simply as choosing in accordance with one's values, but choosing in accordance with the preferred priority of values. The effect of coercion or of unintended negative dominance is to move the point of intersection away from the desired ideal, confronting a person with a choice between the intrinsically worthwhile and the pragmatically necessary, making it almost inevitable that pragmatic necessity will dominate intrinsic value. There might seem to be something of a paradox here. While it seems clear that a coercive agency limits autonomy by presenting a person with a set of choices that are less desirable than those the person faced before the intervention of the coercive agent, it might look as though a person suffered a similar loss of autonomy in the case of positive inducement. The person who can now buy a house because of government subsidy has been acted upon from outside, we might even say manipulated by external forces. But the exercise of power by one person on another is not always detrimental.[24] And autonomy, as we said above, is a capacity and disposition, not an instantaneous state. The example of the government subsidy is, in fact, the exact parallel with regard to the external conditions of autonomy of the liberating and generating of critical reflective abilities discussed earlier. In both cases the source is external but the effect is to enable a person to live, from then on, more autonomously.

But what is the value of autonomy? In the previous chapter I argued, in agreement with other democratic theorists such as Dahl, that autonomy was one of the central values to be appealed to in the normative justification of democracy. But why is it so important? The more thorough analysis of autonomy that has been developed in this chapter enables us to answer this question.

The first value of autonomy is its instrumental value. This should not be under-estimated, particularly because the argument is so convincing. In saying that autonomy has an instrumental value we are saying that it is valuable in terms of its consequences on the realisation of other values. In the case of the external dimension of autonomy this is particularly clear, because that dimension consists in a person's ability to live according to her or his values; more accurately it is the ability to give priority in practice to those values that are given priority in principle. This, by definition, is an essential ingredient in what anyone would consider to be a valuable or worthwhile life.

When we turn to the internal dimension of autonomy the argument is more complex but no less clear in its implications for the value of autonomy. The critical factors here are the ever-present possibility of a person's life being dominated by illusions and unwise desires and values, unwise in the sense that their realisation, though desired, would bring about dissatisfaction, frustration, or other consequences detrimental to a person. The second-order disposition and capacity to distance oneself from one's current first-order beliefs and values by critical reflection is a crucial mechanism of protection that is even more necessary when there is likely to be an external partisan source of beliefs and values.

It can also be claimed, of course, that autonomy, particularly in its internal dimension, is an intrinsic good. We could be intending this as a factual statement about how autonomy is valued by people. We could be asserting with Dahl that the belief that a person's life is only truly worthwhile when it is grounded in autonomous consciousness is deeply entrenched in the Western tradition. It is important to note, however, that the evaluative belief itself is by no means self-evident or universally accepted. Imagine a person who, by accident as it were, had the correct beliefs and the right values, but not the second-order disposition to subject them to critical reflection and did not, to any significant extent, understand the basis of the beliefs and values in question. What would be missing in such a person's life? If we reply that such a person is unprotected against detrimental and, possibly, malign influences that would transform the true understanding of the person into falsity and misconception, we are returning to the instrumental value of autonomy as a crucial mechanism of self-protection. We are not explicating its alleged intrinsic worth. There is a way of explicating this intrinsic value, though admittedly on the basis of a premise that is not itself self-evident either. The premise is the Enlightenment conception of rationality and knowledge as being genuine only if the individual can ground such knowledge in her or his own reason and experience and the acceptance of such a conception as a constitutive element of the self. I am, according to this, only being a person when I am rational and I am only being rational when I ground my beliefs and my values on critical rational reflection. Diderot describes his ideal philosopher as one:

> who, trampling underfoot prejudice, tradition, venerability, universal assent, authority – in a word, everything that overawes the crowd – dares to think for himself, to ascend to the clearest general principles, to examine them, to discuss them, to admit nothing save on the testimony of his own reason and experience.[25]

Such a person cannot consider as legitimately binding, either in the sphere of belief in general or in the particular sphere of value, anything except that which is the product of autonomous understanding.

The front cover of a book entitled *Women, Power and Politics*, shows a picture of a woman carrying a placard bearing the slogan 'The Vote is Not Enough'.[26] I have argued throughout this work that rights of participation without the resources required to fully utilise those rights are almost worthless. The purpose of this long discussion of power, dominance and autonomy has been to emphasise further the inadequacy of equal rights of participation in the political process. If our concern is with equal autonomy, in the first place we need to focus not just on the institutionalised political sphere, but on all spheres of life where disparities of power and domination can occur, partly because of the negative impact of such disparities on equality in the political sphere but mostly because such power and domination is incompatible with that equal autonomy that is postulated as the normative basis of democracy. Secondly, a consideration of the theories of power and domination has highlighted, in both the political and non-political spheres, the intricacies and possible covertness of structures of power and domination. Within a society publicly committed to a creed of equality and even legally conferring political equality on all of its citizens, there can exist groups of people so subordinate to the multi-dimensional power and dominance of others as to almost completely lack autonomy in both the political and the non-political domains. In the case of race and gender, though some transformations are occurring, the evidence of radical subordination is incontrovertible.[27] My purpose has not been to rehearse this evidence in detail but to articulate concepts and theories that help us to understand its nature and persistence. There is, however, another segmentation of society that some democratic theorists have identified as the root cause of an equally pervasive and debilitating system of dominance and subordination, equally detrimental to the realisation of individual autonomy, the economic segmentation of society into owners and controllers of productive assets and non-owners who gain their access to material resources by selling their labour power. That this economic system is in fact inimical to that autonomy that justifies democracy is, however, far from uncontentious. Other theorists see the market economy as the very bulwark of democracy and freedom. It is to the discussion of these opposing viewpoints that we must now turn.

9

Democracy and the economy

The set of problems that we are dealing with here depends upon the assumption that the economic dimension of a society is so important that the manner of its organisation will have a major impact on the political life of the society and on the nature of the life of people generally. We are not, of course, discussing the general question of what impact the economy is likely to have on society and politics. Our concern is with the more limited question of whether an economy organised like the economies of typical modern Western societies will be positively beneficial or harmful to the realisation of democratic ideals. Such economies are usually referred to as market economies, but our first problem must be to identify more precisely their central characteristics.

We sometimes say that such economies are founded on private property; but this, while true, is not specific enough. The institution of private property implies two things, the understanding of which depends upon an appreciation that property ownership is more than a static legal relationship and more than a dyadic relationship between owner and thing owned. Ownership consists in a complex of rights and the rights are rights to act in various ways. Secondly, the point of the rights is not simply to specify the rightful activities of the owner to the things owned but to differentiate the powers of the owner from those of non-owners, some of which powers are powers *against* non-owners. So, particularly in the case of private property, the property relationship is triadic, between owners, things owned, and non-owners. The two factors that constitute the essence of private property are two forms of exclusivity. If A owns X, in the sense of 'owns' that theorists refer to as full liberal ownership,[1] A's rights to use, benefit from and dispose of X exclude from such use, benefit and disposal, both other individual people and the society as collective decision-maker, or to speak more simply, the state. The exclusivity has itself a dual nature; ownership identifies which agent exclusively has the relevant rights and the relevant rights consist partly in the right to exclude others from use, benefit and disposal. A point worth stressing here is that according to this analysis property is power; having property in certain goods is not only the basis of a consequential power that might stem from having those goods at one's disposal but also having property *consists* in having certain differential powers. Though modern market economies are organised around property rights that approximate to full liberal ownership, the crucial factor is not simply private ownership as such, but the private ownership of *productive* property, all of those things required in the production of other goods, in a phrase, the means of production.

Even if we add that the private property in question is property in the means of production, we still do not have an adequate account of modern economies. Producers could privately own the means of production, but all owners could work their own means of production and consume, for the most part, what they produce themselves. This would be what economists call a natural economy. To get closer to a specification of modern market economies we need to add that the privately owned means of production are used primarily to produce goods for the market, for sale at exchange ratios determined by impersonal market forces. The essential elements of the organisation of production and distribution by market principles are firstly, that production is for sale, secondly, that what is produced, what is offered for sale and what is bought is a matter to be decided on by individual economic agents, and thirdly, that the exchange ratios are determined by impersonal market forces, in particular, none of these matters is decided in detail by political decision-making, though there might be general laws that articulate, enforce and protect the market principles, and there might be very exceptional cases of detailed directive intervention.

We have, so far, identified three general organisational principles, namely, private property, property in the means of production and production for the market, with the implied assumption that the above mentioned principles of market organisation predominate in the economy. But such an economy might still be one of independent, individual producers, in which almost everyone owned at least a sufficiency of means of production and worked those means of production themselves. The final element that we need to add to adequately characterise those aspects of modern economies that are relevant to the coming arguments is the simple and evident fact of radical inequality in the ownership of means of production. On the one hand, the vast majority of people in modern market economies have no significant ownership of means of production, while on the other hand a relatively small number of economic agents own vast ranges of productive assets. It is this factor, in the context of the other three, that will turn out to be crucial to the arguments of this chapter. In particular, the inequality of ownership of productive assets has the obvious practical implication that there must be a market in labour. For the vast majority of people, who do not own productive assets, the means of acquiring the money required to purchase economic goods offered for sale on the market consists in selling labour-capacity for a wage or salary to owners, more usually to the agents of owners, of productive assets or means of production. The sale of labour-power, of course, is more in the nature of renting out for a specified period of time. But in some real sense labour-power becomes the property of those who purchase it, with all that this implies in the light of the above analysis of property.

It is not pedantry to insist on identifying and differentiating these four elements of modern market economies. As Dahl, for example, points out in *A Preface to Economic Democracy*, the early republican consensus in America concerning the beneficial democratic consequences of private property assumed that in practice the private owners in question would be independent agrarian producers with roughly equal productive assets.[2] It would be seriously misleading to assume that that consensus and the considerations on which it was based had any direct relevance to arguments concerning modern market economies and the realisation of democratic ideals. In fact Dahl argues, referring to modern economies and assuming that they are constituted by and generate radical inequalities, that;

> . . . an economic order that spontaneously produced inequality in the distribution of economic and political resources acquired legitimacy, at least in part, by clothing itself in the recut garments of an outmoded ideology in which private ownership was justified on the ground that a wide diffusion of property would support political equality.[3]

One final point needs to be made. References to economic inequality are going to be frequent in the arguments to come. But it is essential that we clearly distinguish two different, though often causally interrelated, types of economic inequality, namely: inequality in non-productive assets and inequality in productive assets. All property is power, but there is a specific type of power attaching to ownership of productive resources that is of central relevance to the problem we are considering, the problem of what impact the organisational principles of modern market economies have on the political equality of democratic decision-making and on the realisation of equal autonomy generally.

There is a long tradition associating economic liberalism with democracy, a tradition asserting that democracy and political liberties generally can only take root, survive and flourish in a society characterised by economic freedom. From this perspective the impact of the operation of the economic market on the realisation of democratic ideals is positive and beneficial. I will begin by looking at the main arguments used to support this thesis. Firstly, there is the argument based on historical conjunction. Moves towards the progressive democratisation of political regimes occurred precisely in those areas of the world that were experiencing the emergence of market economies. The argument, of course, goes much further than the mere citing of historical coincidence. In the first place it is noted that the emergence of market economies pre-dated any significant moves towards political democracy. Furthermore, various plausible sociological hypotheses are put forward to explain how and why the economic transformations occurring primarily in Europe from the late middle ages on led to the dissolution of feudal and absolutist regimes and the gradual emergence of more democratic forms of government. While it is not my purpose to discuss in detail the various complex theories of political development,[4] a few salient and relatively uncontentious points can be made. In the first place, the gradual commercialisation, and then industrialisation, of European economies led to the emergence of a new commercial class whose very identity was bound up with the new economic order. Secondly, it was the members of this class that were the first and primary beneficiaries of the growing democratisation of political regimes. Finally, it is at least plausible to suggest that the development of liberal, republican and democratic ideals, together with some transformation in practice of political structures in accordance with these ideals was due, in part, to the social and economic power of this new commercial class.

On a deeper but more amorphous level political theorists at least since the time of John Locke in the seventeenth century have postulated a close relationship between the conceptions of property dominant in a society and the political ideologies articulating theories concerning the rights and tasks of government, the basis of legitimacy of governmental authority and the relationship between the state and its citizens. Locke himself, in his critique of Sir Robert

Filmer's defence of monarchic power, is at pains to point out that Filmer postulated the sovereign's monopolistic ownership of literally all the property within a state as one of the bases of monarchic authority.[5] Hence, the pivotal role played in the *Second Treatise* by the attempt to demonstrate the natural right to acquire property.[6] If a person's property is rightfully held independently of the state and not as an implicit donation from the monarch, which is what ultimate monarchical ownership implies, then the state cannot of its own accord take away the property of its citizens.[7] While this begins simply as limitation on the extent of legitimate power, it results in Locke concluding that when governments have to raise revenues they must do so with the 'Consent of the People, given by themselves'.[8] This is moving close to a conception of governmental power as legitimate only when democratic. C. B. Macpherson claims that the relationship between conceptions of property and political ideology is even closer.[9] Locke, he argues, conceptualises all his postulated basic natural rights as deriving from self-ownership, self-ownership implying that people have a right, within the boundaries of moral law, 'to dispose of their Persons or Possessions'.[10] Hence, just as no agency has the right to commandeer a person's property without consent, consent is required to give any external agency the general authority to command. While the requirement of consent to government is not in itself sufficient to ground the unique legitimacy of democratic decision-making, it is an important first step in formulating the normative basis of democracy. The argument, then, is that the emergence of market economies, involving as it did the emergence of both new patterns of property distribution and new conceptions of property, had a profound impact, both practical and theoretical, on the viability of non-democratic forms of political power, paving the way for the emergence of democracy as ideal and reality.

The second major argument consists in the claim that the freedom and autonomy of individuals within the sphere of economic life itself is maximised by the operation of market principles. There are two stages of the argument. Firstly, it is claimed that by definition the individual transactions that constitute a market economy are free, in the negative sense that implies that they are not the product of external, directive coercion. Famously, in *Capitalism and Freedom*, Milton Friedman argued that in the last analysis economies were either market economies or command economies and that in command economies coercion was the central mechanism of direction.[11] A market economy at least avoids this, conferring negative freedom on economic agents. The second stage of the argument claims in addition that market principles ensure a positive voluntary character to all transactions. As no one is forced into any particular exchange, anyone choosing to engage in some specific exchange must perceive the exchange as positively beneficial; unless the post-exchange situation is seen as better than the pre-exchange situation, no exchange will take place. And this is true of all parties to all exchanges. Hence, equal voluntariness is ensured.

The third argument focuses on democracy within the political sphere and is based on the premise that to hold government really accountable people need two types of independence, both of which are inextricably related to economic liberty. Firstly, a person must have economic independence, the ability to acquire at least the basic means of survival independently of government decision-making. This constitutes a fundamental countervailing power in the absence of which government can easily become tyrannical. Secondly, there is independence of mind and this itself is crucially dependent on there being sources of education, knowledge and opinion free from governmental power. Only in a market society can there be the requisite privately owned, non-state, means of mass communication. State control of communication and people's livelihood is bound, it is argued, to destroy the necessary countervailing power against the state that is itself the prerequisite of democratic accountability. How persuasive are these arguments?

Beginning with the historical argument, it can hardly be doubted that the emergence of market economies was a major factor leading to a more widespread dispersal of political power. The problem with the argument, however, is that it does not establish a continuously positive relationship between the progressive commercialisation of economies and ever higher levels of democratisation. It does not take sufficiently into account degrees of democracy. Imagine the historical argument having been formulated in the middle of the last century when the extent of the franchise in any state that could be plausibly considered democratic at all was extremely narrow. It could be argued that the factor that had led to some minimal degree of democratisation was itself responsible for the limitation of that process. There is a logic to this self-limitation that parallels the postulated practical and theoretical impact of the new forms of property and economy. If economic power in the form of private property is an important part of the leverage by which a group can claim a share of political power, then significant disparities of economic power should be expected to lead to significant disparities of political power. And, indeed, the propertyless were a long time waiting for the minimal democratic right of enfranchisement. On the theoretical level, the Lockean argument would tend to support a neat reversal of the slogan that became popular during the American War of Independence, 'No taxation without representation'. If a person's right to hold the government accountable is based simply on the fact that the government needs the person's consent to raise and dispose of revenue in certain ways, it might seem that there ought to be no representation without taxation, lending weight to the continued exclusion of the propertyless.

If economic liberty and property are important factors leading to the emergence of democracy and contributing to the maintenance of democratic accountability, then radical disparities of wealth would be expected to lead to radical disparities of effective political power. The above arguments can, then, be turned back on themselves. Dahl argues that even in the early days of American republicanism, when the centrality of property was emphasised as necessary for the maintenance of governmental accountability, the inequality of property was seen as a serious threat to political equality.[12] As he says of this perspective:

> Economic resources are to some extent convertible into political resources. If citizens are unequal in economic resources, so are they likely to be unequal in political resources; and political equality will be impossible to achieve.[13]

One of the fundamental problems with the three arguments cited above is that they fail to take sufficiently into account the likely impact of radical inequalities in property. This might have been both understandable and justified in early nineteenth-century America when what Dahl calls 'lucky circumstance'[14] consisting primarily in a land supply of continental proportions resulted in a relatively equal distribution of resources. In circumstances of structurally reproduced inequality of economic assets, the possibility of such inequality having a negative impact on the realisation of democratic ideals must be given serious consideration.

Consider, first, the implications of inequality of assets on the alleged equal freedom and autonomy realised in market transactions. The first stage of that argument consisted in establishing that, seemingly tautologically, transactions in a free market were at least free, in the sense of negative freedom. Far from being a truism, this is in fact false in circumstances of inequality. As I argued in Chapter 5 the absence of a particular constraint leading to a particular type of negative freedom has no logical bearing on the freedom of the person *tout court*. That market exchanges are free from governmental direction does not establish in itself that such exchanges are also free from other constraints that would, if present, constitute serious diminishments of freedom. Further, it can be argued that inequality of assets necessarily results in differential constraint and hence differential levels of freedom and autonomy. Let us go back to the point I made at the beginning of this chapter, namely that property, correctly understood, is power. This implies that inequality of property simply is inequality of power. A owning more than B consists in A having a greater range of powers than B and will almost inevitably result in A having greater powers than B in making 'effective personal choices'.[15] Dahl claims in this context that:

> To the extent that the capacity to make personal choices effective is unequally distributed, then freedom and opportunity are also unequal, and political equality is impaired.[16]

To some extent, the persuasiveness of this argument, depends upon the very general way in which the word 'power' is being used. It is true that if one person has more property than another then that person has a greater range of legal powers and, in general, will have a greater capacity to make effective personal choices. But we have to ask if this is an appropriate sense of differential power in the context of a debate about what we can call interactive constraint. Take the extreme case of two people who each own islands in completely different parts of the world. The first island is large, fertile and well-furnished with a whole range of facilities. The second is a rocky atoll. Assuming that there is no interaction between the two, though it is true that one has greater powers than the other, since there is no interactive constraint, claiming that the first has greater powers seems to be simply another way of making the egalitarian point that the two are unequal in property. If one were committed to equality of outcome in property ownership, then, tautologically, inequality of property would be an undesirable inequality. But this seems to have little direct relevance to specifically democratic commitments. There are however, certain considerations that can re-establish this relevance.

Firstly, the exclusive powers of ownership are also powers to exclude. Consequently, differences in levels of property consist, in part, in different levels of power to exclude, a power that is usually legally articulated and coercively enforceable. When we are talking about inequality of property within a society, this constitutes differential interactive constraint. Secondly, if we are talking, as we are, not just of a system of private property in general but of a market economy, we must take into account the all-pervasive network of anonymous interaction that, in fact, constitutes the market. In this context differential property levels inevitably lead to the type of asymmetrical structural constraint that I illustrated when I introduced that concept. The market universalises competition for resources and the asset rich will dominate the asset poor.

This becomes even more relevant when we concentrate on inequality of productive assets. There are two possibilities here, of which one is a special case of the other. The special case is, in fact, the typical situation in modern market economies, namely, that in which there is such a concentration of productive assets in the hands of a small number of privately owning economic agents that the status of the vast majority is that of employee. It is not just Marxist rhetoric to insist that the employer comes to own, at least temporarily, the labour-power of the employee. Trade unions have negotiating rights and certain countervailing powers and employers are bound by a regulatory legislative framework, but in modern market economies it is still an unquestioned right of employers to hire and fire and, more importantly, to directively dispose of the labour-power they have hired on a day-to-day basis and to benefit from whatever profits are generated by the enterprise. To put the matter more straightforwardly as Dahl does: '. . . with very few exceptions the internal governments of economic enterprises are flatly undemocratic both de jure and de facto'.[17] The point is that such differential property in productive assets leads inevitably within one dimension of the economic sphere itself, the dimension of directing and controlling production and the distribution of surplus, to an authoritarian system of power in which some have the right to order and command the behaviour of others. Such a system, of course, is widely believed to be justifiable precisely on the grounds of the justifiability of the private ownership of property that it depends upon. I will return to this point later.

The more general case is theoretically interesting and will lead on to a consideration of the alleged freedom and voluntariness within the process of the exchange transaction itself. In Chapter 7 of his work *Free to Lose* John Roemer mathematically demonstrates that on the basis of the normal assumptions of neo-classical economics a market society in which productive assets are unequally distributed will result in exploitation of the asset poor by the asset rich, even though there is no market in labour and all economic agents have independent, though unequal, access to productive assets.[18] Roemer is using his own revised definition of exploitation in which exploitation consists simply in the difference between average time worked in the production of the goods an agent trades compared to the average time required to produce the bundle of goods that an agent receives in exchange. His argument, then, concludes that even when no one works for anyone else as an employee, the terms of trade as impersonally determined by market forces will result in the asset poor having to work, on average, longer hours in the production of the goods they exchange than the time represented by the goods they receive in exchange. The reverse, of course, is true of the asset rich. The importance of the argument is that it establishes that, with respect to productive assets and produced goods, market mechanisms result in a clear case of structural domination with respect to a person's ability to effectively and autonomously use what is at the core of a person's powers and will remain always scarce at the margin, namely, a person's energy and time. This is a more formal and more general version of the claim made by C. B. Macpherson that the operations of a capitalist economy necessarily involve the net transfer of human powers.[19] What is interesting about Roemer's version is that it illustrates the possibility of structural dominance and constraint in the absence of the right of the employer to authoritatively direct the activities of the employee and the distribution and use of the generated surplus. Of course, when that right is present and active, the non-democratic nature of decision-making power is clear. In both instances, however, what is ultimately relevant to the argument is the moral justifiability of the inequality of property that in one case leads to structural dominance and in the other to the right to command. I will be returning to this question shortly.

The possibility of structural dominance emerging in 'free' market exchanges brings us directly to the supposed voluntariness of the exchange process itself. As I noted earlier the claim was famously made by Milton Friedman when he said that if individuals are effectively 'free to enter or not to enter any particular exchange' this would bring about the situation in which 'every transaction is strictly voluntary'.[20] In his critical analysis of Friedman's argument, C. B. Macpherson begins by noting that the background condition that would be required to guarantee the full voluntariness of exchange 'is not freedom not to enter into any *particular* exchange, but the freedom not to enter into any exchange *at all*'.[21] He then goes on to show that it is this latter condition that is in fact implicit in the model of simple exchange constructed by Friedman, in which all production units have productive assets that they can use to produce goods for themselves. In that case they are free not to enter into exchange and consequently will do so only if they perceive positive benefits accruing to them from the choice. Macpherson has little difficulty in establishing that, as is the case in capitalist market societies, propertyless workers do not have the option of producing for themselves, and hence they are not free not to enter into exchange, therefore, he concludes 'there is coercion'.[22] As a polemical counter-argument this is reasonably persuasive, though I would argue that it is not rigorous enough and fails to identify the general cause of degrees of involuntariness of choice. The willingness with which one chooses between options one is faced with is dependent on the desirability of the option-set. This, of course, is always a matter of degree and, in any particular case, the undesirability of the options facing a person might be unconnected with other people's choices and actions. Aristotle's merchant, who chooses, though not willingly, to throw overboard his precious cargo in a storm to save the ship is not subject to constraint by others.[23] Systems of property distribution are not, however, 'natural circumstances'. The real weakness in Friedman's argument lies in the weakness of his notion of the voluntary. His explicit account reduces the notion of voluntariness to choice between a multiplicity of options; the multiplicity guarantees that one has a choice. The desirability of the option-set in the case of exchange will depend crucially on the terms of trade. This is the importance of Roemer's thesis. Terms of trade that are highly disadvantageous to one party drastically reduce the voluntariness of the exchange. If this is not just an idiosyncratic accident but results from the patterned unequal distribution of resources it is a clear case of structural dominance, consisting in asymmetric constraint and low levels of autonomy as dependent on external conditions. If the distribution is so unequal that a market in labour is necessary a further dimension of loss of autonomy is added in which the employee comes under the directive authority of the employer. If we undertook to maximise as our primary value equal autonomy, then, as Dahl argues, the right to equal autonomy implies 'a right to govern ourselves democratically within our economic enterprises'.[24]

Dahl, however, arrives at this conclusion, as is the case with Roemer, only after an important normative argument alluded to earlier. A person's sphere of desirable options might be constrained by another's choice, but quite legitimately. If I cannot marry the girl of my dreams because she has decided that she does not want to marry me, then extending the range of desirable options for me by forcing her to marry me would be infringing her right to autonomous choice in this area. But supposing that people can rightfully acquire property and the resultant acquisitions lead to asymmetric constraint. This might be undesirable from the point of view of those constrained, but can it be a legitimate remedy to interfere with other people's fundamental rights? If one person rightfully owns certain productive assets and hires another person to work on these assets, surely it is only fair that the owner of the assets should have at least a greater say in the organisation of the work, in what is done with the assets, than the person hired. The question comes down to the issues of the justification of property rights, the basis of such justification, whether such justification implies any limits or conditions on property ownership and whether property rights, as so justified, can be thought superior to the right to equal autonomy.

There is an extensive and complex literature of this subject[25] that we cannot analyse here in detail, but it would be difficult to find fault with Dahl's assessment, which can be summarised as follows.[26] None of the well-known attempts to provide a firm philosophical foundation for the right to acquire private property is completely and unproblematically intellectually convincing and even if accepted as valid would justify the acquisition of a very limited range of resources to be held in a highly restricted and conditional manner. This is because almost all attempted justifications relate the necessity for property rights to the necessity of access to a sufficiency of material resources required to live a reasonable life and, in particular, to exercise one's autonomy and right to self-government. This, firstly, involves the logical priority of these latter rights and, secondly, does not provide a justificatory basis with any relevance at all to the ownership and control by some of vast ranges of productive assets characteristic of modern business enterprises. If one of the consequences of the operation of the right to acquire, in an unlimited manner, private property in productive assets is that large numbers of people can gain their livelihood only by placing themselves under the detailed directive authority of others in matters that vitally affect their well-being, one would have to conclude that such rights radically conflicted with the rights of equal autonomy. Arguments to the effect that employees of an enterprise voluntarily consent to a relinquishment of autonomy in this sphere and, anyway, are not bound by employers' decisions in the way in which a citizen is bound by governmental decisions, fail to take into account the facts that property rights and their implications are in fact legally enforceable and that the level of voluntariness is minimal when one of the options is the relatively miserable level of existence that unemployment involves. I would, then, concur with Dahl that 'if democracy is justified in governing the state, then it is also justified in governing economic enterprises'.[27]

There are two additional arguments sometimes forwarded to attempt to demonstrate that even if people had a right superior to property in the matter of equal self-government in economic enterprises they might, in fact, be perfectly justified in more or less permanently transferring the agency to exercise that right by consenting to private ownership of productive assets. The first argument is that employee-controlled enterprises will be inevitably so economically inefficient that it might be preferable to barter a modest loss of autonomy for a reasonable standard of living. The second argument contends that the active participation in governing an enterprise is an unrewarding and boring burden that people would do well to 'delegate' to others. Three brief points can be made against these arguments. Firstly, it should be realised that what is being urged here, as it has been urged in the government of the state, is not saved from being undemocratic by the language of consent and delegation. As Rousseau said, sovereignty cannot be delegated, it can only be alienated, and this is particularly true when there are not only no institutional channels of accountability, but when, in addition, the right to decide over the use of productive assets carries with it the enormous power associated with control over fundamental economic resources. As in the case of the Paradox of Popular Sovereignty, the consent to a condition of slavery does nothing to render that condition in its day-to-day operation anything other than what it is, a state of complete subordination. Secondly, though the proposed trade-offs might appear attractive if people could be assured of benevolence, as we have seen in the case of democracy in the state, the fundamental problem is that that assurance cannot be guaranteed. Finally, the two arguments are based on dubious assumptions. There are, in fact, convincing examples of democratically managed enterprises in which workers have not, as it is sometimes assumed they inevitably would, manifested an irresponsible preference for short term benefits over longer-term policies of rational investment.[29] Finally, while conventional wisdom and anyone's experience of participating, in addition to one's everyday work, in the vague meanderings of impotent committees might lead one to conclude that active participation is nothing but a chore, it is at least plausible to suggest that properly prepared for, properly recognised and rewarded responsibility with real power over the immediate circumstances of one's life can be a stimulating and enhancing experience.[30] One final, and very different, consideration must be taken into account before we leave the area of democratic management of economic enterprises. It is evident that the kind of economy envisaged by such writers as Dahl has little if anything in common with traditional state bureaucratic socialism, which, given the latter's abysmal record in terms of efficiency, political freedom and democracy, is just as well. In fact, what Dahl is proposing has long gone under the name of 'market socialism', for obvious reasons. The first point to note is that if such an economic system is in any sense viable, a further major weakness is revealed in an argument such as Milton Friedman's for the proposition that a capitalist market economy is an essential precondition of economic and informational independence from government and a constitutive element of non-coerced economic life. The third possibility of an economy that is neither capitalist nor state socialist is not considered. In an economy of self-managed enterprises there would be numerous loci of non-governmental economic and informational power that would provide that independence from central governmental control that Friedman emphasises, and would provide it in a manner that approximated equality to a far greater extent than is possible in an economy where a relatively small minority controls both the sources of economic independence and the channels of mass communication. But how would such a society fare with respect to the type of equal autonomy threatened by inequalities between the asset rich and the asset poor that are at the centre of John Roemer's thesis? This is a serious problem because the self-management of enterprises is no guarantee of equality of productive assets between enterprises. The only conclusion one can draw, I would argue, is that if the asymmetry of constraint involved in Roemer's exploitation is significant and if, in addition, serious inequality in the economic sphere is likely to have a negative impact on the political equality in the government of the state, then the market between self-governing enterprises would have to be more tempered by central regulation to ensure the appropriate dispersal of economic power than Dahl envisages. The problem is whether the required tempering of the market in the context of a complex economy can itself be the product of genuine self-government. I will be returning to the possible internal limitations on the achievement of genuine democracy that arise from the complexity of organisations in the final chapter.

I want to turn now to the second major strand of the thesis that disparities of economic power are inimical to the achievement of democratic ideals, the strand that concerns the impact of economic inequality on the strictly political sphere. The central question here is how inevitable it is that disparities of economic power become transformed into disparities of political power in the sphere of government. The uncompromising statement that the organs of state power will inevitably be under the sway of the economically dominant class is, of course, the classical Marxist position on this issue; as Marx and Engels famously formulated it in *The Communist Manifesto*, 'the executive of the modern state is but a committee for managing the common affairs of the whole bourgeoisie'.[31] It should be remembered, though, that this statement was made at a time when no modern state had approached even universal manhood suffrage and parties representing working-class interests were in a state of infancy, having no significant impact in the sphere of institutional politics. Furthermore, Marx and Engels in the same manifesto urge the workers to fight for political rights such as enfranchisement as a way of strengthening their collective power and hence, it would seem, did attribute some independent effectiveness to constitutional political structures; a point also supported by Marx's cautious acceptance of the possibility, at least, of a socialist transformation of society through the legal and peaceful capture of state power via electoral support for a socialist party.[32] Could political equality, then, in the form of democratic rights as constitutionally defined, be a countervailing source of power over economic power, restricting its influence and perhaps even transforming its structure and distribution? Despite seemingly powerful evidence in favour of a positive answer to this question, later Marxists almost universally concluded that purely political reforms leading to 'formal' power being extended to the working class were merely a façade behind which the power of the capitalist class remained, though hidden.

The evidence to the contrary is, as I have just said, strong. After a long struggle and against bitter opposition universal manhood (and then universal, that is, including women) suffrage was achieved in a large number of states whose economies were still predominantly capitalist market economies. In addition, working-class political parties became serious competitors for parliamentary power and, of course, have frequently achieved such power in many states.

Furthermore, many highly significant reforms have been introduced in the economic, social and educational spheres, seemingly directly in the interest of working-class people; the legalisation of trade-unions, government regulation of working conditions, health-care schemes, social insurance and unemployment assistance, grant-aided education, all of those measures referred to collectively as 'the welfare state'. Marxists still claim, however, that the economic dominance of the capitalist class is sufficient to undermine the seeming dispersal of political power through the extension of the suffrage so that whether, to use Ralph Miliband's phrase,[33] the government acts at the behest of or merely on behalf of the capitalist class, dominance of the interests of that class undermines the pretensions of representative governments to be significantly democratic; the concrete evidence to the contrary being dismissed as a confusion between radical change and insignificant palliatives.[34]

How has the issue been approached by non-Marxist political scientists? The first non-Marxist thinkers to have a major impact on democratic theory who took a decidedly 'realist' stance on the issue of political structures and processes were the theorists usually referred to as 'the classical elitists', Vilfredo Pareto, Gaetano Mosca and Robert Michels.[35] Though self-confessedly anti-Marxist, their analyses of political power did have one factor in common with the Marxist position, namely, the thesis that the real structure of power rarely ever coincided with the formal constitutional structure. The real structure was always some form of rule by a political elite. The political elite, however, was not envisaged as necessarily related to a distinct non-political group such as an economic class. I will be looking at certain aspects of elite theory in the final chapter, but the theory has no direct relevance to the issue in hand.

Space for the consideration of the possibility of the systematic impact of non-political factors on the processes of political power was created in mainstream political science by the conception of the political system as an integrated part of a wider set of sub-systems constituting a society as a whole, as represented in the seminal work of David Easton.[36] The political system, from this theoretical perspective, is conceived of as, of course, producing outputs having an impact on the other sub-systems of society, but also as depending upon inputs from those sub-systems, inputs that have the capacity to significantly shape the political system in terms of its structure, processes and outputs. Such a high-level theory does not in itself have any specific implications concerning the precise non-political factors likely to have preponderant influence on the political. But the

1950s witnessed a burgeoning of observational research on the structure of community power[37] which gave rise to the neo-elitism that Dahl set out to test in his research for *Who Governs?*, as outlined in the previous chapter. The general conclusion that the community power theorists arrived at was that behind the scenes of 'democratic' rule lurked a relatively small and fairly cohesive elite, who were, by and large, representative of what Dahl refers to as 'the social and economic notables'.[38] Importantly, then, the neo-elitists introduced, independently of the Marxist perspective, the theory of disproportionate effectiveness in the political sphere of economic power.

The vogue for such neo-elitist community power theories was, however, relatively short-lived, subjected as they were to the sophisticated methodological and empirical critiques of theorists such as Dahl, Polsby and Wolfinger.[39] Implicit in the kind of research represented by these theorists is a conception of the day-to-day process of policy formation as subtle, complex and multi-dimensional. While the structure of constitutional power and responsibility is not denied a significant impact, emphasis is placed on the multiplicity of sources of influence and constraint that affect the determination of policy outcomes. Given the hypotheses already mentioned concerning the multiplicity and overlapping nature of interest groups, the plurality of potential political resources and their fragmented dispersal, the classic model of political pluralism, as described previously, is easy to construct. Dahl even ventured, tentatively, to construct a general model of political activism centred on a distinction between 'homo civicus' and 'homo politicus'.[40] The former was a person whose primary goals were 'private'; home, family, career, leisure activities; while 'homo politicus' was the person more or less continuously engaged in active political life. Dahl hypothesises that the life of 'homo civicus' is only touched at the boundaries by political decisions, though infrequently some issue might emerge which becomes of central concern and will transform 'homo civicus' temporarily into 'homo politicus', marshalling her or his resources for the relevant political effort. It is assumed that the vast majority of citizens will be in the category of 'homo civicus', more often than not only minimally involved in active politics. There is the almost explicit assumption here that seeing that almost no one is totally bereft of political resources, long periods as 'homo civicus' are indicative either of the fact that a person is not being significantly affected by political decisions or that the person is satisfied with things as they are. There did, in fact, emerge in this period the hypothesis that apathy leading to low levels of political involvement and participation was positively functional for the operation of democratic politics and, if anything, was indicative of the successful operation of a genuinely democratic structure of power. From the perspective of the problem we are currently dealing with the important element of these pluralist theories was the claim that political resources were non-cumulative and hence no single group could ever even approximate a monopoly of influence on the decision-making process.

As I outlined in the previous chapter, pluralist assumptions themselves came under both methodological and empirical attack and, as Christopher Pollitt notes, many pluralist theorists of the 1960s became in the 1970s and 1980s 'neo-pluralists'.[41] Though the plurality and fragmentation of political resources was never denied, Dahl begins to refer to wealth and economic power as a strategic resource and Lindblom can state:

> It has been a curious feature of democratic thought that it has not faced up to the private corporation as a peculiar organisation in an ostensible democracy.[42]

There has, in fact, been a strange convergence between Marxist and non-Marxist theories of the strategic position of economic power as a determinant of governmental action. While Marxists refuse to relinquish the claim that the overall, long-term interests of the capitalist class dominate policy-making in the last instance, the emphasis on the relative autonomy of the state does imply that certain demands from economically subordinate groups can be responded to, provided that this is compatible with the fundamental interests of capital. On the other hand, despite non-Marxists' insistence that very few interest groups totally lack political resources, it has become more and more common for such theorists to stress the disproportionate effectiveness of well-organised and financially well-endowed groups, which, with some exceptions, are likely to encompass groups controlling as private property large concentrations of productive resources. Axel van den Berg concludes his exhaustive critique of Marxist theories of the state by claiming that, where specific and falsifiable, they are asserting no more than what most liberal democratic theorists have themselves argued.[43]

How do these various groups of theorists envisage the transformation of economic into political power? There are two importantly different types of mechanism postulated;

disproportionate intentional influence and disproportionate structural constraint. With regard to the former, the hypothesis is that significant disparities of wealth will lead in several interlinked ways to differential effectiveness in directly influencing the outcomes of political decision-making. Firstly there is what we could call disproportionality by default, resulting from the wider utilisation of democratic rights by certain groups. As I argued in Chapter 3, if a group is going to have a significant impact in the decision-making process it will need to participate in that process at many levels in an active and informed manner. However, as G. B. Powell states:

> In their seven-nation study, Verba, Nie and Kim found that the individual social and economic resources possessed by citizens were powerful facilitators to political activities of most kinds. The better-off citizens were consistently, in nation after nation, more likely to be informed about politics, to form local organisations, to work with others on community problems, to contribute time and money to political parties, to persuade others how to vote, and so forth.[44]

Given such a conclusion, even if there is no intention on the part of better-endowed groups to have a disproportionate influence, differential political effectiveness as a result of differential participation in the formal decision-making of democratic government is inevitable. Hence the emphasis I placed in Chapter 3 on equality of access to the background resources required to make political equality effective.

Participation in the formal structures of decision-making is not the only or the most important way of influencing decisions. As I have noted previously, the day-to-day process of policy formation is open at many levels to numerous external influences, formal and informal, legal and illegal. It is in this context that we might expect to find the main impact of economic inequality, for what we are dealing with here is not the indirect consequences of such inequality operating through its effect on rates of participation, but the direct and intentional marshalling of resources, particularly money, in the attempt to influence political decisions. The effectiveness of lobbying is not wholly dependent on the organisational efficiency of the lobby; the degree of congruence with already entrenched policy goals and public opinion is, for example, an obviously relevant factor. Nor is organisational efficiency wholly dependent on the level of financial backing; the dedication, enthusiasm and vitality of people intensely committed to a cause could more than substitute for lack of funds. This said, however, it cannot be denied that the availability of financial backing will more likely than not have a very great impact on the effectiveness of a lobby. It was the growing realisation of just this, the strategic nature of wealth as a political resource, that led such theorists as Dahl and Lindblom to reassess their early pluralism. Other resources may be important, even the ability to make a public nuisance of oneself is not only a potential resource but also could, in fact, be ultimately effective. However, as one commentator remarked in the context of a march on Washington by the poor, 'the rich march on Washington all the time', or, to be more accurate, they do not need to march on Washington because they are permanently installed there in well-appointed offices with professional full-time researchers, secretarial staff, publicity agents and lobbyists.

That money can in fact be used effectively to influence government decisions is most clearly demonstrated in the case of illegal influence or corruption. The spectacular revelations of corruption in Japanese and Italian political circles that came to light in 1992–93 are evidence not only of the possibility but also the sometimes widespread reality of disproportionate influence deriving from economic power. There have been numerous empirical studies of the disproportion of influence of well-financed campaigns to influence political outcomes. Two noteworthy instances are M. Crenson's *The Un-politics of Air Pollution* and J. Gaventa's work on power in an Appalachian community.[45] These works present persuasive evidence of the ability of strong economic interests to manipulate the political process to their own advantage. On a more general level, what are referred to as neo-pluralist and corporatist theorists have argued strongly that financially powerful and well-organised groups are, in many areas of policy formation, the major external determinants of political decisions and their mode of implementation, the corporatist version stressing how such effective demand groups come to attain a quasi-official position within the policy-making process.[46]

Can we conclude from all of this work that there is an unquestionable case for the belief that disparities of wealth, particularly in the sphere of productive assets, is a major factor subverting political equality? The conclusion does seem to me to be very strongly supported, though I would enter three cautionary caveats. Firstly, disparity of wealth is not total monopoly and, as I argued above in concurrence with a central theme of Dahl's early pluralism, though economic power may be strategic it is not the only political resource. Consequently, and particularly in the light of the distinction between potential power and actually employed successful power, assertions that major elements of policy outcomes represent the disproportionate influence of economic power need to be backed up by careful empirical research. The second caveat concerns the precise identity of the well-organised, well-financed interest groups. There is no doubt that the private corporation, the large business enterprise and agencies representing coalitions of such organisations constitute major actors in the sphere of influencing governmental decisions. However, other organisations, representing the professions, farmers and labour, for example, do emerge as relatively well-financed and well-placed political influences. This provides a further reason for the necessity of the detailed empirical research just mentioned. The third caveat reinforces this point. Some theorists, notably Eric Nordlinger, have argued that the near consensus among empirical democratic theorists that external societal factors totally dominate the policy-making process is highly implausible. The state is itself a well-endowed organisation, wielding great power and is often 'markedly autonomous . . . even when its preferences diverge from the demands of the most powerful groups in civil society'.[47] This is even compatible with some recent Marxist theories of the state, emphasising the state's relative autonomy.[48] As Jon Elster has argued, if the state is supposed to serve the overall and long-term interests of capital as a whole, as distinct from short-term or factional demands, it must have considerable power to act as it sees fit.[49] But if the state has such autonomous power we cannot reject out of hand the possibility that some particular policy or decision is not the result of pressure from well-endowed interests but, perhaps, a genuine attempt to serve the public interest or to cater for those incapable of organising themselves as a pressure group. This is only a possibility, but it is one that should introduce a note of caution. Even after entering these caveats, however, it is safe to conclude that great concentrations of wealth and economic power are more likely than not to pose a threat to the achievement of equality in the political process; the disadvantaged are likely to be low participants and the advantaged high participants are likely, on the basis of the superior resources they can marshal, to be able to make their voice effectively heard.

But do they even need to make their voice heard? A negative answer to this question constitutes the central element of the theory of structural constraint on governmental decision-making, primarily by the interests of the owners of major productive assets. The general phenomenon that we are considering here has its effect in the impersonal, non-intentional predetermination of the agenda of feasible options facing government in such a way that those options prioritise the partisan interests of some specific group. I am going to argue that, within the limits set by the qualifications that I will make later, firstly, the theory of a structural predetermination of the political agenda is intellectually coherent and, secondly, a strong case can be made that the interests of major productive assets do structurally constrain governments in modern societies.

There are two mechanisms by which partisan interests can come to structurally dominate an agenda: structurally produced partisan over-representation among the agencies that actually articulate the agenda and structural interdependence between different regions of social organisation. I will deal with partisan over-representation first; this is, in fact, a species of structurally produced cultural dominance as discussed in the previous chapter. The mechanism is simple and easy to understand. Various agencies will be involved directly and indirectly in fashioning the basic political agenda of a society at any given time; radio, television, press, political activists, government employees, representatives of interest groups, 'experts' and so forth. Imagine a major divide in society leading to two main sub-groups with partially conflicting interests. The patterned distribution of both resources and attitudes and the organisation of modes of participation in various spheres of social life is such that in those spheres that predominate in the articulation of the basic political agenda one group is over- and the other group greatly under-represented. If we assume that the over-represented group will, perhaps even wholly unconsciously, prioritise its own partisan perspective and interests, the result will be a clear case of a structurally produced pre-determination of the agenda with a bias towards the interests of the dominant group. I have formulated this in a highly schematic fashion, but it is evident that this is, in fact, the mechanism at work in the under-representation of both women and racial and ethnic minorities. There are obvious problems, however, with the thesis that this is the primary mechanism at work in the case of economic class; the organised representatives of the working-class have for nearly a century been major actors in the conventional political arena and, in many states, have frequently attained formal political power; though we cannot wholly discount the theory of 'embourgeoisement' formulated by Robert Michels[50] nor the claims made by theorists such as Ralph Miliband[51] that people of upper-class status are still vastly over-represented in many strategic positions within the state apparatus and other agencies influential in determining the political agenda, I will move on to the second postulated mechanism. Structural interdependence would serve to predetermine the agenda in practice, even if the decision-making agencies were wholly committed to an alternative set or priorities.

The concept of structural interdependence is straightforward. Imagine an economy extensively utilising computer technology and, hence, utilising computer-literate people, hardware engineers, computer scientists, software designers, systems analysts and so forth. The continued functioning of such an economy as so organised would be crucially dependent on an educational system to furnish large numbers of people with the requisite skills. The important point is that such interdependence introduces the possibility of structural compatibility and incompatibility. An educational system training people exclusively in classical Latin would not be compatible with the computerised economy. There are, of course, degrees of compatibility and incompatibility and complex networks of reciprocal interdependence.

It is, I would argue, almost self-evident that the functioning of the political system as organised in a particular way and as undertaking a particular range of tasks will be dependent in certain ways on the economy and its performance. To be more specific, imagine a relatively radical socialist party achieving a solid parliamentary majority in a society whose economy was predominantly capitalist. In the short term such a government's dependence on the efficient functioning of the economy as currently organised is evident. There are many complex lines of dependence that for present purposes can be simplified down to two: the government requires both revenue and material inputs from the economy to ensure its day-to-day functioning and it requires of the economy the provision of employment for a majority of its citizens and the production of goods needed to sustain life and production at 'normal' levels. Whatever its ultimate ideological aims it must give priority to the efficient functioning of the economy, or else be so counter-productive as to risk self-destruction. If an economy is a capitalist economy, the prioritising of the efficiency of the economy involves prioritising the interests of the owners and primary beneficiaries of productive assets. Hence the predetermination of the political agenda of feasible options within parameters set by the interests of the owners of productive assets. The ensuring of the continuous supply of inputs necessary for the functioning of government and the guarantee of a reasonable level of social stability depend upon meeting these requirements. This, I would argue, is the kernel of truth at the core of structural Marxism. But it is only a kernel.

Governments in representative democracies operating within the social matrix of a capitalist market economy will be, whether they are of socialist orientation or otherwise, severely constrained by such dependencies. But constraint should not be confused with automatic causal determinacy or inevitable teleological functionality. Furthermore, we always have to keep in mind firstly, that compatibility and incompatibility are matters of degree and, secondly, that structural interdependence is, according to the argument, short term. I will briefly explain these points.

There is nothing in social systems generally that remotely resembles a Darwinian environment that selects the 'fittest', the functionally adapted, nor is there anything sufficiently analogous to the mechanisms of automatic and detailed genetic inheritance. We could imagine a government whose policies were so dysfunctional in economic terms that it was 'eliminated' either by social upheaval or electoral defeat. But it could equally well destroy the economy. Or it could be eliminated and be replaced by a competitor that was equally dysfunctional; and so on. In fact, the impact of the requirement of compatibility is mediated through human knowledge, which, of course, is fallible. There is very little in this whole complex of interrelationships that is strictly automatic. There is no guarantee that the functional will necessarily emerge.

Of more relevance to practical matters, compatibility, as I said is a matter of degree. There would, in principle, be nothing impossible in the idea of a socialistically inclined government acutely assessing the level of incompatibility feasible in specific circumstances, implementing policies that partially realised its ideals while maintaining some acceptable level of compatibility, but also, in the meantime, gradually transforming the economy so as to lessen the government's dependence on the efficiency of the capitalistic sector. Even conceding all of the above, it does seem to me, however, that the argument from structural constraint does establish that, in practice, there is a very high probability of the partisan interests of the owners of major productive assets being given, willy-nilly, high priority in the determination of the political agenda. Whatever a government's genuine ideals may be, the habituating effect of even relative conformity to the constraints generated by economic interests in the never-ending short term cannot be underestimated.

We have been examining in this chapter the relationship between modern market economies, in particular the concentration of the ownership of productive assets, and the realisation of democratic ideals. Though nothing like logical conclusiveness is possible in such areas the weight of evidence seems to me to point to the conclusion that such concentration of economic power is directly inimical to equal autonomy in the economic sphere itself and a significant and continuous threat to genuine political equality in the government of the state.

10

The logical limits of democracy

It is often said that the Athenian city-state from the time of Kleisthenes' constitution in 508 BC to its final incorporation into the Macedonian empire of Alexander the Great almost two hundred years later was, leaving aside the limitation of the franchise, as near as a political community has ever come to complete democracy. For its 30,000–40,000 citizens the political system afforded not only generalised equality of voice in the governing of the state, but it satisfied the law of requisite variety in involving citizens at all stages of the decision-making process from the determination of the agenda by the Council of Five Hundred, to the debate and decision in the Assembly, to the implementations of policy by the Boards of Magistrates and the popular Juries. It is easy to identify those features of the system that constituted its internally complex equality in the exercise of political power. Political rights were based simply on citizenship and not on property ownership, nobility, military rank and so forth. The exercise of political power was direct, the basic decisions being made by the Assembly at which all adult male Athenians had the right to attend, to speak and to vote. All other offices were open to all citizens and selection was by random lot. The shortness in terms of office, the non-re-eligibility rules, the very multiplicity of offices and practice of payment, even for attendance at the Assembly, ensured high levels of involvement. The accountability of officials was guaranteed by the mandatory yearly audit in which all officials were required to produce a detailed account of their actions. Even for those offices that were not filled by lot, such as the post of General or Strategos, appointment was by election, on a yearly basis and incumbents could be, and were, held to account for their actions by the Assembly.[1]

In comparing Athenian democracy to the government of modern states, the sheer size, populousness and complexity of the latter, it is argued, render Athenian-type institutions wholly inappropriate and the adoption of the civic ideal of 'happy versatility' and active participation can be seen as either idle romantic idealism or dangerous *naïveté*. Referring to the one element of direct democracy that is still used in the modern state, the referendum, Robert Michels alludes to the verdict of the socialist Edouard Bernstein as saying:

> with good reason that even if none but the most important political and administrative questions are to be submitted to the popular vote, the happy citizen of the future will find every Sunday upon his desk such a number of interrogatories that he will soon lose all enthusiasm for the referendum.[2]

It seems evident that the possibility of democracy in the modern state depends upon electoral representation and a professional, but accountable, civil service. Furthermore, the efficiency of electoral representation itself seems to require those organisations that have become central to the political life of democracies, namely, political parties. It is here, however, that we run up against what are claimed as the logical limits of democracy. In the previous two chapters we examined the theory that the putative political equality inscribed in a democratic constitution could be subverted by various types of extra-procedural inequalities. The argument we are concerned with now is that even if all of these inequalities were to be eliminated the democratic ideal would still remain a forever unattainable aspiration. Neither modern society as a whole nor those institutions supposedly designed to render government democratic, political parties, can function without organisation. In the opinion of Robert Michels we encounter here 'an iron law' deriving from the 'tactical and technical necessities' of organisation that not only renders complete democracy unachievable but also in fact, transforms all attempts to implement it into its opposite. As he puts the matter in the final chapter of *Political Parties*:

> It is organisation which gives birth to the dominion of the elected over the electors, of the mandataries over the mandators, of the delegates over the delegators. Who says organization, says oligarchy.[3]

Democracy will always remain a façade behind which one political elite or another wields the real power. 'Historical evolution mocks all the prophylactic measures that have been adopted for the prevention of oligarchy.'[4]

Along with Pareto and Mosca, whom he acknowledges as his forerunners,[5] Michels bases his argument for the inevitability of oligarchy on three assumptions: 'the objective immaturity of the mass' which 'is not a mere transitory phenomenon which will disappear with the progress of democratisation ...' but 'derives from the very nature of the mass as mass';[6] the superiority of leaders and the subversion of any desire to be genuinely accountable to the mass that comes about as a result of the experience of power and leadership;[7] and the technical necessities of organisation.[8] As we will see, however, it is the third assumption that is basic and, to a very large extent, underlies the first two.

While it is true that Michels' language is redolent with what might appear as an intellectual arrogance that dismisses the ordinary person, on the basis of very little systematic evidence, as congenitally crass and stupid, a more careful analysis would reveal that the fundamental argument underlying his position is somewhat different and far more difficult to contest. The incompetence of the mass derives from its atomistic multiplicity and the inevitable gulf separating the detailed knowledge of the full-time professional from that of even the most informed amateur. The core of Michels' thesis lies in his reference to 'the very nature of the mass as mass'.[9] The very same argument can be seen in Mosca's rejection of the time-honoured classification of constitutions in terms of number as falling into one of the three categories of rule by the one, the few or the many. In Mosca's opinion rule is always rule by the few. The reasoning behind this is easy to explain. One is too few, all is too many. Michel Foucault has famously and persuasively argued that power as positive control is co-extensive with the capacity for surveillance. The management and organisation of a populous and vastly complex society involves the gathering, marshalling, appraisal, processing, storage and use of a huge quantity of detailed information. It is inconceivable that a single individual could have this capacity. Of course, an individual might have advisers and subordinates to whom the tasks of monitoring and surveillance are delegated. But here again delegation will inevitably involve alienation; if the titular head of an organisation had the capacity to monitor in detail the monitoring of the monitors, delegation would not have been required in the first place. The mass does not suffer this incapacity; its numerousness would enable it to gather and process all the pieces of information required for rule. The problem here is one of disaggregation. Knowledge can only be the basis of a unitary ruling power if it itself is unified. Unification requires a pooling of information that is only possible in a group whose members can engage in constant and detailed reciprocal communication. This places a relatively low upper limit on the possible size of such a group. Even then there will be a certain amount of disaggregation. Only in very simple matters could there be a literal collective rule.

It is what I referred to above as the atomistic multiplicity of the mass, the inability of members of a highly numerous group to be in reciprocal communication, each with all, that is the basis of the need for organisation. And it is from the necessity of organisation that the superiority of the leaders derives. Elite theorists do sometimes assume a natural superiority in leaders. And Michels in particular discusses at length 'the exercise of power and its psychological reaction upon the leaders',[10] resulting in a greed for power and a complete unwillingness to relinquish it once it has been attained.[11] The supposed superiority of leaders and the corrupting effects of power are relatively secondary elements in the process by which organisation becomes oligarchic and leaders attain a position in which they become 'STABLE and IRREMOVABLE'.[12] It is again the logic of organisation that is at work here.

'Organisation' is an ambiguous word. In one sense it refers to any relatively stable and complex pattern of action, and particularly, interaction. In a second sense it refers to the planning and implementation process intended to produce organisation in the first sense. Thirdly, it can refer to an institution, a group of people whose actions and interactions are fairly tightly governed by regulations that define roles, functions and tasks for each individual and the organisation as a whole. The basic logic of Michels' position is that in almost all matters of complexity organisation in the behaviour of vast numbers of people requires active organising; organisation in the first sense requires organisation in the second sense. Furthermore, this active organising, to be efficient, requires an organisation in the third sense. If the matters being dealt with are complex, such an organisation, to be efficient, will need to be permanent and professional and, for the same reason that organisation was required in the first place, it will need some form of hierarchical structure that will itself involve concentrated loci of power within the organisation. Those who occupy these loci of power will be in a radically asymmetric position with respect to the 'ordinary' members of the organisation and an even more asymmetric position with respect to the members of the mass whose activity is being organised. The asymmetry consists not just in the fact that they are the leaders and the others are the led, but in what this implies, namely, the concentration of administrative, financial and, in particular, cognitive resources. They may be formally accountable to the mass, there may be institutions that are intended to guarantee that accountability such as elections, but the co-extensiveness of power and the capacity for surveillance emerges again here. Neither the mass as mass nor any individual member of the mass has the capacity for the continuous monitoring that is required for countervailing control and real holding to account. Michels argues strongly, as we have seen, that leaders will almost inevitably develop a self-protective mentality, a desire to hold on to power and the freedom of manoeuvre that the ability to protect one's position requires. This might be because their professional livelihood depends upon maintaining their position, or because they have developed a taste for power or even because they genuinely believe in the goals of the organisation and consider themselves indispensable in the leading of the organisation. The real basis, however, of what Michels calls the stable and irremovable position of the leaders is the above-mentioned asymmetry. Power in this case implies the capacity to preserve itself.

But surely, though there might be some grain of truth in Michels' theory and that of the elite theorists generally, to say that oligarchy is inevitable is in large measure exaggerated rhetoric. In the first place, the basic logic of Michels' argument rests on a series of links, each one specifying a functional requirement. Organisation needs organisation that needs an organisation which needs an internal integrating power. But what guarantees that such needs will be met? Michels' answer to that question is competition. On one level, as we have seen, Michels' argument is grounded in reflection on the logic of organisation as such, but the organisations that he is specifically concerned with are political parties either in an electoral representative system or more generally in the context of a struggle for political power. 'The modern party is a fighting organisation in the political sense of the term, and must as such conform to the laws of tactics.'[13] Though the existence of competition does not automatically generate the conditions required for success, it eliminates the least efficient and, as mediated by human consciousness, stimulates the creation of the characteristics it requires.

Suppose we accept that there is a strong tendency towards oligarchy in the political party, as John Plamenatz pointed out there is still a crucial gap in Michels' argument.[14] The political party is not society as a whole, and society as a whole is not a single unitary organisation in the technical sense. It is made up of individuals and a multiplicity of organisations, but these are not branches of some unitary overall organisation in the way in which the marketing, the production design, the research and development and the accounts department of a firm, for example, are all integral parts of a single organisation. While these points are true they are, I would argue, largely irrelevant to Michels' thesis. Society may not be an organisation, but in numerous ways vitally important to them individual members of society are organised by means of authoritatively binding rules that issue from an organisation that is the ensemble of state apparatuses. Furthermore, the successful political party becomes the incumbent governing party at the hub of those state apparatuses. Democratic control over the rules and conditions produced by government decisions depends in a representative system on control by citizens over political parties, both in the process whereby such parties formulate their policies and in the implementation of those policies by the ruling party of the day. If all political parties inevitably develop an oligarchic core that is immune from control by its supporters and ordinary members, does this not imply that representative party 'democracy' completely fails to afford its citizens any significant level of control over government decisions and is in fact an illusion, 'nothing but a continuous fraud on the part of the dominant class'.[15]

But has not Michels simply overstated his case both with regard to intra-party democracy and democracy in the government of the state? It is a plain fact of life that leaders are removed and that ruling political parties sometimes lose elections; they are held to account. Is not Michels failing to take into account the crucial role of competition between parties in the maintenance of democratic accountability? It has to be admitted that Michels sometimes states his thesis in an exaggerated fashion. Though famously he talks of 'the iron law of oligarchy'[16] he is at times prepared to speak of a *tendency* towards oligarchy and even to discuss the possibilities of mitigating this tendency.[17] Furthermore, when he says that leaders are irremovable, he does not mean either that specific top individuals in a political party are literally irremovable or that, over a period of time, the political elite of a society cannot lose its position of power. If it is thought that these concessions significantly aid the democratic case, however, this is because of a too narrow construal of 'leaders', and a misconception of the process by which leaders and political elites can be replaced. When he talks of 'leaders' he is referring not to the one or two top figures in a party, but to the solid core of permanent and active party members. Michels is prepared to accept some limited validity for Pareto's theory of the circulation of elites, but it is a process that involves a minuscule number of people, compared to the total population of the state, and is more in the nature of a struggle for predominance *within* the political elite.

Top figures, powerful subgroups including sometimes even the core dominant element of a political party, and political elites as a whole are removable. But by what process? Consider the key strategic power-holders in an organisation and assume that Michels is correct in his claim that they will be, in general, extremely reluctant to relinquish power. Though not strictly irremovable this group is in a very powerful position, as we have seen, to maintain its hegemony. How could it be successfully challenged? Certainly not by a lone individual nor by the disaggregated mass as a whole. Its overthrow will have to be carefully planned and tightly orchestrated by an efficiently organised group with the capacity to topple the current leadership and then to secure its own position by the continued successful running of the organisation: in a word, a counter-elite. If this is the process by which dominant sub-groups or political elites as a whole are replaced, it is not democracy but elite competition.

What if the elite competition is electoral, that is, the current political class is toppled by the counter-elite persuading enough of the electorate to change its allegiance? The role of competition between political parties might be thought to be the central factor in ensuring government accountability and hence a significant degree of democratic control by ordinary citizens. Michels employs several arguments on the basis of which he rejects the concept of 'government by the masses' as impossible. In the first of these he cites the writings of radical democratic theorists and anarchists from Rousseau to Malatesta to the effect that delegation of power, either within a party or through the representative system in the state, is always the alienation of power over which the delegators immediately lose control.[18] He would admit that the exercise of the right to vote is a power through which, with universal suffrage and equal vote weighting, political equality in this moment of decision-making is realised. This, however, the one and only power people exercise in a representative system, is a power the exercise of which destroys itself:

> Under representative government the difference between democracy and monarchy, which are both rooted in the representative system, is altogether insignificant – a difference not in substance but in form. The sovereign people elects, in place of a king, a number of kinglets.[19]

His argument is based in the first instance on the undoubted legal fact that after an election the 'sovereign people' have no constitutional powers of direction over the elected delegates. An elected representative will 'regard himself as authorised arbiter of the situation, and really is such'.[20]

His second argument is meant to deal with a possible objection to the first based on the distinction between constitutional power and informal control and influence. Constitutionally a deputy is a free agent, but in reality there will always be among the electors some who can influence, perhaps even directively control, the representative. His reply is that these sources of influence are 'the big guns of the constituency or the local branch of the party. In other words, they are persons who . . . have in fact come to form part of the ruling oligarchy'.[21] The whole detailed, intricate and sprawling mass of legislation and administration that constitutes the day-to-day business of modern government is the almost completely exclusive province of the professionals and permanent activists that constitute the political elite, albeit, in modern society, an elite with significant internal factions. The power of electors, exercised through the blunt instrument of the vote, carries, it is said, constitutionally no weight in the directive control of government and, informally, almost as little.

It might be argued that this conclusion totally neglects what has become a central element of the theory and practice of representative government. By the law of anticipated reaction, it is not the last election that exercises controlling power over the government of the day and the various parties competing for power, but the anticipation of the next election. The possible effectiveness of anticipated reaction is well-understood in the theory of power and was cited, though cautiously, by Bachrach and Baratz as one possible species of the second face of power.[22] The mechanism of its operation is simple. A person who is the active, explicit decision-maker in a particular sphere is aware of others whose interests and preferences are likely to be affected by the decisions and is aware that these and others have the power to act detrimentally, if they so choose, to the interests of the active decision-maker. The active decision-maker, then, is likely to anticipate these possible reactions and attempt to avoid negative reactions by giving due consideration to the interests and preferences in question, even if these are not explicitly articulated. The most famous use of this type of argument in support of the thesis that the decisions of representatives, whose interest lay in ensuring future electoral support and, hence, power, would tend to coincide with the wishes of at least a majority of the people, was in James Mill's *Essay on Government*[23] Michels' contention that such considerations cannot provide a basis for any significant directive power on the part of the masses returns us once more to the central core of his theory. Bachrach and Baratz's own caution in appealing to this type of second-dimensional power derived from their awareness that such supposed power became tenuous in the extreme the more the anticipated reaction was merely a construal and the less it was grounded in the detailed knowledge and expressed preferences of the alleged holders of this power concerning the complex of measures adopted by the explicit decision-maker. In the absence of detailed knowledge, can we be talking about anything more than an amorphous pressure to rule in a fashion that will not appear to people generally as too irresponsible or too neglectful of the requirement to rule benevolently? In discussing the possibility of direct democracy and the use of the referendum Michels first identifies what he sees as the fundamental problem, 'the incompetence of the masses and the lack of time'.[24] Though the lack of time referred to here is the time required to put even the most important political and administrative decisions to direct popular vote, it is closely related to the 'incompetence' factor. As I noted above, Michels' argument does not require the thesis that the ordinary person is inferior in terms of general intellectual capacity. The incompetence is simply the obverse of the detail and complexity both of society and the decisions that have to be made. This is the hard rock of contemporary democracy. Positive, directive control requires knowledge and the motivation to use it and the cybernetic law of requisite variety requires a complexity in control of inputs that matches the possible variety of desired outputs.[25] The conspicuous absence in the representative government of modern states of both of these is interlinked and just how interlinked they are will become apparent shortly. Lack of requisite variety in input control results in democratic politics becoming, for the most part, a spectator sport and, at that, one that attracts a minuscule audience except in the short time surrounding elections or in periods of political scandal.

It is part of the conventional wisdom of representative democratic theory that the multiplicity of political parties, together with the multiplicity of other loci of critical opposition guaranteed by political freedoms generally, have significant democratically beneficial effects particularly relevant to the problem of what we will call, technically, cognitive variety. Political parties, critical investigative journalists and, sometimes, dedicated specialists who devote practically their whole lives and energies to the sceptical monitoring of government performance do increase the flow of relevant information and 'simplify' things for the ordinary citizen.

We encounter again, though, the problems inherent in the delegation of responsibility, particularly the responsibility for critical monitoring. I do not wish to deny the possible beneficial effects that can come about as the result of the plurality of centres of opposition legitimated by political freedoms. The question is not whether there are beneficial effects but whether these beneficial effects raise, to any significant extent, the level of detailed knowledge, and thence, the possibility of democratic control in the hands of the ordinary citizen. This can be doubted when the downward communication from the informed professional opposition to the ordinary citizen is, for the most part, reduced to the party slogan, the one-word headline and the sound-bite.

The problems of significant levels of citizen participation in the government of a modern state are not, it should be obvious, simply questions of space and geography. The democratic potential of the latest interactive telecommunications technology should not be exaggerated. The problems of the physical co-presence of millions of people can be overcome by such technology, as could the problems of providing the citizen with access to the complex and extensive mass of information concerning government action that is required as a necessary background for appraising that action. But the problem of the individual human being assimilating this information is hardly addressed at all. Any one person can still only communicate with a few others at any one time and teletext has to be read one page at a time. The critical problem is not the channels of communication, but human capacity to assimilate and process the information, and one of the crucial dimensions of that problem is simply time. There is the problem of the initial capacity for assimilation and appraisal and the problem of the background training and education required to render assimilation and appraisal appropriately critical, which itself involves the problem of time indirectly. A total solution to these problems seems impossible, but the inability to solve a problem completely does not imply that significant progress cannot be made. Perhaps Michels was guilty of uncritically assuming that the limits of the educational and informational capacity of ordinary citizens has been reached and was so pitifully inadequate to the task of even guarding the guardians as to render representative government as inexorably elitist as Plato's Republic.

If the critical factor is information what are the possibilities of increasing not just its potential availability but also the capacities of assimilation and appraisal? Firstly, we would have to return to our discussion in Chapter 3 of those background resources there identified as necessary prerequisites of effective political equality; in general, these involve relatively high levels of educational and cultural development and the conditions of daily life, time and leisure that are essential to both the opportunity to acquire political competence and the motivation to do so. It certainly does not seem literally impossible to achieve very significant improvements here. But what about the utilisation of these background resources in the actual day-to-day informed involvement in political affairs? Do we not here run up against a logically, or at least humanly, insuperable information ceiling? If we keep in mind that we are not necessarily looking for some unachievable 'total' knowledge, and, though, as I have been arguing all along, radical delegation of responsibility results in its virtual transfer, a moderate specialisation and division of labour among the already multi-competent could ensure a maintenance of a relative independence and autonomy, then here again very significant improvement is possible. Possible, but how likely? If we admit the possibility, the probability depends upon motivation. And here we encounter another central problem of contemporary democratic theory.

I mentioned when discussing the law of requisite variety the links between cognitive or informational variety and the variety of control over inputs. One obvious interdependence consists in the strategic importance of information; having available multiple input controls but no knowledge of how to utilise them or what outputs might be desirable is pointless. The links that I wish to concentrate on now, though, travel in the reverse direction; I want to look at the effects of impoverished input control on knowledge. The first effect is directly causal and easy to understand. Imagine that a person's direct control input into the decision-making process was limited to the casting of a single vote for one or other candidate belonging to one or other of a small number of political parties in elections held every four or five years or so; the typical situation of the vast majority of citizens in modern representative systems. A crucial dimension would be lacking in such a person's political knowledge, the dimension of practical experience that derives from involved and responsible exercise of power. It is, I would argue, the lack of such sustained experience that Schumpeter is referring to when he assesses the thinking about politics of the ordinary citizen as 'infantile', 'associative', 'affective' and lacking 'a sense of reality'.[26] As I mentioned when discussing Schumpeter in Chapter 1, it is perfectly plausible to argue that this 'incompetence' is a result of the lack of opportunity for responsible involvement rather than a justification for the permanent denial of such opportunity. If the range of inputs was enlarged, the channels for involvement multiplied and each individual's real responsibility for outcomes increased, then both practical experience and a sense of reality would be the likely outcome. The basic problem that such suggestions encounter, however, in the context of the centrally governed modern nation-state is the problem of the dilution of power to the level of the insignificant. The most famous version of this problem in modern political theory is that formulated by Anthony Downs as the paradox of rational voting.[27] Though this particular version of the problem is specific to electoral voting in populous representative systems, it is well-recognised as having much wider implications concerning the motivation to participate in collective action.[28]

In his seminal work, *An Economic Theory of Democracy*, Anthony Downs sets out to construct a model of the operation of representative democratic systems based on the assumption that in such systems there were two types of rational agents, political parties seeking electoral support and a set of individual voters each of whom was seeking to choose, by voting, a political party with a package of policies that was as near as possible to her or his own preferences for political outcomes. The assumption of rationality enables the theory to predict how various agents will choose in specified circumstances. It is, consequently, of vital importance that there is as precise as possible a specification of the postulated principles of rational choice. It is assumed that there are three determinants of the rationality of a choice: the relative values of the possible outcomes, the cost of each choice of option, and the probability of the chosen option effectively producing the value attaching to the option. To explain the point and mode of operation of these determinants, imagine first of all an agent faced with three options, A, B and C, with the respective numerical representation of preference-values 10, 7 and 3. If we neutralise conditions two and three by assuming that no cost is involved in making certain in each case that the choice of an option will bring about the ascribed value, then rationality would imply choosing A over B and C. This is what, by definition, the fully informed rational agent would choose.

We complexify the situation slightly if we introduce differential costs. With the same outcome values the rational choice of option would be different if, for example, A involved incurring a cost of 9, B a cost of 5 and C zero cost. The preference schedule would be inverted, since the net value to the agent of A, B and C would be, respectively, 1, 2 and 3. We complexify matters greatly if we introduce the third dimension of uncertainty. The best examples to illustrate the effects of differential uncertainty are those of ordinary gambling, say, the laying of bets on horses. By staking a pound on a horse that was being given odds of 100–1, a person *could* win a hundred pounds. But that might not be a particularly rational choice if the person was almost certain that the horse would lose. To go back to our original schematic illustration, how would the preference-structure of a rational agent be affected by the introduction of differential probabilities? Suppose the probability of the choice of C being effective was almost zero, while there was a reasonable probability, say fifty/fifty, of the choice of B being effective. The probability of the choice of A being effective is positive, but relatively low, let us say one in a hundred. The first point to note about the introduction of uncertainty and probability is that it is no longer simply possible net value that is at issue; there is the question of what we could call the lay out cost that is put at risk by the levels of uncertainty, and, of course, the levels of probability themselves. Thus, C has the greatest net value and, though its probability is low, it is still a relatively attractive option because its lay-out cost is zero; nothing is put at risk. A is not particularly attractive, it has a low probability and a low pay-out compared to B and C. In fact, we could not think of a reason why anyone, even a great gambler, would choose A over B. B looks like the most attractive option. Though choosing C has no direct cost, there is the opportunity cost of forgoing a fifty/fifty chance of a reasonable return for a modest outlay. The introduction of uncertainty, then, obviously introduces complexity, but with specified ranges of probability and suitably defined discount rates and rates of risk-willingness, a rational choice theory can at least assign probabilities to choices.

How is this relevant to Downs' democratic theory? The individual voter is postulated as a rational agent making a choice between political parties on the basis of what Downs calls 'party differential', the degree of closeness between the policy packages of the parties and the voter's own preferences, the differential being the distance between the parties as determined by a particular voter's preferences. Imagine a voter choosing between, to simplify matters, two parties, one which is much closer to the voter's preferences than is the other. It seems that the obviously rational choice is the nearest party. But how is the choice effected? Again, quite obviously, by casting a vote for the chosen party. How do cost and uncertainty enter this kind of choosing situation? What is the cost of casting a vote for the party of one's choice? It looks to be fairly minimal; for most people, a small amount of time, perhaps a minimum of inconvenience, and, as all commentators add, the cost of shoe leather. It is with probability that the problems begin to emerge. The vote is construed as an action intended to bring about a desired effect, the election of the preferred party and, hopefully, the implementation of the preferred policies. Just like the laying of a bet on a horse it is a chosen means to an end. As with the laying of a bet, the choosing of the means does not guarantee the successful effecting of the end. What, for any individual voter, is the probability that this particular action, the casting of this vote, will be effective in bringing about the desired goal? The precise answer would depend upon the size of the electorate, the turn-out and the specific electoral system used, but in any typical modern state the probability will not approach the level of statistical significance. The fact that it is statistically extremely improbable that a single vote will be decisive in determining an election means that there is little or no point in any individual voter voting at all. We might argue that since the cost is minimal, we are here in a situation similar to the choice of option C in our schematic example. C has zero cost, a low probability of effectivity, but a high pay-off if it occurs. So, why not choose it? If we were to be pedantic and mathematical, it would be noted that there is a minimal cost in actually casting a vote and even a small number will begin to approach infinity when it is divided by one approaching zero, which is what the probability of a single vote being decisive is approaching. But this is not where the real significance of the argument lies. Its real significance lies in its implications for the motivation to acquire the requisite knowledge to vote rationally. Downs himself formulates the paradox in terms of the thesis that, even with fairly low costs, the statistical insignificance of the probability of a single vote being effective implies that it is irrational to vote.[29] I would prefer to say that it is irrational to vote rationally. Some equivocation is being introduced intentionally here to highlight the paradox and what seems to me to be its real significance. I will explain the second sense of 'rational' that I have introduced.

The notion of rationality as so far defined is, to put it non-technically, a matter of making a sensible choice in terms of outcomes, costs and probabilities. But there is a broader notion of rationality that is also relevant; this broader notion is, to all intents and purposes, identical with the concept of autonomy introduced in Chapter 8. The central element in this broader notion is information or belief formation, at least if we extend belief to cover a person's values and preferences. In the limited sense of rational choice a specific set of preferences are taken as given, they fix the rank-ordering of the outcomes and it is assumed that the person 'knows' that ordering, the costs and the probabilities of effectiveness. But clearly in any particular case a person might, in terms of current beliefs, make a perfectly rational choice, but looked at in a broader perspective, could be acting irrationally. A person who puts a thousand pounds on a 100-1 horse with three legs may be making a 'rational choice' if he or she firmly believes that despite the odds and the lack of a leg the horse, without any doubts, is certain to win. But we might judge the person far from rational if we discovered that the certainty was based on the calculation that the horse's name, when transcribed into numbers and divided by the date of the race was equal to Π to the fourth decimal place. Though, as with autonomy, we are always talking about relative degrees of rationality, we can say that in the broader sense action is rational when it derives from appropriate information concerning preferences and circumstances, when such information is appropriately scrutinised by critical reflection. It is not always rational, of course, to insist, before making any particular choice, that one has absolutely exhaustive information subject to completely thorough critical scrutiny. The level of appropriateness is dependent on the importance of the choice; but the importance of the choice is itself dependent not just on the weightiness of the matters being decided but on the probability of the individual's choice being effective. Put simply, if there is no chance of my choice being effective, it does not greatly matter whether I make the right choice. If we defined a choice as rational in the abstract when it was based upon fully scrutinised relevant information, we then arrive at the conclusion that it is not always rational to choose rationally in the abstract sense. This brings us back to my reformulation of Downs' paradox: it is not rational to vote rationally, which has the more shocking implication that it is rational to vote irrationally, if it is rational to vote at all.

Many theorists have recognised that the importance of these considerations lies in their implications for the motivation to become politically informed.[30] Downs' own original claim that it is irrational to vote is easily dealt with. As I pointed out in Chapter 7, a person's reason, and quite rational reason, for voting might be that it is a public statement of equal citizen status. Not all rational action need be directly and instrumentally rational. But if people want their votes to be informed inputs into the decision-making process, the votes must be based on relevant information. It can be accepted that the business of becoming politically informed need not necessarily be thought of as nothing but a burden and a cost. There could be a culture that ascribed high intrinsic value to political awareness. We do, however, come back to the paradoxical conclusion that were this the case, with respect to any particular individual, if all of this information is to be channelled through a single vote that is one of millions the likelihood of its being effective is practically zero.

It should be pointed out that though these considerations were originally put forward in the context of a theory of electoral representative systems, their implications apply with equal force to direct democracy. To go back to Bernstein's comments referred to above about the citizen of the future being swamped under a sea of interrogatories, or, in the age of interactive telecommunications, being permanently chained to the mini-tel, it is easy to appreciate how such a person might conclude that since a response was highly unlikely to be effective, it was not worth making one. Would it be worth bothering to find out what one was being asked to respond to? Size and populousness produce two factors whose interplay can lead to the political paralysis of the individual: the complexity of the information needed to make informed choices and the extremely low probability of any individual choice being effective. If power in a large group is distributed equally, the equal effectiveness of all will inevitably result in each individual being equally ineffective. It is, perhaps, this which leads, as Macpherson put it, to the conclusion that:

> To those furthest removed from the sources of information the rational decision will be not to pay the cost of informing themselves, but to let some interested agency pay the cost, and accept biased information from it. Hence if all men act rationally their influence on policy must be very unequal.[31]

Is there any solution to this problem?

The seemingly obvious solution is geographical decentralisation. We can specify this with mathematical accuracy: the less populous the autonomous unit, the greater will be the effectiveness of an equal share of power. But the reason why collective decision-making is required, in the first place, to ensure equal autonomy is the inescapability of significant and possibly detrimental interaction. Hence the appropriate scope of a decision-making process will be determined by the networks of likely significant interaction. We might be easily persuaded that the individual, the household, the street, the local district, the town or city, the country, the province were of too narrow a scope; if there are significant interdependencies between such units, '*de jure*' autonomy will result in '*de facto*' domination and subordination.

The one possible solution can be found, paradoxically enough, by a more thorough working out of the implications of what I argued earlier was the core of truth in Mosca's and Michels' basic thesis. As I formulated it earlier, in matters of great complexity one is too few and all is too many. Efficient control requires relatively systematic coordination and some unitary direction or integration, which, according to Michels, implies organisation, or, more accurately, *an* organisation. But if matters increase in complexity the inevitable result will be a certain level of disaggregation in the controlling organisation. If complexity increases further, what is required is not an organisation but organisations. The awareness of this lies behind the insights of the pluralist and neo-corporatist theories of the modern state. For the same reason that a single individual cannot autonomously exercise positive directive control, neither, when matters become massively complex, can a single, relatively small unitary elite. The modern state is itself an ensemble of apparatuses and neither the executive core nor the separate elements of this ensemble can rule without extensive dependence on, for both information and implementation, a large number of groups and organisations. We can accept Eric Nordlinger's thesis that the state and the distinct apparatuses that constitute it is itself a major actor.[32] But it seems to me undeniable that outputs are the result of multi-channel inputs.

Dahl's original pluralist theory, particularly as it was formulated in the 'minorities rule' thesis, suggests that we might already have found in the theory of pluralistic inputs an informal solution to the problem of equal, and real, political effectiveness.[33] Firstly, as we saw before, there is the plausible assumption that not everyone's interests are all equally affected by every single political output. I am affected somewhat by a penny increase in a pint of milk but not at all to the same extent as the dairy producer. Secondly, the very multiplicity of organisations and groups means that the ordinary members are much closer to the elites that constitute the professional representatives of various interests than they could be to some single elite imagined as ruling in splendid isolation at the top of a massive unitary pyramid of power. A person does not have to be continuously monitoring every conceivable decision in every region of society; a certain limited number of areas will be especially important and in those areas delegation of responsibility to professional representatives can be real, accountable delegation because of the relative closeness of the ordinary member to the members of the elite. Do these considerations constitute a satisfactory solution to the problem of effective political equality?

There are four problems with this solution, some of which we have seen before. Firstly, some of these organisations are vastly more powerful than others and represent the partisan interests of relatively small minorities. Secondly, if the organisations in question are relatively large, the elite of the organisation can quite easily become oligarchic. Thirdly, the ordinary citizen is to a very large extent affected by centralised decision-making, control over which needs to be exercised through the formal political system, in which, as we have seen, the single individual is doomed to ineffectiveness. This problem can, in fact, be seen to be exacerbated by a fourth point, namely, the significant power in the political process of the non-governmental and quasi-governmental groups and organisations to which we are referring. The mass of ordinary citizens has no direct control over the elites of most of these organisations. Such organisations have a relative autonomy from government and the ordinary individual has no significant control over government anyway.

It is precisely this set of considerations that leads Dahl to the conclusion referred to earlier that the most formidable problem of contemporary democracy is the dominance of elite groups of specialists in the sphere of public policy-making. I mentioned earlier Dahl's proposal of a 'mini-populus' for each major decision-making sphere, but a more thorough and radical solution is that proposed by John Burnheim in his work *Is Democracy Possible?*[34] There are two central elements to Burnheim's proposal, both more radical versions of the elements of Dahl's solution: they are, firstly, thorough and extensive functional decentralisation and, secondly, control over the disaggregated functions by decision-making bodies whose members would be selected by lot from those with a 'material interest' in the sphere in question and who would serve for relatively short periods of office.[35] The functional decentralisation that Burnheim suggests is intended to be radical, it involves the abolition of the centralised nation-state. It is hard to disagree with Burnheim's assessment of the dismal record of the nation state,[36] but the democratic reasoning behind the proposed disaggregation of functions is plausible.[37] We need, say, an agency to lay down regulations concerning nuclear power and another agency to determine allowable food additives. Why should these both be the same agency, and, at the same time, the agency that organises the educational system and the road-network of the country? In effect, of course, there is already a large amount of disaggregation, but it is assumed that for popular control of such bodies they need to be hierarchically subordinated to the central state. But our whole argument has been that this does not guarantee effective popular control. If such bodies were autonomous, but representative of the people because there were staffed through random selection with fairly rapid turnover, effective control, motivation to become informed and, not equal ineffectiveness, but real and responsible effectiveness of decision makers would be the result.

Such functional decentralisation would, in itself, facilitate regional decentralisation precisely by means of separating out those spheres in which regions are interdependent from those in which there could be genuine regional autonomy. Two regions that exchange food products, for example, might in that respect be bound by the regulations of a food quality board, but there is no necessity for them to have absolutely identical educational or health-care systems. There are, no doubt, attaching to Burnheim's as to Dahl's proposals problems of professionalism, coordination and possible hierarchical interdependence that might require such institutions as regional councils with more general functions. But along with democratic control of economic enterprises we are being offered a vision of a society in which people would be capable of exercising genuine responsibility in an equal and effective way over their lives and destiny. Is it simply a utopian dream? Utopian thinking has an honoured place in the tradition of political thought. A utopian society may not be realisable, but its description can provide a vantage point for the criticism and reform of the status quo, habituation to which can all to easily lead us to the blinkered conclusion that we have already achieved the limits of the possible. More cynically, drawing out the logical implications of an ideal such as real political equality can reveal to us hidden priorities and, perhaps, hypocrisies. In the end, we all might prefer to sacrifice the opportunity that effective equality would afford us to take responsibility for ourselves for the sake of a quiet life of passive consumption of both goods and political decisions. But there is also the hope that the utopian vision might lead us to look with a more disillusioned eye on systems of government in which the many are condemned to the impotent role of observers and political power and prestige are the prerogative of the self-important few.

Notes

Notes to chapter 1

1 Richard Wollheim, 'On the theory of democracy', in Bernard Williams and Alan Montefiore (eds), *British Analytical Philosophy* (London, Routledge & Kegan Paul, 1967), pp. 247–66.

2 Alfred J. Ayer, *Language, Truth and Logic*, 2nd edn, (Harmondsworth, Middx, Penguin, 1971). For a clear and succinct analysis of the impact of logical positivism on political theory see Raymond Plant, *Modern Political Thought* (Oxford, Basil Blackwell, 1991), pp. 1–22.

3 Ludwig Wittgenstein, *Philosophical Investigations*, trans. by G. E. M. Anscombe (Oxford, Basil Blackwell, 1968), p. 49e. For an exposition and critique of analytic philosophy as overly meta-linguistic see Ernest Gellner, *Words and Things* (London, Routledge & Kegan Paul, 1979). A lucid account of the theories of value and morality developed within the British tradition of philosophy from the turn of the century up to the 1960s can be found in W. D. Hudson, *Modern Moral Philosophy* (London, Macmillan, 1970). For an overview of more recent attempts to develop theories of value in the context of political theory see Will Kymlicka, *Contemporary Political Philosophy* (Oxford, Clarendon Press, 1990). Arnold Brecht, *Political Theory: The Foundations of Twentieth Century Political Thought* (Princeton University Press, 1968), gives a more wide-ranging account of the background to the problems of normative political theory.

4 Richard Wollheim, 'On the theory of democracy', in Williams and Montefiore, *British Analytical Philosophy*, p. 248. The work of Weldon's being referred to is Thomas D. Weldon, *The Vocabulary of Politics* (London, Penguin, 1953). It was one of the classic statements of the death of traditional political theory.

5 Aristotle, *The Athenian Constitution*, trans. by P. J. Rhodes (Harmondsworth, Middx, Penguin, 1984).

6 As quoted in Aristotle, *The Politics*, trans. by J. A. Sinclair (Harmondsworth, Middx, Penguin, 1962), p. 24.

7 Aristotle, *The Nicomachean Ethics*, trans. and intro. by David Ross (Oxford University Press, 1925), pp. 1–2.

8 For an account of the notion of a human practice modelled on the Greek concept of *techné*, see Alasdair MacIntyre, *After Virtue* (London, Duckworth, 1981), pp. 181–203.

9 See Friedrich von Hayek, *Law, Legislation and Liberty*, Vol. 2 (London, Routledge & Kegan Paul, 1976), p. 83, where he says: 'While an equality of rights under a limited government is possible and an essential condition of individual freedom, a claim for equality of material position can be met only by a government with totalitarian powers.'

10 Joseph Schumpeter, *Capitalism, Socialism and Democracy* (London, Allen and Unwin, 1976).

11 Ibid., p. 262.

12 Graeme Duncan and Steven Lukes, 'Democracy restated' in Henry S. Kariel (ed.),

Frontiers of Democratic Theory (New York, Random House, 1970), pp. 188–212.
13 Hayek, *Law, Legislation and Liberty*, p. 83.
14 Isaiah Berlin, *Four Essays on Liberty* (Oxford University Press, 1969), pp. 118–72.
15 Plato, *The Republic*, trans. Desmond Lee (London, Penguin, 1987), Bks IV and IX. For a good introductory discussion of Plato's account of the tripartite soul, see George Klosko, *The Development of Plato's Political Theory* (London, Methuen, 1986), pp. 64–80.
16 For a discussion of this point, see Mogens H. Hansen, *The Athenian Democracy in the Age of Demosthenes*, trans. by J. A. Crook (Oxford, Basil Blackwell, 1991), pp. 74–81,
17 Robert Nozick, *Anarchy, State and Utopia* (Oxford, Basil Blackwell, 1974).
18 Bernard Williams, *Ethics and the Limits of Philosophy* (London, Fontana, 1985); Michael Walzer, *Spheres of Justice* (Oxford, Basil Blackwell, 1985); Charles Taylor, *Sources of the Self* (Cambridge University Press, 1989).
19 Berlin, *Four Essays on Liberty*, p. 171.
20 Thomas Hobbes, *Leviathan*, ed. Richard Tuck (Cambridge University Press, 1991), pp. 117-29. David Gauthier, *The Logic of Leviathan* (Oxford, Clarendon Press, 1969) stresses this interpretation of Hobbes; Gauthier himself in David Gauthier, *Morals by Agreement* (Oxford, Clarendon Press, 1986) attempts to justify a system of ethical rules as being in the actual self-interest of all ethical agents in a community.
21 Brian Barry, *Democracy, Power and Justice* (Oxford, Clarendon Press, 1989), p. 423.
22 Ibid., p. 423.

Notes to chapter 2

1 Robert A. Dahl, *Democracy and Its Critics* (New Haven, Yale University Press, 1989), p. 2.
2 Ibid., p. 2.
3 For the classic attack on notions of 'essentialism' see Karl R. Popper, *Conjectures and Refutations: The Growth of Scientific Knowledge* (London, Routledge & Kegan Paul, 1963), pp. 18–21 and pp. 103–114.
4 Arne Naess *et al.* claim, in fact, to have identified 311 different meanings of 'democracy' in Western literature since the first use of 'demokratia' by Herodotus. Arne Naess, Jens A. Christopherson and Kjell Kvalo, *Democracy, Ideology and Objectivity* (Oxford, Basil Blackwell, 1956).
5 Mogens H. Hansen, *The Athenian Democracy in the Age of Demosthenes*, trans. by J. A. Crook (Oxford, Basil Blackwell, 1991).
6 See entry on 'Definition' in Paul Edwards (ed.), *The Encyclopaedia of Philosophy*, Vol. 2 (London, Collier-Macmillan Ltd, 1967), pp. 314–24, for a summary of philosophical theories of definition.
7 See Hansen, *The Athenian Democracy in the Age of Demosthenes*, pp. 86 and 125–60.
8 Joseph Schumpeter, *Capitalism, Socialism and Democracy* (London, Allen & Unwin, 1976); Crawford B. Macpherson, *Democratic Theory: Essays in Retrieval* (Oxford, Clarendon Press, 1977); John Burnheim, *Is Democracy Possible?* (Cambridge, Polity Press, 1988).
9 Schumpeter, *Capitalism, Socialism and Democracy*, p. 269.
10 Burnheim, *Is Democracy Possible?*, pp. 1–18.
11 Macpherson, *Democratic Theory: Essays in Retrieval*, pp. 3–23.
12 Ludwig Wittgenstein, *Philosophical Investigations*, trans. by G. E. M. Anscombe (Oxford, Basil Blackwell, 1968), pp. 32e-6e; For a discussion of this theory of conceptual unity see Renford Bambrough, 'Universals and family resemblances' and Haig Khatchadourian, 'Common names and "family resemblances" ' in George Pitcher (ed.), *Wittgenstein: The Philosophical Investigations* (London, Macmillan, 1968).
13 Herodotus, *Histories*, trans. by A.D. Godley (Cambridge, Mass., Loeb Classical Library, 1990), Book VI, 131.
14 See W. G. Forrest, *The Emergence of Greek Democracy: The Character of Greek Politics*,

800–400 B.C. (London, Weidenfeld & Nicolson, 1978), pp. 45–66 and 178–89.

15 The fullest and most up-to-date account can be found in Hansen, *The Athenian Democracy in the Age of Demosthenes*, pp. 125–295.

16 A discussion of Carnap's conception of constructional definition can be found in Nelson Goodman, 'The significance of Der Logische Aufbau der Welt' in Paul A. Schlipp (ed.), *The Philosophy of Rudolf Carnap* (La Salle, Illinois, Open Court, 1963), pp. 545–58.

Notes to chapter 3

1 Jean-Jacques Rousseau, *The Discourse on Inequality*, trans. by Maurice Cranston (Harmondsworth, Middx, Penguin, 1984), pp. 57–8.

2 Robert A. Dahl, *Democracy and Its Critics* (New Haven, Yale University Press, 1989), p. 233.

3 See Mogens H. Hansen, *The Athenian Democracy in the Age of Demosthenes*, trans. by J. A. Crook (Oxford, Basil Blackwell, 1991), pp. 304–20.; see also, Moses I. Finley, *Politics in the Ancient World* (Cambridge University Press, 1983), pp. 70–96.

4 John Stuart Mill, 'Considerations on representative government' in John Gray (ed.), *On Liberty and Other Essays* (Oxford University Press, 1991), pp. 326–45.

5 Austin Ranney and Wilmoore Kendall, 'Basic principles for a model of democracy', in Charles F. Cnudde and Deane E. Neubauer (eds), *Empirical Democratic Theory* (Chicago, Markham Publishing Company, 1969), pp. 41–63.

6 James Bryce, *Modern Democracy* (New York, The Macmillan Company, 1924), Vol. 1, p. 26.

7 Ranney and Kendall, 'Basic principles for a model of democracy', in Cnudde and Neubauer, *Empirical Democratic Theory*, p. 47.

8 Ibid., p. 49.

9 Ibid., p. 50.

Notes to chapter 4

1 Chester G. Starr, *The Birth of Athenian Democracy: The Assembly in the Fifth Century B.C.* (Oxford University Press, 1990).

2 Ibid., p. 33.

3 Ibid., p. 34.

4 Ibid., p. 34.

5 Ibid., pp. 33–4.

6 For versions of such liberal inclusion principles see Jack Lively, *Democracy* (Oxford, Basil Blackwell, 1975), and Robert A. Dahl, *Democracy and Its Critics* (New Haven, Yale University Press, 1989), pp. 193–209.

7 Joseph Schumpeter, *Capitalism, Socialism and Democracy* (London, Allen & Unwin, 1976), pp. 244–5.

8 Aristotle, *The Politics*, trans. and intro. by J. A. Sinclair (Harmondsworth, Middx, Penguin, 1962), pp. 37–8.

9 Robert A. Dahl, *A Preface to Democratic Theory* (University of Chicago Press, 1956); Jack Lively, *Democracy*; Austin Ranney and Wilmoore Kendall, *Democracy and the American Party System* (New York, Harcourt, Brace & World, 1956).

10 Lively, *Democracy*, pp. 16–27.

11 Dahl, *A Preface to Democratic Theory*, pp. 37–8.

12 Lively, *Democracy*, pp. 16–27.

13 Dahl, *A Preface to Democratic Theory*, pp. 65–151. See also Robert A. Dahl, *Pluralist Democracy in the United States: Conflict and Consent* (Chicago, Rand McNally, 1967). For a good exposition and critique of the basic assumptions of pluralism see William A. Gamson, *The Strategy of Social Protest* (Homewood, Illinois, The Dorsey Press, 1975).

14 See Gamson, *The Strategy of Social Protest*, pp. 130–43; Peter Bachrach and Morton S. Baratz, *Poverty and Power: Theory and Practice* (Oxford University Press, 1970).

15 James M. Buchanan and Gordon Tullock, *The Calculus of Consent* (Ann Arbor, University of Michigan Press, 1962), pp. 155–8.
16 Thomas Hobbes, *Leviathan*, ed. Richard Tuck (Cambridge University Press, 1991), p. 62.
17 For an argument very similar to the one presented here see P. Jones, 'Intense preferences, strong beliefs and democratic decision making', in *Political Studies*, 36:1, March 1983.
18 George Bernard Shaw, 'Essays in Fabian Socialism', in *The Works of Bernard Shaw*, Vol. 30 (London, Constable And Co., 1932), pp. 89–98.
19 Arend Lijphart, *Democracy in Plural Societies: A Comparative Exploration* (New Haven, Yale University Press, 1977).

Notes to chapter 5

1 Friedrich von Hayek, *Law, Legislation and Liberty* (London, Routledge & Kegan Paul, 1976), Vol. 2, p. 83. See also by Hayek, *The Constitution of Liberty* (London, Routledge & Kegan Paul, 1960) and the early classic statement of his position that I will refer to most in this chapter, *The Road to Serfdom* (London, George Routledge & Son, 1944).
2 Hayek, *The Road to Serfdom*, p. 52.
3 Robert A. Dahl, *Democracy and Its Critics* (New Haven, Yale University Press, 1989), p. 333.
4 Hayek, *The Road to Serfdom*, p. 31.
5 Ibid., p. 91
6 Ibid., p. 89.
7 Ibid., p. 90.
8 Ibid., p. 148.
9 Dahl, *Democracy and Its Critics*, p. 333.
10 Ibid., p. 335.
11 Ibid., p. 340.
12 Mogens H. Hansen, *The Athenian Democracy in the Age of Demosthenes*, trans. by J. A. Crook (Oxford, Basil Blackwell, 1991), p. 227.
13 Ibid., pp. 178–224.
14 Ibid., pp. 225–6.
15 Ibid., pp. 240–1.
16 Giovanni Sartori, *Democratic Theory* (New York, Frederick A. Praeger, 1965), p. 261.
17 Ibid., p. 254.
18 E. Laboulaye, *L'État et ses limites* (Paris, 1871); Fustel de Coulanges, *La Cité antique* (Paris, 1864); Benjamin Constant, *Political Writings*, ed. and trans. by Biancamaria Fontana (Cambridge University Press, 1988).
19 Sartori, *Democratic Theory*, p. 225.
20 See, for example, G. E. M. de Ste Croix, *The Class Struggle in the Ancient Greek World* (London, Duckworth, 1981); Moses I. Finley, *Democracy Ancient and Modern* (London, Chatto and Windus, 1973); A. H. M. Jones, *Athenian Democracy* (Oxford University Press, 1957).
21 Sartori, *Democratic Theory*, p. 373.
22 Ibid., p. 263.
23 Ibid., p. 272.
24 Ibid., pp. 250 and 268.
25 Ibid., p. 257.
26 Hayek, *The Road to Serfdom*, pp. 156–7.
27 Quoted in Charles Taylor, *Sources of the Self* (Cambridge University Press, 1989), p. 323.
28 Taylor, *Sources of the self*, pp. 3–107.
29 Hayek, *The Road to Serfdom*, p. 156.
30 Jean-Jacques Rousseau, *The Social Contract*, trans. by Maurice Cranston (Harmonds-

worth, Middx, Penguin, 1968), pp. 72–83.

31 For a famous interpretation of Rousseau along these lines see Jacob L. Talmon, *The Origins of Totalitarian Democracy* (London, Secker & Warburg, 1952).

32 Hayek, *The Road to Serfdom*, p. 80.

33 Anthony Giddens, *A Contemporary Critique of Historical Materialism* (London, Macmillan, 1981), pp. 1–48.

34 My own translation; for the original Greek see the bi-lingual Thucydides, *History of the Peloponnesian War*, trans. by C. A. Smith (Cambridge, Mass., Harvard University Press, 1921) Loeb Classical Library, 110, p. 158

Notes to chapter 6

1 Henry David Thoreau, 'On the duty of civil disobedience', in *Walden and 'Civil Disobedience'* (New York, New American Library, 1960), p. 236.

2 For a thorough historical survey of the anarchist tradition, see George Woodcock, *Anarchism* (Harmondsworth, Middx, Penguin, 1963); for a more discursive analysis see David Miller, *Anarchism* (London, J. M. Dent & Sons, 1984).

3 William Godwin, *Enquiry Concerning Political Justice*, ed. I. Kramnick (Harmondsworth, Middx, Penguin, [1793] 1976).

4 David Miller (ed.), *The Blackwell Encyclopaedia of Political Thought* (Oxford, Basil Blackwell, 1987), p. 381.

5 Thoreau, *Walden and 'Civil Disobedience'*, p. 223.

6 Ibid., p. 230.

7 Robert Paul Wolff, *In Defense of Anarchism* (New York, Harper Colophon, 1976).

8 Keith Graham, *The Battle of Democracy: Conflict, Consensus and the Individual* (Brighton, Wheatsheaf Books, 1986), pp. 75–94.

9 Jacob L. Talmon, *The Origins of Totalitarian Democracy* (London, Secker & Warburg, 1952).

10 Jean-Jacques Rousseau, *The Social Contract*, trans. by Maurice Cranston (Harmondsworth, Middx, Penguin, 1968), p. 60.

11 John Locke, *Two Treatises of Government*, ed. Peter Laslett (Cambridge University Press, 1991).

12 Thomas Paine, *Political Writings*, ed. Bruce Kuklick (Cambridge University Press, 1989); *The Portable Thomas Jefferson*, ed. Merrill D. Peterson (Harmondsworth, Middx, Penguin, 1977).

13 Locke, *Two Treatises of Government*, pp. 269–78.

14 Ibid., pp. 285–302.

15 Ibid., p. 362.

16 Ibid., pp. 277–8.

17 Plato, *The Republic*, trans. by H. D. P. Lee (Harmondsworth, Middx, Penguin, 1955), p. 369.

18 Niccolo Machiavelli, *The Prince*, trans. by Russell Price, eds Russell Price and Quentin Skinner (Cambridge University Press, 1988), p. 54.

19 For an overview of communitarian and neo-contractarian theories see Will Kymlicka, *Contemporary Political Philosophy* (Oxford, Clarendon Press, 1990), pp. 50–94 and 199–237. Habermas develops his notion of the 'ideal speech situation' in Jürgen Habermas, *Communication and the Evolution of Society*, trans. by T. McCarthy (Boston, Mass., Beacon, 1979).

20 Robert A. Dahl, *Democracy and Its Critics* (New Haven, Yale University Press, 1989), p. 175.

21 Ibid., p. 180.

22 Ibid., p. 182.

23 Ibid., pp. 97–105.

24 Ibid., p. 114.

Notes to chapter 7

1 William N. Nelson, *On Justifying Democracy* (London, Routledge & Keegan Paul, 1980).
2 John Dunn (ed.), *Democracy: The Unfinished Journey* (Oxford University Press, 1992), pp. 239–66.
3 Joseph Schumpeter, *Capitalism, Socialism and Democracy* (London, Allen & Unwin, 1976), p. 242.
4 Ibid., p. 242.
5 Thucydides, *History of the Peloponnesian War*, trans. by C.A. Smith (Cambridge Mass., Harvard University Press, 1921), Loeb Classical Library Vol. 108, pp. 319–41. In addition to Mogens H. Hansen, *The Athenian Democracy in the Age of Demosthenes*, trans. by J. A. Crook (Oxford, Basil Blackwell, 1991), see also Cynthia Farrar, *The Origins of Democratic Thinking: The Invention of Politics in Classical Athens* (Cambridge University Press, 1988).
6 Thucydides, *History of the Peloponnesian War*, pp. 319–41.
7 Robert A. Dahl, *Democracy and Its Critics* (New Haven, Yale University Press, 1989), p. 84, p. 31.
8 Ibid., p. 85.
9 Ibid., p. 86.
10 John Locke, *Two Treatises of Government*, ed. Peter Laslett (Cambridge University Press, 1991), p. 304.
11 Jeremy Bentham, 'An introduction to the principles of morals and legislation', Mary Peter Mack (ed.), *A Bentham Reader* (New York, Pegasus, 1969).
12 John Rawls, *A Theory of Justice* (Oxford University Press, 1972), pp. 22–33. For a wide-ranging critical discussion of Rawls, see Norman Daniels (ed.), *Reading Rawls: Critical Studies of 'A Theory of Justice'* (Oxford, Basil Blackwell, 1975). See also Brian Barry, *The Liberal Theory of Justice* (Oxford University Press, 1977). I refer to Rawls in this context because of the widespread influence that his work has had, but a much more thoroughgoing attempt to base morality on rational self-interest can be found in David Gauthier, *Morals by Agreement* (Oxford, Clarendon Press, 1986).
13 Rawls, *A Theory of Justice*, pp. 150–61.
14 Ibid., pp. 118–92.
15 See Daniels (ed.), *Reading Rawls* and Barry, *The Liberal Theory of Justice*.
16 John Rawls, 'A Kantian conception of morality', *Cambridge Review*, Vol. 96 (1975).
17 Charles Taylor, *Sources of the Self* (Cambridge University Press, 1989), pp. 3–107.
18 Ibid., pp. 73–107.
19 For a good introduction to ancient Stoic philosophy see John N. Rist, *Stoic Philosophy* (Cambridge University Press, 1969).
20 Immanuel Kant, *Groundwork of the Metaphysic of Morals*, trans. by H. A. Patton (New York, Harper & Row, 1964), p. 17.
21 Georg W. F. Hegel, *Phenomenology of Spirit*, trans. by A.V. Miller (Oxford, Clarendon Press, 1977), pp. 104–19. For an illuminating study of the master/slave relationship in Hegel's thought see Richard Norman, *Hegel's Phenomenology: A Philosophical Introduction* (London, Sussex University Press, 1976).
22 See John Plamenatz, *Man and Society*, Vol. 2 (London, Longmans Green, 1963), pp. 188–90.
23 See Anton Powell, *Athens and Sparta: Constructing Greek Political and Social History from 478 B.C.* (London, Routledge, 1988), pp. 96–135, 214–62.
24 Jon Elster, 'The possibility of rational politics' in David Held (ed.), *Political Theory Today* (Cambridge, Polity Press, 1991), pp. 115–42.
25 Dahl, *Democracy and Its Critics*, p. 86.
26 Ibid., pp. 52–79.
27 Ibid., p. 75.
28 Ibid., p. 93.
29 Crawford B. Macpherson, *Democratic Theory: Essays in Retrieval* (Oxford, Clarendon

Press, 1977).

30 See Terence H. Irwin, *Aristotle's First Principles* (Oxford, Clarendon Press, 1988), chs 13–21; Amelie Oksenberg Rorty, *Essays on Aristotle's Ethics* (Berkeley, University of California Press, 1980).

31 Nelson, *On Justifying Democracy*, pp. 20–4.

Notes to chapter 8

1 Karl Marx, 'On the Jewish question', in David McLellan (ed.), *Karl Marx: Selected Writings* (Oxford University Press, 1977), p. 46.

2 Crawford B. Macpherson, *Democratic Theory: Essays in Retrieval* (Oxford, Clarendon Press, 1973), pp. 10–12.

3 Robert A. Dahl, *A Preface to Economic Democracy* (Cambridge, Polity Press, 1985), p. 111.

4 Robert A. Dahl, *Who Governs?: Democracy and Power in an American City* (New Haven, Yale University Press, 1961), p. 6.

5 Ibid., pp. 270–5.

6 Robert A. Dahl, 'The concept of power', *Behavioural Science*, 2 (1957), 201–15.

7 Dahl, *Who Governs?*, p. 333.

8 Ibid., p. 334.

9 Ibid., p. 189.

10 Ibid., p. 228.

11 Peter Bachrach and Morton S. Baratz, 'The two faces of power', *American Political Science Review*, 56: 4 (Dec. 1962), 947–52.

12 Peter Bachrach and Morton S. Baratz, *Poverty and Power: Theory and Practice* (Oxford University Press, 1970).

13 Bachrach and Baratz, 'The two faces of power', 948.

14 Robert A. Dahl, *After the Revolution* (New Haven, Yale University Press, 1970), p. 114.

15 Ibid., p. 27.

16 Steven Lukes, *Power: A Radical View* (London, Macmillan, 1974), p. 23.

17 Ibid., p. 27.

18 Ibid., pp. 21–2.

19 Jon Elster, 'Belief, bias and ideology', in Martin Hollis and Steven Lukes (eds), *Rationality and Relativism* (Oxford, Basil Blackwell, 1982), pp. 123–48.

20 See Julia O'Faolain and Lauro Martines (eds), *Not in God's Image* (London, Temple Smith, 1973); Eva Figes, *Patriarchal Attitudes* (London, Panther Books, 1972); Susan Brownmiller, *Femininity* (London, Paladin Grafton Books, 1986), Andrea Dworkin, *Pornography: Men Possessing Women* (London, The Women's Press, 1981); Susan Moller Okin, *Women in Western Political Thought* (London, Virago, 1980); Gordon W. Allport, *The Nature of Prejudice* (New York, Doubleday, 1958); J. Dollard, *Caste and Class in a Southern Town* (New Haven, Yale University Press, 1937); Frantz Fanon, *The Wretched of the Earth*, trans. by Constance Farrington (London, MacGibbon and Kee, 1965); Edward W. Said, *Culture and Imperialism* (London, Chatto and Windus, 1993).

21 Robert A. Dahl, *Democracy and Its Critics* (New Haven, Yale University Press, 1989), p. 91.

22 Gerald Dworkin, *The Theory and Practice of Autonomy* (Cambridge University Press, 1988), p. 30.

23 Willard Van Orman Quine, *Word and Object* (Cambridge, Mass., The MIT Press, 1960), p. 3.

24 See Peter Morriss, *Power: A Philosophical Analysis* (Manchester University Press, 1987), pp. 32–5.

25 Quoted in Charles Taylor, *Sources of the Self* (Cambridge University Press, 1989), p. 323.

26 Margaret Stacey and Marion Price, *Women, Power and Politics* (London, Tavistock Publications, 1981).

27 See Stacey and Price, *Women, Power and Politics*; P. Norris, *Politics and Sexual Equality*

(Brighton, Wheatsheaf Books, 1987); V. Randall, *Women and Politics*, 2nd edn (London, Macmillan, 1987); J. Lovenduski and J. Hills (eds), *The Politics of the Second Electorate* (London, Routledge & Kegan Paul, 1981); E. Haavio-Mannila (ed.), *Unfinished Democracy* (London, Pergamon, 1985); Cynthia Fuchs Epstein, *Woman's Place* (Berkeley, University of California Press, 1970); Gunnar Myrdal, *An American Dilemma*, 2nd edn, Vol. I: *The Negro in a White Nation*; Vol. II: *The Negro Social Structure* (New York, McGraw-Hill, 1964).

Notes to chapter 9

1 Lawrence C. Becker, *Property Rights: Philosophic Foundations* (London, Routledge & Kegan Paul, 1979), p. 7.
2 Robert A. Dahl, *A Preface to Economic Democracy* (Cambridge, Polity Press, 1985), pp. 69–73.
3 Ibid., p. 73.
4 See Gianfranco Poggi, *The Development of the Modern State: A Sociological Introduction* (London, Hutchinson, 1978).
5 John Locke, *Two Treatises of Government*, ed. Peter Laslett (Cambridge University Press, 1991), pp. 156–71.
6 Ibid., pp. 285–303.
7 Ibid., pp. 355–63.
8 Ibid., p. 363.
9 Crawford B. Macpherson, *The Political Theory of Possessive Individualism* (Oxford University Press, 1962), pp. 194–262.
10 Locke, *Two Treatises of Government*, p. 271.
11 Milton Friedman, *Capitalism and Freedom* (Chicago University Press, 1962).
12 Dahl, *Preface to Economic Democracy*, pp. 68–70.
13 Ibid., p. 68.
14 Ibid., p. 70.
15 Robert A. Dahl, *After the Revolution* (New Haven, Yale University Press, 1970), p. 106.
16 Ibid., p. 106.
17 Dahl, *Preface to Economic Democracy*, p. 55.
18 John Roemer, *Free to Lose* (London, Hutchinson, 1988), pp. 99–106.
19 Crawford B. Macpherson, *Democratic Theory: Essays in Retrieval* (Oxford, Clarendon Press, 1973), pp. 16–18.
20 Friedman, *Capitalism and Freedom*, p. 14.
21 Macpherson, *Democratic Theory*, p. 146.
22 Ibid., p. 146.
23 Aristotle, *The Nicomachean Ethics*, trans. and intro. by David Ross (Oxford University Press, 1925), Bk. 3, Ch. 1.
24 Dahl, *Preface to Economic Democracy*, p. 135.
25 See Becker, *Property Rights*; Robert Nozick, *Anarchy, State and Utopia* (Oxford University Press, 1972); Ronald Dworkin, 'What is equality? Equality of welfare and equality of resources', *Philosophy and Public Affairs* (Summer–Autumn, 1981); G. A. Cohen, 'Nozick on appropriation', *New Left Review*, 150 (1985); G. A. Cohen, 'Self-ownership, world ownership and equality, part 2', *Social Philosophy and Policy* 3: 2 (1986).
26 Dahl, *Preface to Economic Democracy*, pp. 74–83, 134–5.
27 Ibid., p. 135.
28 Jean-Jacques Rousseau, *The Social Contract*, trans. by Maurice Cranston (Harmondsworth, Middx, Penguin, 1968), pp. 69–70.
29 See Derek Jones and Jan Svejnar (eds), *Participatory and Self-managed Firms: Evaluating Economic Performance* (Lexington, Mass., D. C. Heath, 1982); John Simmons and William Mares, *Working Together* (New York, Knopf, 1983).
30 Carole Pateman, *Participation and Democratic Theory* (Cambridge University Press, 1970).

31 Karl Marx and Frederick Engels, 'The Communist Manifesto', in David McLellan (ed.), *Karl Marx: Selected Writings* (Oxford University Press, 1977), p. 233.
32 Ibid., p. 594.
33 Ralph Miliband, *Marxism and Politics* (London, Oxford University Press, 1977), p. 74.
34 See Axel van den Berg, *The Immanent Utopia: From Marxism on the State to the State of Marxism* (Princeton University Press, 1988), pp. 135–79.
35 For a good introductory discussion of the classical elitist school see Geraint Parry, *Political Elites* (London, Allen & Unwin, 1969).
36 David Easton, *The Political System: An Enquiry into the State of Political Science* (New York, Alfred A. Knopf, 1953).
37 See C. Wright Mills, *The Power Elite* (London, Oxford University Press, 1958); H. D. Lasswell, *The Comparative Study of Elites* (Stanford University Press, 1952); F. Hunter, *Community Power Structure* (Chapel Hill, University of North Carolina Press, 1953).
38 Robert A. Dahl, *Who Governs? Democracy and Power in an American City* (New Haven, Yale University Press, 1961), pp. 63–84.
39 Dahl, *Who Governs?*; N. W. Polsby, *Community Power and Political Theory* (New Haven, Yale University Press, 1961); R. Wolfinger, 'Reputation and reality in the study of community power', *American Sociological Review*, Vol. 25.
40 Dahl, *Who Governs?*, pp. 223–8.
41 Christopher Pollitt, 'Democracy and bureaucracy', in Christopher Pollitt and David Held (eds), *New Forms of Democracy* (London, Sage Publications, 1986), pp. 158–91.
42 Charles Lindblom, *Politics and Markets* (New York, Basic Books, 1977), p. 356.
43 van den Berg, *The Immanent Utopia*, pp. 464–519.
44 G. Bingham Powell, *Contemporary Democracies* (Cambridge, Mass., Harvard University Press, 1982), p. 112. The study referred to is Sydney Verba, Norman H. Nie and Jae-on Kim, *Participation and Political Equality* (Cambridge University Press, 1978).
45 M. A. Crenson, *The Un-politics of Air Pollution* (Baltimore, John Hopkins Press, 1971); John Gaventa, *Power and Powerlessness: Quiescence and Rebellion in an Appalachian Valley* (Oxford University Press, 1980). See also Thomas R. Dye and Harmon Zeigler, *The Irony of Democracy: An Uncommon Introduction to American Politics* (Pacific Grove, California, Brooks/Cole, 8th edn, 1990); W. A. Gamson, *The Strategy of Social Protest* (Homewood, Ill., Dorsey Press, 1975).
46 See Grant McConnell, *Private Power and American Democracy* (New York, Alfred Knopf, 1967); Theodore J. Lowi, *The End of Liberalism: Ideology, Policy and the Crisis of Public Authority* (New York, Norton, 1969); Stein Rokkan, 'Norway: numerical democracy and corporate pluralism', in Robert A. Dahl (ed.), *Political Opposition in Western Democracies* (New Haven, Yale University Press, 1966).
47 Eric A Nordlinger, *On the Autonomy of the Democratic State* (Cambridge, Mass., Harvard University Press, 1981), p. 1.
48 See van den Berg, *The Immanent Utopia*, pp. 181–356.
49 Jon Elster, *Making Sense of Marx* (Cambridge University Press, 1985), pp. 411–28.
50 Robert Michels, *Political Parties: A Sociological Study of the Oligarchical Tendencies of Modern Democracy*, trans. by Eden and Cedar Paul (New York, Dover Publications, Inc., 1959), pp. 205–14.
51 Ralph Miliband, *The State in Capitalist Society* (London, Weidenfeld & Nicolson, 1969), pp. 51–62.

Notes to chapter 10

1 See Mogens H. Hansen, *The Athenian Democracy in the Age of Demosthenes*, trans. by J. A. Crook (Oxford, Basil Blackwell, 1991), pp. 125–259.
2 Robert Michels, *Political Parties: A Sociological Study of the Oligarchical Tendencies of Modern Democracy*, trans. by Eden and Cedar Paul (New York, Dover Publications, 1959), p. 336.

3 Ibid., p. 401. A lucid and critical account of Pareto, Mosca and Michels can be found in Geraint Parry, *Political Elites* (London, Allen & Unwin, 1969).
4 Michels, *Political Parties*, p. 406.
5 Ibid., pp. 377–9.
6 Ibid., p. 404.
7 Ibid., pp. 205–14.
8 Ibid., pp. 400–8.
9 Ibid., p. 404.
10 Ibid., p. 203.
11 Ibid., pp. 205–31.
12 Ibid., p. 401.
13 Ibid., p. 41.
14 John P. Plamenatz, *Democracy and Illusion* (London, Longman, 1973), pp. 52–83.
15 Michels, *Political Parties*, p. 38.
16 Ibid., pp. 377–92.
17 Ibid., pp. 404–8.
18 Ibid., pp. 36–9.
19 Ibid., p. 38.
20 Ibid., p. 39.
21 Ibid., p. 39.
22 Peter Bachrach and Morton S. Baratz, 'Two faces of power', *American Political Science Review*, 56: 4 (Dec. 1962), 947–52.
23 James Mill, *Essay on Government*, ed. and intro. by Currin V. Shields (New York, Bobbs-Merrill, 1955), pp. 66–82.
24 Michels, *Political Parties*, p. 336.
25 For an account of this law see Ross Ashby, *An Introduction to Cybernetics* (London, Methuen, 1964), pp. 202–14.
26 Joseph Schumpeter, *Capitalism, Socialism and Democracy* (London, Allen & Unwin, 1976), p. 262.
27 Anthony Downs, *An Economic Theory of Democracy* (New York, Harper and Brothers, 1957).
28 Mancur Olson, *The Logic of Collective Action* (Cambridge, Mass., Harvard University Press, 1971); Brian Barry, *Sociologists, Economists and Democracy* (London, Collier-Macmillan, 1970).
29 Downs, *An Economic Theory of Democracy*, pp. 240–1.
30 Michael Laver, *The Politics of Private Desires* (Harmondsworth, Middx, Penguin, 1981); Alan J. Ware, *The Logic of Party Democracy* (London, Macmillan, 1979).
31 Crawford B. Macpherson, *Democratic Theory : Essays in Retrieval* (Oxford, Clarendon Press, 1973), p. 189.
32 Eric A. Nordlinger, *On the Autonomy of the Democratic State* (Cambridge, Mass., Harvard University Press, 1981).
33 Robert A. Dahl, *A Preface to Democratic Theory* (Chicago University Press, 1956), p. 133.
34 John Burnheim, *Is Democracy Possible?* (Cambridge, Polity Press, 1985).
35 Ibid., pp. 100–24.
36 Ibid., p. 33.
37 Ibid., pp. 19–50.

Index